OXFORD ENGLISH MONOGRAPHS

General Editors

The Art of Hunger

*Aesthetic Autonomy and the
Afterlives of Modernism*

ALYS MOODY

OXFORD
UNIVERSITY PRESS

OXFORD

UNIVERSITY PRESS

Great Clarendon Street, Oxford, OX2 6DP,
United Kingdom

Oxford University Press is a department of the University of Oxford.
It furthers the University's objective of excellence in research, scholarship,
and education by publishing worldwide. Oxford is a registered trade mark of
Oxford University Press in the UK and in certain other countries

Published in the United States of America by Oxford University Press
198 Madison Avenue, New York, NY 10016, United States of America

British Library Cataloguing in Publication Data
Data available

Library of Congress Control Number: 2018940199

ISBN 978–0–19–882889–1

Printed and bound by
CPI Group (UK) Ltd, Croydon, CR0 4YY

Acknowledgments

One of the themes of this book is that even the most apparently isolated project is ultimately a social and even a collective endeavor. It is therefore a pleasure to be able to acknowledge the social and institutional ties that have shaped this book.

Above all else, this book is the product of the endlessly stimulating conversations that I have been privileged to have had—and to still be having—about modernism, aesthetics, politics, and the history of theory with many brilliant scholars, including (but not limited to) Becky Roach, Kaitlin Staudt, Stephen J. Ross, Kevin Brazil, Ben Etherington, Sean Pryor, Alexis Becker, and Angus Brown. Similarly, Ankhi Mukherjee's brilliant, intellectually generous doctoral supervision and her on-going friendship and mentorship have profoundly shaped my work and my thinking, and have opened new vistas in my research. To these people who have formed me as a scholar and who have helped me to think the thoughts that became this book, I am deeply grateful.

These thoughts have been realized with help from the careful readings granted this book by so many of my peers. I am grateful to Angus, Sean, Alexis, Helen Rydstrand, Baylee Brits, Louise Mayhew, and Paul Sheehan for their attentive, rigorous, and thoughtful readings of individual chapters. Parts of this book were presented at the New Zealand Modernist Studies Consortium, the United States Studies Center's American Cultures Workshop, and the University of New South Wales Centre for Modernist Studies in Australia. The feedback I received at each was enormously valuable, and I am grateful to those who invited me and to those who attended these sessions. I owe particular debts to Jacob Edmond, Erin Carlston, and Thomas Adams for comments that stimulated me to think through or rethink key parts of this project. Ankhi Mukherjee, Jean-Michel Rabaté, Laura Marcus, and Oxford University Press's anonymous readers provided intensive, rigorous, and generous readings of complete manuscripts at different stages. Their advice has profoundly shaped this book. Above all, to Becky and Kait, who read every word, often more than once: thank you. This book is as much yours as it is mine.

The Art of Hunger had its genesis at the University of Oxford, and was drafted while I was employed in the English Departments of the University of Waikato, New Zealand, and Macquarie University, Australia. Much of my thinking about this project has emerged from classroom discussions at all three institutions, and I am grateful to have had supportive colleagues and inspiring students at each. Beyond those already mentioned, I am particularly grateful to Charlotta Salmi, Alice Taylor, Ed Sugden, Julie Taylor, Paulina Kewes, Sarah Shieff, Kirstine Moffatt, Shaynah Jackson, Alex Lodge, Laura Haughey, Stephanie Russo, Louise D'Arcens, and all my students, who made my time at these institutions so conducive to completing this project. Even further back, the initial idea for this project began with my Masters and Honours theses at the University of Sydney, and I remain grateful to Melissa Hardie and Mark Byron for their generous stewardship of these projects and for the formative role they played in my early intellectual development. In my more recent life in Sydney, I owe much to the people who have provided a warm return. Many thanks to those friends in Sydney and elsewhere who cheered me on in the final stages of this book (and before): Robyn Stuart, Nick Garner, Mitali Tyagi, Iyanoosh Reporter, Anya Poukchanski, Emma Dunlop, Rose Vickers, and too many academic friends and colleagues to count— your enthusiasm and support has sustained me.

This book relies on archival research undertaken in the New York Public Library's Berg Collection, the Columbia University Archives, the British Library, and the Harry Ransom Center at the University of Austin at Texas. I am grateful to the archivists and librarians at these institutions, whose expertise has been an enormous help at every stage of this research. Jesus College and the Faculty of English at the University of Oxford, the Faculty of Arts and Social Sciences at the University of Waikato, and the Faculty of Arts at Macquarie University all funded travel that enabled me to undertake this archival research. I am particularly grateful for an Andrew Mellon Foundation Research Fellowship at the Harry Ransom Center, which offered the financial support and intellectual environment that allowed me to undertake the research that forms the basis of Chapter 4. Paul Auster, who generously agreed to meet with me early in this project, has offered support and information that substantially advanced this research.

The initial doctoral research on which this book is based was funded by the Clarendon Trust, an Oxford Australia James Fairfax Award, a Jesus College Old Members' Prize, a Jesus College Graduate Scholarship, and an Overseas Research Award from the UK government. Cornell's School of Criticism and Theory gave me a tuition scholarship, which allowed me to develop my thinking on modernism in relation to the German philosophical tradition, and the University of Trier offered me a summer scholarship, which provided necessary language training for this project. These generous sources of funding made the research that went into this book possible, and I remain deeply indebted to these institutions for that support.

I am grateful to the staff and editors of Oxford University Press, whose labour has brought this book to fruition, and especially to Ellie Collins, without whom this book would never have seen the light of day.

For permission to quote from unpublished materials, I am grateful to Paul Auster; J. M. Coetzee; The Berg Collection of English and American Literature, The New York Public Library, Astor, Lenox and Tilden Foundations; and the Harry Ransom Center, the University of Texas at Austin. Parts of Chapter 2 appeared initially as part of "The *Non-Lieu* of Hunger: Post-War Beckett and the Genealogies of Starvation," in *Samuel Beckett Today/Aujourd'hui*, and I am grateful to Brill for permission to reprint these extracts.

Last and most, thank you to my family: Cath, Evan, Jemma, Lilly, and Rose. You make everything possible.

Contents

Introduction

The Aesthetics of Hunger

Hunger as a metaphor for art is a surprisingly pervasive trope in modernism. Arthur Rimbaud's sonorous, "Ma faim, Anne, Anne" of his 1872 poem "Fêtes de la faim" and the quiet death by starvation of Herman Melville's Bartleby inaugurate this tradition in proto-modernist writing, but the trope resonates in a peculiarly vivid way within—or more accurately, on the margins of—modernism proper. For Norwegian writer Knut Hamsun, it was the key figure of his first semi-autobiographical novel, *Hunger*. For Kafka, it provided one of his most potent metaphors of artisthood in his 1922 short story "A Hunger Artist." The trope was taken up by many of their successors, particularly the Parisian surrealists and the American Lost Generation. In post-war and contemporary literature, the metaphor of writing as a kind of starvation continues to resonate in the works of writers grappling with their relation to modernism, from Samuel Beckett, to Paul Auster, to J. M. Coetzee.

This book argues that this tradition—what I call, following Auster, "the art of hunger"—uses the figure of hunger to dramatize and work through a set of aesthetic problems. More specifically, I argue that the art of hunger emerges as a figure for aesthetic autonomy in crisis; a figure, that is, for aesthetic autonomy that has failed to secure the social consensus that would make autonomy legible. Without this social assent, the link between aesthetic autonomy and freedom—which has long been one of its most pervasive and powerful justifications—disappears. The art of hunger instead imagines the aesthetic as a realm of unfreedom and physical suffering, marked by a refusal to bow to necessity that nonetheless fails to end in liberation. This aesthetic stance negates most familiar justifications for art—it is neither free nor pleasurable, neither politically or morally edifying nor intrinsically satisfying—and in this sense it drama-tizes the loss of social assent by radically assenting to be as unredeemable as art's most vehement critics assume it to be. Nonetheless, from this position of failure and negation, the art of hunger imagines a novel aesthetics that sees the body as the point of mediation between art and society, between necessity and negation. In doing so, it offers a way of thinking art beyond the requirement of freedom, and of testing what an unfree art might be capable of.

The art of hunger is best understood as a fundamentally modernist trope, in the sense that, in its dramatization of aesthetic autonomy, it stages the crisis of one of modernism's signature aesthetic positions. Modernism's association with autonomy has been one of its most controversial characteristics, often fuelling attacks on the writing of this period and on its heirs. Much modernist scholarship since the field's resurgence in the 1990s—work on gender and race, on the middlebrow, on modernism's relationship to media and popular culture, and on its relationship to celebrity and the literary marketplace—has implicitly or explicitly sought to redeem modernism (or to undermine it) by unpicking the apparently inviolable connection between modernism and autonomy, revealing new, less autonomous modernisms and exposing the less autonomous flipside of high modernism.[1] This work has demonstrated the extent to which modernism's association with autonomy has been the result of a narrow canon—often disproportionately European, male, and white—and of a too-hasty willingness to take authors from this canon at their word when they have espoused positions of autonomy. It has shown that modernism was a larger tent than previously assumed, and that the espousal of aesthetic autonomy constituted only a single strand within this complex literary-historical picture. Nonetheless, a more recent wave of scholarship, typified by Andrew Goldstone's *Fictions of Autonomy* and Lisa Siraganian's *Modernism's Other Work*, has sought to swing the pendulum back, reaffirming the centrality of aesthetic autonomy to modernist literature, by arguing that autonomy is less formalist, less apolitical, and less asocial than we have tended to assume. The art of hunger is a modernist practice in the sense that, like the modernist writing examined by Goldstone and Siraganian, it interrogates writing's relationship to autonomy. *The Art of Hunger* seeks to contribute to the revival of interest in modernist autonomy from the besieged and beleaguered position implied by the art of hunger.

While the art of hunger is a modernist trope, its tentacles reach not only back into the nineteenth century but forward to the very end of the twentieth. This book traces the modernist art of hunger's contemporary

---

[1] See, for example, Lawrence Rainey, *Institutions of Modernism: Literary Elites and Public Culture* (New Haven: Yale University Press, 1998); Aaron Jaffe, *Modernism and the Culture of Celebrity* (Cambridge: Cambridge University Press, 2005); Rita Felski, *The Gender of Modernity* (Cambridge, MA: Harvard University Press, 1995); Houston A. Baker Jr, "Modernism and the Harlem Renaissance," *American Quarterly* 39, no. 1 (1989): 84–97.

legacies, focusing primarily on writing between 1945 and 1990, particularly the work of Samuel Beckett, Paul Auster, and J. M. Coetzee. In orienting myself towards the writing of the late twentieth century, I am less interested in arguing that these later writers should be classed as modernist, than in tracing modernism's legacies in more recent writing. Aesthetic autonomy after modernism has a checkered history, retaining much of its earlier prestige in certain circles, but also experiencing a series of profound crises and shocks that challenged its on-going viability as an aesthetic position. Throughout these travails, aesthetic autonomy was consistently understood as a modernist position, and modernism's fate was insistently linked to that of aesthetic autonomy. Modernism as an idea in the late twentieth-century literary imagination was thus intimately bound up with the idea of aesthetic autonomy. When late modernists like Beckett, postmodernists like Auster, and postcolonial writers like Coetzee draw on the art of hunger, they do so in dialogue with its earlier modernist manifestations. This tradition therefore becomes a path by which post-war and contemporary writing negotiates its relationship to modernism, and works through the fate of aesthetic autonomy beyond the modernist era. It offers an alternate version of aesthetic autonomy—less certain of its social position, and less utopian in its claims—that remains more tenable during moments of aesthetic autonomy's most acute crises, as modernist autonomy seems, repeatedly, to enter what feels like its death throes, losing (and then regaining) its prestige without losing its centrality to many writers' conceptualizations of the aesthetic.

1. AESTHETIC AUTONOMY WITHOUT SOCIAL ASSENT

If the art of hunger represents a failure of social assent to aesthetic autonomy, it confronts an immediate objection, in that we do not typically think of aesthetic autonomy as a social phenomenon. While its critics have worried over its apparent irresponsible refusal of the social, however, theorists of aesthetic autonomy have repeatedly emphasized that it relies upon social assent. The communicability of apparently subjective aesthetic judgements—what he calls "common sense"—is a central tenet of Kant's definition of the aesthetic in the *Critique of Judgement*, usually taken as the inaugural document of aesthetic autonomy.[2] In "The Crisis in Culture," Hannah Arendt foregrounds this dimension of Kant's writing,

---

[2] Immanuel Kant, *Critique of Judgement*, ed. Nicholas Walker (Oxford: Oxford University Press, 2007), 68, 69.

arguing that "the ability to see things not only from one's point of view but from the point of view of all those who happen to be present" is central to Kantian aesthetics.[3] Arendt's reading of Kantian judgement shifts his aesthetics somewhat, insisting that it is not the universality of Kantian "common sense" but the more limited, more context-bound assent of "all those who happen to be present" that defines the sociality of aesthetic experience, but they share a conviction that aesthetics requires social assent for its operations.

Pierre Bourdieu, who has traced the emergence of an autonomous literary field in France in the late nineteenth century, makes the most sustained and influential case for aesthetic autonomy as an inherently social phenomenon, arguing that the "society of artists" produces a market that has "the virtue of assuring a form of social recognition for those who otherwise appear (that is, to other groups) as a challenge to common sense."[4] Bourdieu's sociological analysis of this literary field is made possible by his understanding of autonomy as a social category that declares its separation from—even opposition to—the wider society, even as it generates its own social dynamics. His work offers a conceptual framework for more recent analyses of modernist autonomy, such as Andrew Goldstone's reading of it as "a shared social-aesthetic project" in which, he argues, "fictions of autonomy change according to what they seek to be autonomous from."[5] Despite the sometimes fairly dramatic differences in their positions, these theorists all agree that aesthetics in general, and aesthetic autonomy in particular, are inherently social phenomena, and that art can only meaningfully be autonomous if this autonomy is grounded in the community's assent, be that the assent of the presumptively educated bourgeoisie implied by Kant's "common sense" or that of Bourdieu's oppositional "society of artists." Moreover, as both Bourdieu and Goldstone suggest, aesthetic autonomy as we know it today has achieved its most influential and stable social context in the communities and coteries of modernism.

The art of hunger presents a special case of aesthetic autonomy as a social phenomenon, however, because it dramatizes the breakdown of this assent. The authors discussed here experience the loss of the sociality of the aesthetic on two fronts. On the one hand, they confront a public that does not grant the autonomy of the aesthetic. On the other, they

---

[3] Hannah Arendt, *Between Past and Future: Six Exercises in Political Thought* (New York: The Viking Press, 1961), 221.

[4] Pierre Bourdieu, *The Rules of Art: Genesis and Structure of the Literary Field*, trans. Susan Emanuel (Stanford: Stanford University Press, 1995), 58.

[5] Andrew Goldstone, *Fictions of Autonomy: Modernism from Wilde to de Man* (Oxford: Oxford University Press, 2013), 15.

experience art as an intensely isolated and isolating experience, stripped of the alternative social recognition of Bourdieu's "society of artists." I do not mean to confuse this collapse of sociality with earlier understandings of aesthetic autonomy that deny the importance of the social to this concept entirely. With Rita Felski, I agree that, "Art works must be sociable to survive, irrespective of their attitude to 'society'."[6] This book is interested, however, in a tradition whose problematic attitude to "society," and whose sense of society's equally complicated relationship to its authors, pushes its artworks to the limits of their ability to survive (the art of hunger, after all, is a figure for art that approaches death). My work offers a gentle corrective, from the margins, to claims like Lisa Siraganian's insistence that, "Autonomy from the world was never, for the modernists, a failure of relation to it."[7] I argue that, for the tradition of modernism that I examine here, autonomy from the world *did* imply a failure of relation, but that this was neither triumphant nor desired—and did not, whatever the difficulties it threw up, exempt them from seeing autonomous art as a social phenomenon. Instead, the writers I discuss in this book experience their writing's failure of relation to society as a traumatic collapse of context and purpose. The art of hunger is the tradition, I suggest, that seeks to explore the possibilities that remain available for art when a writer's aesthetics entail a collapse of their social context.

One way of understanding this position is to see the art of hunger as the desocialization of the more familiar trope of the starving artist. Bourdieu notes that, "the invention of the pure aesthetic is inseparable from the invention of a new social personality, that of the great professional artist who combines, in a union as fragile as it is improbable, a sense of transgression and freedom from conformity with the rigor of an extremely strict discipline of living and of work, which presupposes bourgeois ease and celibacy."[8] The starving artist typifies this new professional artist, his starvation signifying both prongs of this "personality": starving is simultaneously a form of discipline, as in the practice of fasting; and the visible manifestation of the poverty that signals the artist's refusal to conform to the strictures of the marketplace. He (these artists are always presumptively male) is a familiar figure in modernist self-representation: he is the protagonist of autobiographies from Henry Miller's *Tropic of Cancer* to Ernest Hemingway's *A Moveable Feast*, and appears with enough frequency in surrealist self-mythologization that Mina Loy felt moved to

[6] Rita Felski, *The Limits of Critique* (Chicago: University of Chicago Press, 2015), 166.
[7] Lisa Siraganian, *Modernism's Other Work: The Art Object's Political Life* (Oxford: Oxford University Press, 2012), 4.
[8] Bourdieu, *The Rules of Art*, 111.

satirize it with her novel *Insel*. But all these starving artists, however taciturn and wilfully unpleasant, are embedded within a bohemian social milieu that makes their behavior intelligible as a form of aesthetic practice. Indeed, for many of them, the social is precisely the point: *A Moveable Feast* is above all a portrait of the social world of 1920s expatriate Paris; *Insel* above all the story of a friendship. In these cases, adopting the persona of the starving artist is understood to cement a writer's or artist's position *within* bohemia, rather than to cast them out of it.

The art of hunger that I examine in this book both is and is not part of this starving artist tradition. Like the starving artist, the writers of the art of hunger combine social transgression with intense discipline; they aspire, that is, to become the kind of "social personality" capable of embodying the autonomy of art. But, in an important sense, they fail—fail in part because aesthetic autonomy requires an audience that is not available to them, a society of artists that is neither an uncomprehending mass audience nor the complete absence of an audience. The difference between a figure like Kafka's hunger artist, who ends as a lonely and unrecognized (and dead) failure, and one like Henry Miller or Ernest Hemingway, who is able to leverage his performance of starving autonomy to cement his position within a literary field, is, in large part, one of positioning. Those writers most centrally involved in elaborating the art of hunger—Hamsun, Kafka, and Beckett, for instance—stand persistently at the margins of modernism. Socially, ethnically, geographically, or historically, they are all notably peripheral to the main game of Anglo-American "high modernism," and to the other major modernisms flourishing in Germany and France in the early twentieth century. They sit, like Hamsun, on Europe's underdeveloped edges; like Coetzee, in its "provincial" colonies (and at its extreme historical margins); or, like Kafka, as part of a marginal and displaced minority, writing in another culture's language, producing what Deleuze and Guattari have called his "minor literature."[9] Or, like Beckett and Auster, they are in the right place at the wrong time, writing a second- or third-generation expatriate Parisian modernism, long after the expatriates have all left Paris. On these historical and geographical peripheries, where European modernism's hegemony fizzles out, the autonomous literary field as Bourdieu describes it does not exist to provide the kind of well-developed social milieu that he finds in late nineteenth-century Paris. Out here, aesthetic autonomy is only an aesthetic principle, not a social dynamic. And without the social organization that validates and elucidates the principle, the starving artist is less a

---

[9] Gilles Deleuze and Félix Guattari, *Kafka: Towards a Minor Literature* (Minneapolis: University of Minnesota Press, 1986).

recognizable "social personality" than a choleric old crank, refusing to eat for no reason at all.

These writers, then, are marginal—but not *too* marginal. The canon of hunger artists, at least insofar as hunger functions as a reliable and readable trope for aesthetic autonomy, is an exclusively white male one, and for good reason. As a large body of scholarship has recognized, self-starvation has a long association with women and with femininity. As a result, female hunger artists—Emily Dickinson or Simone Weil would be strong candidates—are inevitably read as participating in a tradition that is deeply invested in the political, social, and religious roles of women.[10] Similarly, poverty became increasingly racialized in many parts of the English-speaking world during the twentieth century, both domestically within countries like the US, the UK, and Australia, and globally as the concept of "world hunger" emerged, foregrounding extreme poverty in regions such as Africa and South Asia. In this context, the starving bodies of people of color developed their own inescapable set of cultural meanings, inscribing them within a narrative that linked poverty to race, as I discuss in the context of South African apartheid in Chapter 4. Because starvation has such strong political and cultural associations for both women and people of color, it is only white men whose starvation can reliably be read as a purely aesthetic gesture, and therefore only white men for whom hunger can reliably function as a trope for autonomy. This caveat ought to remind us that the art of hunger tradition is not exempt from the older criticisms that have been mounted against aesthetic autonomy: that it tends to be a privilege, like other forms of autonomy, reserved for white men, and that its canonization has tended to disproportionately exclude women, people of color, and working-class writers from its ranks.[11] Indeed, it is particularly important to bear in mind the racialized and gendered nature of this tradition as I move, in the pages that follow, to conceptualize its relation to freedom and embodiment.

One of the curious side effects of these writers' combination of white masculinity with a marginal modernism has been to make them sometimes

---

[10] Sandra M. Gilbert and Susan Gubar, *The Madwoman in the Attic: The Woman Writer and the Nineteenth-Century Literary Imagination* (New Haven: Yale University Press, 1979); Sigal Gooldin, "Fasting Women, Living Skeletons and Hunger Artists: Spectacles of Body and Miracles at the Turn of a Century," *Body and Society* 9, no. 2 (2003): 27–53; Walter Vandereycken and Ron van Deth, *From Fasting Saints to Anorexic Girls: The History of Self-Starvation* (London: Athlone Press, 1994).

[11] For a feminist critique of autonomy, see Mary Devereaux, "Autonomy and Its Feminist Critics," in *Encyclopedia of Aesthetics*, ed. Michael Kelly (New York: Oxford University Press, 1998); for a discussion of autonomy's difficult relationship to its racial others, see Simon Gikandi, *Slavery and the Culture of Taste* (Princeton: Princeton University Press, 2011).

appear to critics as towering, isolated geniuses, even as contemporary criticism has theoretically abandoned such affectations. Despite on-going work that seeks to place them in their historical moments, scholarly communities around authors like Beckett and Coetzee continue to read the oppositionality of their aesthetic position as making them into ahistorical figures who somehow transcend their social contexts. One of the claims of this book is that the crisis of aesthetic sociality that is crystallized in the art of hunger is itself a social position, and that the historical, discursive, and social contexts out of which these authors write shape their aesthetics more profoundly than much criticism has acknowledged. This book is interested in how the crises that confront the legacies of modernism in the latter half of the twentieth century place aesthetic autonomy under siege in these new discursive environments. Locating Beckett within the debates around aesthetic autonomy in post-war France, Auster in the intellectual and political foment of post-1968 US and France, and Coetzee in the hyper-politicized literary field of late apartheid South Africa, I argue that each of these authors stakes a claim to autonomy and seeks to affiliate themselves to modernism in literary fields that no longer straightforwardly recognize such claims. They therefore adopt positions that, while oppositional, are best understood within the debates out of which they arise. Moreover, by tracing these debates, I suggest that we get an insight into the travails of aesthetic autonomy itself over the twentieth century, and a sense of the extent to which modernism set the terms for late twentieth-century thinking on art and aesthetics.

2. TASTE AND TASTELESSNESS: AGAINST CULINARY ART

But why turn to hunger to describe this crisis of aesthetic autonomy? Part of the answer, which I explore in more detail in Chapter 1, lies in its capacity to dramatize the less-than-glamorous stakes of being outside the protection of society and its economic arrangements. Another part of the answer is more philosophical. The art of hunger is in key respects the bastard child of German Idealist aesthetics, which invented the concept of aesthetic autonomy through the systematic exclusion of food from the categories of art and beauty. This tradition emerges in opposition to eighteenth-century British taste philosophy, in which the concept of aesthetic taste was initially developed by analogy to literal or bodily taste.[12] Hume, for instance,

---

[12] For a much more detailed account of this philosophical tradition, and its impact on British Romanticism, see Denise Gigante, *Taste: A Literary History* (New Haven: Yale University Press, 2005).

draws upon "the great resemblance between mental and bodily taste" to derive a definition of the all-important "delicacy of imagination" from a story, taken from *Don Quixote*, about the ability of Sancho Panza's relatives to distinguish faint overtones of metal or leather in a barrel of wine.[13] This definition rests on the assumption that aesthetic taste is something like bodily taste applied to a different object. It takes place in the context of a broad assumption that aesthetics is principally a question of sensation—that is, that it is phenomenological and acts on the body.

Kant's *Critique of Judgement*, the foundational document of aesthetic autonomy, represents the decisive break from this tradition, the moment at which food is exiled from the realm of art and beauty. Writing out of and against the British tradition, Kant retains the concept of taste as the faculty by which aesthetic judgements are passed, but draws a bright line between its aesthetic and bodily manifestations.[14] This distinction becomes the foundation upon which Kant builds one of the most distinctive and influential aspects of his theory of aesthetics, that of the disinterestedness of the aesthetic. For Kant, "*Taste* is the faculty of judging an object or a mode of representation by means of a delight or aversion *apart from any interest*. The object of such a delight is called *beautiful*."[15] Kant develops this definition of the aesthetic by arguing that the beautiful is devoid of both sensory interest in the agreeable and conceptual interest in the good. If Hume and other taste philosophers could derive properties of aesthetic taste by exploring its analogy with bodily taste, Kant instead takes eating and physical taste as paradigmatic examples of the agreeable. Thus, Kant uses "a dish that stimulates the sense of taste with spices and other condiments" as his example of that which is agreeable but not good, and illustrates the inherently particular nature of the agreeable by observing that the claim "Canary-wine is agreeable" always implies only, "It is agreeable *to me*."[16] The agreeable—with the pleasures of dining as its principal manifestation—is neither disinterested, nor universal, nor purposive without purpose, nor necessary, failing on each of Kant's four definitions of the beautiful. It stands therefore for everything that he seeks to exclude from the category of the aesthetic, leading him to found the principle of aesthetic autonomy on an opposition between aesthetics and eating.

Kant's repudiation of eating, however, is not an embrace of hunger. For Kant, eating is only one manifestation of the whole realm of bodily

---

[13] David Hume, *Four Dissertations*, Eighteenth Century Collections Online (London: printed for A. Millar, 1757), 216–17.

[14] Kant uses the German term *Geschmack*, which retains the double sense of the English. He makes only one, rather disingenuous, reflection on the derivation of the word in its aesthetic sense, observing that bodily and aesthetic taste both require singular judgements, not derivable from general principles. Kant, *Critique of Judgement*, 114–15.

[15] Ibid., 42.   [16] Ibid., 39–40, 43.

experience and desire that maintains the subject in an interested relation to the physical world. Hunger, another manifestation of bodily interest, is similarly excluded. Indeed, in a rare elision between physical and mental taste, Kant opposes hunger to all kinds of taste, arguing that it removes the faculty of discrimination on which aesthetic taste is founded. As a result, he concludes, "only when people's needs have been satisfied can we tell who among the crowd has taste or not."[17] Hunger in this sense emerges as a paradigm of interest, an experience of investment so strong that it erases everything outside itself. Moreover, its inimicality to either taste or a properly disinterested aesthetic is also, crucially, the mechanism that preserves the class structure of Kant's aesthetic theory, ensuring that the poor, those whose needs have not yet been satisfied, are by definition excluded from entry into the bourgeois realm of Kantian taste.

Kant's formulation of aesthetic autonomy has been enormously influential for post-Kantian philosophers, artists, and audiences, standing at the foundation of discussions of aesthetic autonomy wherever it appears. This influence, however, has frequently carried within it the implicit opposition between eating and aesthetics. Writing in the wake of Kant, aesthetic philosophers have had constant recourse to this trope in their attempts to establish art's autonomy. Where Kant is interested in the subjective processes that allow us to make aesthetic judgements, understood broadly to include not only artistic but also and primarily natural beauty, Hegel's aesthetics shifts the focus to the nature of art itself. For Hegel, art is a particular expression of *Geist* and therefore "has the vocation of revealing *the truth* in the form of sensuous artistic shape."[18] Nonetheless, like Kant, Hegel opposes this truth-embodying sensuous shape to "purely sensuous apprehension," where the latter has much in common with the Kantian category of the agreeable. For Hegel, art is opposed to desire, which he defines as an "appetitive relation to the outer world." Echoing and extending Kant's profession that the aesthetic must be divorced from any interest in an object's actual existence, Hegel emphasizes that, "desire requires for itself not merely the superficial appearance of external things, but themselves in their concrete sensuous existence. Mere pictures of the wood that it wants to use, or of the animals that it wants to eat, would be of no service to desire."[19] Here Hegel draws an explicit distinction between real objects capable of inciting desire and art which, deferring the object's actual existence, also defers its relation to desire.

[17] Ibid., 42.
[18] Georg Wilhelm Friedrich Hegel, *Introductory Lectures on Aesthetics*, ed. Michael Inwood, trans. Bernard Bosanquet (London: Penguin, 1993), 61.
[19] Ibid., 41.

Here, as in Kant, eating returns as one of the key examples of such desire. In fact, as Hegel's editor, Michael Inwood, suggests in his commentary, Hegel's arguments in this section seem "more appropriate to the desire to eat than to e.g. sexual desire," suggesting that Hegel's conception of the desire that he posits as antithetical to art takes the desire for food as its exemplary and informing instance.[20] While for Hegel the determining feature of art is its sensuous embodiment of truth, this sensuousness remains opposed, as in Kant, to bodies that eat or that desire to eat.

Arthur Schopenhauer, Hegel's rival and fellow post-Kantian Idealist, adopts an even stricter and more thoroughgoing view of the separation of art and appetite. For Schopenhauer, the true value of art lies in its suspension of the will, which he sees as the source of all suffering, the desiring property that motivates and corrupts all (phenomenal) existence. Art presents Ideas, which, like the Platonic idea or Kantian thing-in-itself, constitute the true nature of the world, divorced from the impulses of the will. As the bearer of these will-less Ideas, art therefore promises to still the will. The desire to eat, in contrast, is one of the principal manifestations of what Schopenhauer at one point calls the "hungry will," and he makes extensive use of examples drawn from the domain of food and eating to illustrate its malevolent force.[21] In his definition of the charming—a rough analogue to the Kantian agreeable—Schopenhauer extends this exclusion to specifically prohibit the depiction of food in art, singling out Dutch still life painting for "err[ing] by depicting edible objects." This misstep, Schopenhauer suggests, negates their very status as art, for, "By their deceptive appearance these necessarily excite the appetite, and this is just a stimulation of the will which puts an end to any aesthetic contemplation of the object."[22] Schopenhauer, radicalizing the exclusion of eating from the aesthetic, insists that anything that might give rise to even the *thought* of eating compromises proper aesthetic detachment, stirs the will, and thus undermines art's true function.

Despite his firm rejection of hunger that is oriented towards an object, Schopenhauer, alone among the Idealists, reserves an important place for self-starvation. In the fourth book of *The World as Will and as Representation*, Schopenhauer sets out his ethics, which are supposed to achieve what Schopenhauer's aesthetics cannot: a permanent renunciation of the will, in place of the temporary reprieve offered by art. Here, he advocates an asceticism whose aim "is to serve as a constant mortification of the will,

---

[20] Ibid., 126.
[21] Arthur Schopenhauer, *The World as Will and Representation*, trans. E. F. J. Payne, vol. 1 (New York: Dover Publications, 1969), 154.
[22] Ibid., 1:207–8.

so that satisfaction of desires, the sweets of life, may not again stir the will, of which self-knowledge has conceived a horror"—a practice that finds one of its highest expressions in the renunciation of the will to eat.[23] Schopenhauer is, however, careful to keep his embrace of asceticism separate, both structurally and conceptually, from his aesthetic rejection of eating. The reasons for this derive from the Idealists' shared conception of aesthetic autonomy: aesthetics, for Schopenhauer, as for Kant and Hegel, is a purely mental phenomenon. This is the source of its strength as a site for the Kantian play of faculties, Hegelian revelation of truth, and Schopenhauerian suspension of the will. It also means, however, that the price of this autonomy is its exile from the everyday life of either artist or spectator, as well as from the realms of bodily experience and sensation. Art, in such a model, can have as little to do with hunger as with eating, for both are experiences that must be lived out from within a body and both therefore necessarily violate the relegation of the aesthetic to the mental, on which its autonomy is constructed. In this context, the art of hunger might be understood as a calculated misreading or parody of German Idealism's opposition between eating and aesthetics, an attempt to rein-scribe aesthetic autonomy in the material realm from which the Idealists exclude it.

In this sense, Friedrich Nietzsche can be read as an early philosophical precursor to the art of hunger. The German Idealist tradition excludes eating from the realm of art in order to develop a theory of aesthetic autonomy that is not bound to the body. Nietzsche, whose aesthetics tend towards the heteronomous and embodied, develops a counter-metaphor, figuring modern art as a form of starvation. For Nietzsche, the playwrights of late Greek drama are "emaciated epigones," whom he condemns to "Hades so that there you can for once eat your fill on the crumbs of the masters of a previous age."[24] In their humiliating starvation, they are, he claims, the forebears of modern culture, whose "uncanny agitation" is nothing more than "the starving man's craven grasping and snatching for food."[25] For Nietzsche, starvation is a sign of belatedness and derivative-ness, of an excessive reliance on "history and criticism," and of a general-ized cultural enervation. He rejects aesthetic autonomy, and the literary historical and critical traditions that he associates with it, on the grounds of its deleterious effects on the body. While the writers I discuss in this book do not share Nietzsche's skepticism of aesthetic autonomy or his

[23] Ibid., 1:381–2.
[24] Friedrich Nietzsche, *The Birth of Tragedy*, trans. Douglas Smith (Oxford: Oxford University Press, 2000), 62.
[25] Ibid., 123.

repudiation of bodily weakness, they nonetheless carry forward the claim that modern art is undergoing a crisis, linked to its belatedness, and that hunger offers a way of inscribing that belatedness on the body.

Together, these philosophers from Kant to Nietzsche constitute a tradition whose influence on modernist art and aesthetics has been immense. In different ways, each of these thinkers has articulated and pioneered some of modernism's key ideas. Kant's model of autonomous art underpins many modernist theories of aesthetics, while Hegel's claim that modern art had reached or passed a critical endpoint is an early expression of the sense of crisis that pervades modernism. Schopenhauer's alternate articulation of the central importance of art, which places music at its heart, was similarly influential throughout the nineteenth century and beyond, while Nietzsche has frequently been read as one of the great aestheticians of modernism.[26] These philosophers' ideas, and the models of aesthetic autonomy that they embrace (or, in Nietzsche's case, reject), pervade the modernist period and underpin much of its artistic production.[27]

Modernist writers continue to make use of both German Idealism's exclusion of food from the realm of the aesthetic and its coupling of this unconsuming art with the notion of aesthetic autonomy. Examples of the modernist disdain for appetitive art are numerous, and span modernism's stylistic and ideological range. Bertolt Brecht, in one of the most influential formulations of this trope, despairs of "our existing opera" which, he argues, "is a culinary opera... To every object it adopts a hedonistic approach."[28] Henry James similarly dismisses those readers whose aesthetic taste too closely resembles its literal counterpart in "The Art of Fiction," complaining that, "The 'ending' of a novel is, for many persons, like that of a good dinner, a course of dessert and ices, and the artist in fiction is regarded as a sort of meddlesome doctor who forbids agreeable aftertastes."[29] George Orwell reprises the metaphor in *Keep the Aspidistra Flying*, where Gordon Comstock expresses his disgust for the "soggy, half-baked trash" of the popular novel, imagining it as "pudding, suet pudding. Eight hundred slabs

---

[26] On Schopenhauer's influence on modern literature, see David E. Wellbery, *Schopenhauers Bedeutung für die Moderne Literatur* (Munich: Carl Friedrich von Siemens Stiftung, 1998).

[27] Robert Pippin goes further, arguing that Kant was the "first thoroughgoing 'philosophical modernist'" and that the post-Kantian German tradition as a whole is characteristically modernist in its attempts to grapple with the "deepest assumption in modernity's self-understanding (the assertion of autonomy)": Robert B. Pippin, *Modernism as a Philosophical Problem*, 2nd edn (Malden: Blackwell, 1999), 11, 10.

[28] Bertolt Brecht, *Brecht on Theatre: The Development of an Aesthetic*, ed. and trans. John Willett (London: Eyre Methuen, 1964), 35.

[29] Henry James, "The Art of Fiction," in *Norton Anthology of Theory and Criticism*, ed. Vincent B. Leitch, 2nd edn (New York: Norton, 2010), 747.

of pudding walling him in—a vault of puddingstone."[30] Bloomsbury's chief aestheticians, whose aesthetics were strongly influenced by Kantian ideals of disinterest and aesthetic autonomy, were similarly united in their insistence that art and appetite belong to irreconcilable realms. Roger Fry writes dismissively of mass-market novels, "which supply every day their pittance of imagined romantic love to hungry girl clerks and housemaids," while Clive Bell ridicules psychoanalysts by professing that, "if Cézanne was forever painting apples, that had nothing to do with an insatiable appetite for those handsome, but to me unpalatable, fruit."[31] Even Katherine Mansfield, who is on the whole more receptive to food imagery than her male counterparts, complains of "these little predigested books written by authors who have nothing to say."[32]

The modernist scorn for culinary art, like that of the German Idealists, reflects a commitment to aesthetic autonomy. It suggests that art that is too readily consumed is unserious and unaesthetic, and seeks to demarcate a zone of high art, uncontaminated by the temptation of easy pleasures or the desires of the flesh. For these modernists, digestible or "predigested" art, with its "agreeable aftertastes," occupies a position similar to Kant's category of the agreeable and Schopenhauer's of the charming, in that they are all forms of cultural production whose excessive ability to satisfy removes them from the sphere of the aesthetic. The modernists, however, turn this philosophical heritage towards their own concerns, inscribing it within the opposition between modernism and mass culture. As Andreas Huyssen has argued, "Modernism constituted itself through a conscious strategy of exclusion, an anxiety of contamination by its other: an increasingly consuming and engulfing mass culture."[33] Modernists used their disdain for edible, consumable art as one of the key tropes through which they figured this exclusion. Moreover, as Fry's reference to "hungry girl clerks and housemaids" suggests, the modernist scorn for culinary art preserves the gender politics of the modernism/mass culture distinction. As Huyssen has shown, "political, psychological and aesthetic discourse around the turn of the century consistently and obsessively genders mass culture and the masses as feminine, while high culture, whether traditional or modern, clearly remains the privileged realm of male activities."[34]

---

[30] George Orwell, *Keep the Aspidistra Flying* (San Diego: Harcourt, 1956), 4–5.
[31] Roger Fry, *The Artist and Psycho-Analysis* (London: Hogarth Press, 1924), 11; Clive Bell, "Dr. Freud on Art," *The Nation and the Athenaeum* 35 (1924): 690.
[32] Katherine Mansfield, *The Collected Letters of Katherine Mansfield*, ed. Vincent O'Sullivan and Margaret Scott, vol. 5: *1922–23* (Oxford: Oxford University Press, 2008), 225.
[33] Andreas Huyssen, *After the Great Divide: Modernism, Mass Culture, Postmodernism* (Bloomington; Indianapolis: Indiana University Press, 1986), vii.
[34] Ibid., 47.

Within this gendered framework, the girlish treats, superficial pleasures, and domestic labor suggested by the culinary arts perpetuate the modernist contempt for feminized mass culture and preserve an austere and ascetic masculinity as the site of high culture.

The modernist rewriting of culinary art as mass art has had a pervasive influence on twentieth-century theory and criticism. Theorists as different as Hans Robert Jauss and Q. D. Leavis have written against the corrupting influence of "'culinary' or entertainment art" and the "detrimental diet" of bestsellers.[35] No doubt the most influential theoretical formulation of this anti-culinary trope, however, comes from Adorno, in his staunchly anti-populist defense of aesthetic autonomy. For Adorno, mass culture is characterized by its "pre-digested quality... It is baby-food: permanent self-reflection upon the infantile compulsion towards the repetition of needs which it creates in the first place."[36] Because it offers no roughage, no resistance, mass culture has an infantalizing effect on its audiences. It limits their ability to "digest" things for themselves, their ability to analyze and confront new texts. In this context, Adorno argues, art is the antidote to the passive consumption promoted by capitalism and symbolized by the too-easily digested. Following Kant, who, he argues, "snatched art away from that avaricious philistinism that always wants to touch it and taste it," Adorno elaborates an anti-capitalist aesthetic autonomy.[37] For Adorno, art's difficulty is key to its ability to hold off the voracious hordes: "the absorption of resistant material and themes opposes the culinary consumption of art even if, given the general ideological tendency to integrate everything that resists integration, consumption undertakes to swallow everything up whole, however repulsive it might seem."[38] Adorno combines elements of Kantian autonomy with the new modernist privileging of art's unfamiliarity or difficulty, in order to revise both traditions from a Marxist perspective. Eliding the difference between the consumption of food and capitalist consumption, he uses the trope of anti-culinary art to figure art's critical stance towards capitalist commodity culture at large.

---

[35] Hans Robert Jauss, *Toward an Aesthetic of Reception*, trans. Timothy Bahti (Brighton: Harvester Press, 1982), 25; Q. D. Leavis, *Fiction and the Reading Public* (London: Chatto and Windus, 1939), 54.

[36] Theodor Adorno, *The Culture Industry: Selected Essays on Mass Culture*, ed. J. M. Bernstein (London: Routledge, 1991), 67.

[37] Theodor Adorno, *Aesthetic Theory*, ed. Gretel Adorno and Rolf Tiedemann, trans. Robert Hullot-Kentor (London: Continuum, 1997), 12.

[38] Ibid., 121.

The conceptual link between hunger and aesthetic autonomy that is the subject of this book comes out of this philosophical tradition. Pitting autonomous art against culinary art, and aesthetic autonomy against the pleasures of a good meal, the philosophers and critics traced above pave the way to imagine hunger as the natural mode of aesthetic autonomy. When Adorno declares that, "the bourgeoisie want art voluptuous and life ascetic; the reverse would be better," or when Nietzsche imagines the modern artist as "eternally hungry," they suggest that hunger and asceticism lie at the heart of the modern and modernist understanding of art.[39] The art of hunger might be understood as an attempt to take this conceptualization of aesthetic autonomy both seriously and literally. Like the philosophers traced above, the writers in this tradition are committed to aesthetic autonomy. This attachment leads them to pit high art against the pleasures of mass culture, and to imagine art as, in its essence, an unsatisfying and difficult undertaking. They do so, however, by translating aesthetic autonomy back into the realm of the body, thus seeking to dramatize an art that, contra Kant and his post-Kantian friends, suffers through its own embodiment.

The aesthetic autonomy that emerges from the tradition outlined above is in many respects a different beast to the Bourdieusian notion of autonomy with which I began. While Bourdieu conceives of autonomy as a social phenomenon, in which a literary field establishes its social position by opposing itself to the commercial demands of popular and mass art, the tradition I trace here is a philosophical one. It is committed to an ideal of autonomy that is an intrinsic property, not of a literary field, but of art or aesthetic appreciation as such. The art of hunger, as an art that stages the loss of aesthetic autonomy's social context, relies upon this less contextually bound understanding of autonomy for its viability. In various ways, all the authors I discuss in these pages write themselves into the tradition above, using it, and the tradition of the art of hunger itself, as an *ersatz* literary field, an alternate context in which aesthetic autonomy can find its guarantor. Autonomy for these writers, therefore, is both a social condition, as Bourdieu claims, *and* a particular philosophical idea about the nature of literature. Indeed, the crisis of autonomy that I am associating with the art of hunger is the direct result of the disjuncture between the idea of autonomy traced above and its social milieu. The art of hunger, that is, is a position that dramatizes the painful failure of these different modes of autonomy to coincide, through the isolated, victimized, and spectacular body of the autonomous artist.

---

[39] Ibid., 16; Nietzsche, *The Birth of Tragedy*, 4.

3. THE ART OF HUNGER IS AN UNFREE ART

The attempt to persevere with an autonomous art in a social environment where aesthetic autonomy is disputed or disparaged throws into question its capacity to produce freedom. To strip aesthetic autonomy of its association with freedom, however, is a strange and difficult move, cutting against almost every extant defense of the concept. As Stephen Best and Sharon Marcus have observed, "many of our most powerful critical models see criticism as a practice of freedom by locating autonomy, self-reflexiveness, detachment and liberatory potential either in the artwork itself or in the valiant labor of the critic."[40] Aesthetic autonomy is a particularly influential instance of this association between criticism and liberation, and has been theorized from its inception as a practice of freedom. Kant's characterization of aesthetic judgement as the "free play" of the faculties opens the way for this association, and it is brought into an early political formulation in Friedrich Schiller's 1794 treatise *On the Aesthetic Education of Man*, which argues that "To bestow freedom by means of freedom is the fundamental law" of what he calls the "aesthetic State."[41]

This association between aesthetic autonomy and freedom persists into more recent accounts, and across remarkably different political ideologies. It is foundational to Jacques Rancière's work on aesthetics, which maintains that, "The scenario depicted by aesthetic revolution is one that proposes to transform aesthetics' suspension of the relations of domination into the generative principle for world without domination."[42] In her book, Lisa Siraganian makes a liberal version of this claim, arguing that, "The freedom of the art object not from the world generally but from the reader's meaning specifically presents a way to imagine an individual's complicated liberty within yet enduring connection to the state."[43] Nicholas Brown, in Marxist terms, argues that in the contemporary not only is "the assertion of aesthetic autonomy . . . in itself, a political position," but that "a plausible claim to autonomy is in fact the precondition for any politics at all."[44] Even Adorno, whose aesthetics, grounded in

[40] Stephen Best and Sharon Marcus, "Surface Reading: An Introduction," *Representations*, no. 108 (2009): 13.

[41] Friedrich Schiller, *On the Aesthetic Education of Man, In a Series of Letters*, ed. and trans. Elizabeth M. Wilkinson and L. A. Willoughby (Oxford: Oxford University Press, 1982), 215.

[42] Jacques Rancière, *Aesthetics and Its Discontents*, trans. Steven Corcoran (Cambridge: Polity Press, 2009), 36–7.

[43] Siraganian, *Modernism's Other Work*, 4.

[44] Nicholas Brown, "The Work of Art in the Age of Its Real Subsumption under Capital," *Nonsite.org*, March 13, 2012.

writers like Kafka and Beckett, steers closest to the art of hunger, and who insists on "the unfreedom in all art," nonetheless ultimately sees art as pointing, however darkly, to a kind of freedom beyond—"By their negativity, even as total negation, artworks make a promise"—in which their autonomy allows them a limited critical distance from the relentless unfreedom of contemporary society.[45]

The writers I discuss in this book forcefully undercut this connection between aesthetic autonomy and freedom, portraying their art as unfree and unchosen. For some of the writers of the art of hunger, this lack of freedom takes the form of a literal loss of liberty: Bartleby starves to death in jail; Kafka's hunger artist spends the story living in a succession of cages. For others, it is signaled by an ending that purports to introduce real freedom, in contrast to the unfreedom of the art of hunger: Hamsun's narrator finishes *Hunger* by signing on as crew on a ship, liberating himself from starvation and writing in one fell swoop; Rimbaud provides the real counterpart to Hamsun's fictionalized account, famously giving up poetry for life as a French colonialist. In her book *The Hunger Artists*, Maud Ellmann posits a connection between starving, writing, and imprisonment, arguing that, "Writing and fasting both attempt to rise above the flesh in order to escape its mortal bounds."[46] While the writers of my study are deeply invested in this connection between writing and fasting, however, they imagine it to be of a piece with the loss of freedom, not the path out of it.

Despite the prevalence of prisons and cages in these texts, the art of hunger's unfreedom is not the denial of freedom by the state or by society at large. It does not participate in the tradition of critique that has driven symptomatic readings of literature as a record of oppression. The art of hunger, while not an art of freedom, is also not an art of oppression. Instead, it is troubled by the negotiations aesthetics makes with necessity, and by the constant failure to achieve what political philosophers call "positive liberty"—that is, the freedom of self-actualization.[47] The ambivalence around the artist's will, typified in Bartleby's famous slogan "I would prefer not to," is characteristic of the art of hunger. Neither involuntarily imposed on the artist by external forces, nor freely chosen by the artist himself, it forces us to think about art beyond the binary of freedom and oppression.

[45] Adorno, *Aesthetic Theory*, 18, 135.

[46] Maud Ellmann, *The Hunger Artists: Starving, Writing and Imprisonment* (London: Virago Press, 1993), 92.

[47] For the foundational articulation of this idea, see Isaiah Berlin, *Liberty, Incoporating Four Essays on Liberty*, ed. Henry Hardy (Oxford: Oxford University Press, 2002), 166–217.

The chief—and, to many readers, no doubt the most disturbing—consequence of this claim is that these writers deny themselves not only the occasion to read art as free, but also the possibility that that allows to turn aesthetic autonomy into a political act. The art of hunger, that is, stages the unthinkability of politics outside of society. This claim would not come as a surprise to most of the theorists who seek to link aesthetic autonomy to freedom. For writers as different as Rancière, Siraganian, and Brown, the politics of aesthetic autonomy is grounded in the ways in which it models an ideal social world, or in which autonomy itself can be understood as a (sometimes minimally or oppositionally) social act. Nonetheless, it is not uncommon to read many of the writers discussed in the pages that follow—perhaps most commonly, to read Kafka, Coetzee, and Melville's Bartleby—as figures for or writers of a utopian (or at least a progressive) politics. At least in the texts I discuss, such a reading would require the construction of an asocial, anti-social, or extra-social politics, something that, as I argue in Chapters 1 and 4, is neither supported by the texts nor a sound political strategy. As Bruno Latour has argued, "emancipation . . . does not mean 'freed from bonds,' but *well*-attached."[48] The art of hunger provides a negative demonstration of this claim, showing the unfreedom that arises in the absence of social bonds.

To claim that the art of hunger does not provide a political model or depict a sound political goal is not, however, to suggest that it is devoid of political implications, although the nature of these implications shifts over the period under consideration in this monograph. For the hunger artists writing in the modernist period (and, in a different register, for people like Brown in the twenty-first century), the unfreedom of art manifests primarily in the tension between autonomy and the market. If refusing the market is what makes art art, the art of hunger nonetheless suggests that it does not make art or the artist free. On the contrary, if turning away from the market ends in starvation (as well it might for the writer who is not independently wealthy), this refusal simply reveals the artist's subjugation to the more basic and banal necessities of life: food, and an income to buy it with. The art of hunger, and the associated figure of the starving artist, therefore represent not autonomy as freedom, but the double bind produced by aesthetic autonomy's disavowal of the necessities of life. As the twentieth century wore on, doubts about the viability of aesthetic autonomy as a position from which to write were joined by waves of criticism that argued that aesthetic autonomy was not only financially unviable, but also irresponsible, neglecting the political responsibilities of the writer to

---

[48] Bruno Latour, *Reassembling the Social: An Introduction to Actor-Network-Theory* (Oxford: Oxford University Press, 2005), 218.

produce engaged, socially relevant art. In these new contexts, the art of hunger's ambivalence over the question of freedom starts to look like an advantage to defenders of autonomy, allowing authors to resist the linking of art to the cause of freedom, without becoming complicit in oppression.

Instead of imagining art as a practice of freedom, the art of hunger offers up the spectacle of the starving, suffering body. Indeed, if these writers offer an affirmative definition of what their aesthetics might look like, it lies in the primacy of the body itself. Put this way, the art of hunger is an attempt to think through the tension between embodiment and aesthetic autonomy—which has been imagined, since Kant, as a largely disembodied practice. The writers of the art of hunger put this distinction into question, by imagining the struggle to achieve aesthetic autonomy as one that plays out on the body of the artist, his body suffering and finally dying in the approach towards autonomy. Its impossibility and its failure lies in the attempt to reconcile these irreconcilable terms, in the recognition that the only fully autonomous body—autonomous even from food itself—is a dead body. In a sense, then, the art of hunger represents the violent return of the old eighteenth-century connection between aesthetics and the sensuous, translated in modernism into a radically new affective register that sees art not as pleasure but as suffering. Where Lisa Siraganian's study of autonomy could take the breath as its animating trope, implying that art is life, the writers studied here take a much grimmer view of autonomy: for these writers, the art of hunger is the figure for aesthetic autonomy in its death throes.

In their emphasis on the materiality of the starving body, the authors I discuss in this book imagine hunger in quite unusual terms. Theorists of self-starvation such as Maud Elllmann and Leslie Heywood are united in seeing hunger as a form of disembodiment, a process whereby the body is subjugated to mind, spirit, language, or will.[49] There is a reciprocity in this exchange that has something of the ascetic about it, in Geoffrey Harpham's "loose sense" of the term: "any act of self-denial undertaken as a strategy of empowerment or gratification."[50] Indeed, acts of self-starvation are necessarily read against a cultural background in which asceticism, as Harpham's book shows, has a pervasive, structuring influence. Nonetheless, the authors in my study cast doubt both on the viability of the term "self-denial," in a context where characters are

---

[49] Ellmann, *Hunger Artists*, 4; Leslie Heywood, *Dedication to Hunger: The Anorexic Aesthetic in Modern Culture* (Berkeley: University of California Press, 1996), xii.

[50] Geoffrey Galt Harpham, *The Ascetic Imperative in Culture and Criticism* (Chicago: University of Chicago Press, 1987), xiii.

curiously deprived of will; and on the feasibility of transcendence, be it religious, linguistic, or rational. The art of hunger instead offers a model of asceticism stripped of its emancipatory power and of any possibility of disembodiment, a process that Sloterdijk identifies with the modern "despiritualization of asceticisms."[51] Where an aesthetic asceticism would hold starvation and art in a reciprocal relationship, such that the more one starves, the more capable one is of achieving the higher states necessary for art, these writers strive instead to collapse that distance, to produce an art that is identical with the act of starvation. Substituting embodiment for disembodiment and immanence for transcendence, these writers retain the forms of practice associated with asceticism but strip it of asceticism's emancipatory power, imagining the body instead as the final frontier of necessity and human finiteness.

By replacing the disembodiment of asceticism and post-Kantian aesthetics with a more embodied, materialist art, the art of hunger reflects a historical shift in the conceptualization of the body. As Vanita Seth has shown, the "Classical age" of the seventeenth and eighteenth centuries believed that "human corporeality was detached from Man's more exalted status as a knowing, reasoning, free-willed subject."[52] In this context, "the significance of the body was essentially disavowed," in favour of a focus on the self-determining human subject.[53] Kantian and post-Kantian thought, emerging at the tail end of this period, reflects the disavowal of the body in its attempt to produce a disembodied aesthetics that belongs exclusively to the mental realm. Its rejection of food and eating therefore takes place as part of a larger devaluation of the body, and an attempt to develop a dualistic subjectivity in which imagination, not the body, served as the telos of the subject.

The nineteenth century saw a significant shift in the way the body was imagined. Like the Classical Age, the nineteenth century saw the body as an object, devoid of agency, but in this later period it was now "accorded an immutability and intransigence that is resistant to the inconstancy and variability of time."[54] The body, that is, ceases to be pliable and malleable, subject to the whims of the free Enlightenment subject, and instead becomes understood as one of the chief limits to human potential. While this historical shift is clearly discontinuous, with both asceticism and a disembodied post-Kantian aesthetics retaining much of their purchase

---

[51] Peter Sloterdijk, *You Must Change Your Life: On Anthropotechnics*, trans. Wieland Hoban (Cambridge: Polity Press, 2013), 61.
[52] Vanita Seth, *Europe's Indians: Producing Racial Difference, 1500–1900* (Durham, NC: Duke University Press, 2010), 199.
[53] Ibid., 204.   [54] Ibid., 175.

today, the nineteenth century nonetheless makes available a counter-discourse. This new worldview imagines the body as a fixed and immovable limit, just at the moment when the art of hunger is first beginning to emerge as a way of dramatizing a new aesthetic position.

A new attention to hunger stands at the center of this re-evaluation of the body. T. R. Malthus's wildly influential *Essay on the Principle of Human Population* (1798), for instance, locates human misery in "the constant tendency in all animated life to increase beyond the nourishment prepared for it"—that is, in the incommensurability between human reproduction and our need to eat.[55] Such an account produces a vision of the human body as what Seth calls an "untranscendable, immutable object," by imagining hunger as one of its chief limitations.[56] This way of understanding hunger as a limiting factor runs counter to the ascetic imaginary, in which self-starvation and other practices of bodily mortification are thought to allow us to transcend the limitations of our bodies. In the Malthusian framework, bodily suffering does not do away with the body, so much as it foregrounds the body's inescapability, its insistent materiality, and its untranscendability. As Catherine Gallagher has shown, Malthusian ideas, via the intermediary text of James Frazer's *The Golden Bough*, shaped important aspects of modernism in general.[57] This book argues that the theory of the body that such ideas produced is particularly important in the modernist writing associated with the art of hunger, with its skepticism about transcendence and its tendency to use starvation to magnify rather than reduce the role of the body.

This newly limited and limiting conceptualization of the body shapes the aesthetic possibilities of the art of hunger in crucial ways. On the one hand, the nineteenth-century body is a perversely appropriate site on which to inscribe aesthetic autonomy. This theory of the body sees it as providing "constancy and temporal immutability," a welcome counter, in the Victorian mind, to the inescapable historicity of most other aspects of human experience.[58] The body is no longer subject to history, but is now imagined as the limit that history butts up against. In this sense, it shares aesthetic autonomy's resistance to the vagaries of historical, social, and political experience. If the body is a transhistorical phenomenon, marked by its intransigent immutability, then the art of hunger—an aesthetic

---

[55] T. R. Malthus, *An Essay on the Principle of Population, Or, A View of Its Past and Present Effects on Human Happiness; with an Inquiry into the Prospects Respecting the Future Removal or Mitigation of the Evils Which It Occasions* (London: J. Johnson, 1803), 2.

[56] Seth, *Europe's Indians*, 211.

[57] Catherine Gallagher, *The Body Economic: Life, Death, and Sensation in Political Economy and the Victorian Novel* (Princeton: Princeton University Press, 2006), 170.

[58] Seth, *Europe's Indians*, 217.

position grounded in this recalcitrant body—can be understood as the translation of aesthetic autonomy's resistance to historical change into the sphere of material, embodied existence. Instead of locating art's autonomy in the free play of the mind, the art of hunger finds it instead in the historical intransigence of the body.

On the other hand, though, this preservation of aesthetic autonomy carries with it the aesthetic problems that I have already associated with the art of hunger. Imagining aesthetic autonomy as manifesting through an intransigent body creates problems for art's relationship to society. As Catherine Gallagher has argued, "Malthus's theory destroyed the homological relationship between individual and social organisms by tracing social problems to human vitality itself."[59] The art of hunger—despite being entirely uninterested in human vitality—develops in a moment in which the body's status as a synecdoche for society is under pressure. In this context, the starving body becomes available as a spectacle of individual and idiosyncratic failures, and of failures that are marked primarily through the exclusion of the body's bearer from the realm of the social. For this reason, as I have argued, the art of hunger is able to make use of the spectacle of starving bodies to dramatize the experience of espousing an aesthetic position—the position of aesthetic autonomy—which fails to achieve social assent.

Dramatizing the collapse of social autonomy through this newly intransigent body, the art of hunger also makes the body into one of the causes of its unfreedom. If the Classical Age saw the body as mutable, pliable and subject to human agency, it did so in order to guarantee the freedom and free will of the subject. The revision of the body that made it immutable and intransigent therefore also posited it as one of the most important limits to human freedom. By figuring aesthetic autonomy through the untranscendable and unfree body, the writers of the art of hunger strip this post-Kantian position of all possibility of freedom. They equate the aesthetic—long imagined to be a site of freedom—with the body that poses a limit to freedom, and in doing so, they produce a theory of art that sees it as autonomous but not free.

The disavowal of art's capacity to produce freedom, and of its political efficacy more broadly, makes the art of hunger into a singularly unheroic aesthetic position. Walter Benjamin's claim that "To do justice to the figure of Kafka in its purity and its peculiar beauty one must never lose sight of one thing: it is the purity and beauty of a failure" holds true for all

---

[59] Catherine Gallagher, "The Body Versus the Social Body in the Works of Thomas Malthus and Henry Mayhew," *Representations* 14 (1986): 84.

the writers of this study.[60] The art of hunger is an art of failure, as we often say of Beckett, and an art of the impossible, as Yves Bonnefoy has said of Rimbaud.[61] It reflects the failure both of collectivist models of liberty, such as most Marxist accounts, as well as of individualist models, such as those commonly found in liberalism. If the writers of the art of hunger do not find freedom in social bonds, they also cannot find it in themselves, as art is experienced as a state that is unchosen and unwilled. In this sense, the art of hunger fails, it lacks the possibility of freedom, because it imagines art as a solitary activity in which the artist exercises only the most limited agency, and an agency that is almost always negative.

4. HISTORIES OF AUTONOMY: MODERNISM AND METHOD

The lineages I have traced here see the art of hunger as emerging from a specific intellectual history, the confluence of shifting understandings of the body in the nineteenth century with a long tradition of aesthetics that defines art's autonomy through its exclusion of food. Both of these historical trajectories culminate in the modernist period, which is marked by a fascination with the materiality of the body and a commitment to practices of aesthetic autonomy. In this sense, I have been suggesting, the art of hunger is a modernist tradition. In the light of the long time span of this concept, however—both its pre-history in eighteenth- and nineteenth-century thought, and its afterlife in post-1945 literature—it is worth paying a little more attention to what I mean here by the term modernist, and how I see it relating to the conglomerate of ideas I call the art of hunger.

This book is interested above all in modernism as a retrospective construct. In tracing this formation, it offers a partial intellectual history of the intertwined fates of aesthetic autonomy and modernism in the second half of the twentieth century. More specifically, it is a history of how modernism came to be understood as the literary mode of aesthetic autonomy. I focus particularly on three moments—France in the aftermath of World War II; the US and France in the wake of the 1968 student protests; and South Africa in the dying days of apartheid—when this version of modernist autonomy was least secure in its position in the literary field. This is not to suggest a straightforward or linear trajectory for

[60] Walter Benjamin, *Illuminations: Essays and Reflections*, ed. Hannah Arendt, trans. Harry Zohn (New York: Schocken Books, 1968), 144–5.
[61] Yves Bonnefoy, *Rimbaud par lui-même* (Paris: Éditions du Seuil, 1951), 169–78.

the fates of either modernism or aesthetic autonomy. On the contrary, there are as many times and places since modernism that have resoundingly endorsed a theory of aesthetic autonomy as there are those that have denigrated or attacked it. My claim is not that aesthetic autonomy or even modernism entered a uniform decline in the years after World War II, but that, in specific moments and at specific places, both came to seem illegitimate, precarious, or simply unpopular. The history of modernism as a retrospective construct and as a specter haunting contemporary writing has its roots at least as much in the moments of its delegitimization as it does in the moments of its canonization. In tracing some of the most momentous blows to modernism's hegemony in the post-World War II period, I therefore seek to provide a history of what has become today the commonplace association between aesthetic autonomy and modernism.

The art of hunger is part of this historical arc in that, like modernism itself, it is a retrospective construction. Unlike the post-World War II writers who form the focus of the better part of this book, the modernist hunger artists that I discuss in Chapter 1 did not know each other and can only peripherally be said to have influenced each other's work. They come from significantly different historical times and geographic places. Several of them—Melville and Rimbaud, most importantly—are not even usually considered modernist, although they share something that we are tempted to call a modernist sensibility and, like the tradition of aesthetic autonomy, are widely acknowledged to have left major and lasting impacts on modernism. In this unlikely context, what makes these writers modernist—and what makes them a tradition—is their reception from the 1930s through to the present. Scholars and writers, centrally among them writers like Paul Auster and J. M. Coetzee, have tended to read them together, and to read them, in this context, as modernist. Through these readings, later writers have produced the art of hunger as a kind of modernism of the last resort—a marginal, precarious tradition, which can both dramatize the sense of crisis that attends modernism and aesthetic autonomy in the historical moments I consider, and provide a way of imagining the persistence of both traditions. In this sense, the way in which the earlier writers come into focus as a modernist tradition—as the art of hunger—is a product of the way in which modernism and its canons have been constructed from late modernism onwards.

In understanding modernism as a retrospective construct that circulates as both a product of and participant in contemporary literary discourse, we might learn something from the way scholars of the Middle Ages have theorized the concept of medievalism. As recent work on the topic has shown, the Middle Ages persist into the modern period as a syncretic concept that is as much a construction of the present as an excavation of the past. As Louise D'Arcens argues, "the 'found' and the 'made' Middle Ages...cohabit" in many medievalist texts, producing a notion of the medieval that arises from the interplay between presentist preconceptions and historical texts and artefacts.[62] A similar claim could be made for the role of modernism in the contemporary academy and within the contemporary high art and literary worlds. In these contexts, modernism persists both as a set of actually existing texts and artefacts, and as a concept that conditions our readings as much as it is conditioned by them. I am suggesting, therefore, that modernism as it appears in this monograph has more in common with medievalism than with the study of the medieval period per se. This constructed modernism is the subject of this book and the referent of the "modernism" of my title.

This way of thinking about modernism's contemporary legacies takes its impetus from recent attempts to rethink historicism's role in literary criticism more broadly. In her recent polemic on the state of literary studies, Rita Felski calls for us to abandon models of historicism that "serve as the equivalent of cultural relativism, quarantining difference, denying relatedness, and suspending—or less kindly, evading—the question of why past texts matter and how they speak to us now."[63] Instead, she advocates for attention to "cross-temporal networks" that "mess up the tidiness of our periodizing schemes," asking "us to acknowledge affinity and proximity as well as difference, to grapple with the coevalness and connectedness of past and present."[64] This book takes up this challenge, seeking to understand what modernism has meant to writers in the second half of the twentieth century by tracing the circulation of an idea that, in many contexts, comes to define modernism—the idea of aesthetic autonomy. In this sense, I am less interested in what aesthetic autonomy "really" meant in the modernist period, or what the art of hunger "really" looked like from the vantage point of 1922 or 1890, than I am in how these ideas have been constructed and produced in the latter half of the twentieth century. I argue that the art of hunger offers post-war and contemporary writers a way of thinking with and through modernism and its texts, in order to approach pressing questions about the status and function of the aesthetic in their own historical moments.

The attempt to trace modernism's circulation beyond its period of origin has required a rather historicist approach to the moments of its reception. As a result, there is a methodological bifurcation at the center of

---

[62] Louise D'Arcens, "Introduction: Medievalism: Scope and Complexity," in *The Cambridge Companion to Medievalism*, ed. Louise D'Arcens (Cambridge: Cambridge University Press, 2016), 5.

[63] Felski, *The Limits of Critique*, 156.   [64] Ibid., 159.

this book. Chapter 1, which focuses on the art of hunger as it emerged in modernism, operates according to a logic of retrospectivity. In this chapter, I seek to derive a theory of the modernist art of hunger from its key texts, focusing not only on the moments of production but also on their circulation and reception, and asking what reading these disparate but thematically linked texts together tells us about the intellectual coherence and aesthetic stakes of the art of hunger, understood as a tradition and an aesthetic position. Chapters 2–4 each follow a single exemplary practitioner of the art of hunger—Beckett, Auster, and Coetzee respectively—and seek to locate his deployment of the art of hunger as a response to larger debates about modernism and aesthetic autonomy in his respective literary field. The goal in these chapters is to understand the ways in which modernism in general and the art of hunger in particular persist as sites and occasions for the contestation of ideas about aesthetic autonomy, by developing a richly textured sense of the historical debates that condition the re-emergence of the art of hunger at specific historical junctures.

Taken together, the book as a whole seeks to trace how modernism's relationship to aesthetic autonomy, and with it the minor modernism of the art of hunger, have emerged as transhistorical and transnational phenomena. I am interested in how these ideas, texts, and tropes circulate across different historical moments: how they become new in new times and accumulate meaning through their different iterations, as well as how they are retrospectively gathered together, written and rewritten to constitute a tradition. Here, my dual definition of aesthetic autonomy as both a social condition and a philosophical idea becomes important. By emphasizing its double-edged nature, I'm able to understand autonomy's persistence diachronically. I see earlier social milieus as producing particular forms and definitions of aesthetic autonomy, which are then reprised not as history but as theory, to be contested or debated anew in new times. As such, I read autonomy as both an idea that circulates transnationally with the spread of modernism and a condition of a social milieu, and understand its specific manifestations to arise in part from the disjunctures and the departures between these different understandings of autonomy. In this transhistorical frame, aesthetic autonomy's pre-existing value as an aesthetic ideal serves to reinforce and bolster writers in later periods where autonomy is newly contested or delegitimized, even as the forms that aesthetic autonomy adopts to survive these perilous moments condition future understandings of the term.

This retrospective model of modernism's relationship to contemporary literature breaks with some of the more influential frameworks for understanding modernism's dissemination and transmission beyond early twentieth-century Europe and the US. While these frameworks have often partaken of the expansive movement that Douglas Mao and Rebecca Walkowitz identify with the "new modernist studies," this book is not primarily concerned with expanding modernism's definitional scope, or with reconceiving contemporary literature as modernist.[65] My model should, therefore, be distinguished from most theories of global modernism, including Susan Stanford Friedman's attempt to develop a theory of planetary modernisms by conceiving of modernism as "the *expressive dimension of modernity*."[66] This definition has allowed Friedman to expand modernism's scope temporally as well as spatially and thus in theory allows us to redefine much contemporary literature as modernist. But Friedman's approach—in common with other more modest theories of global modernism—understands the new modernisms that she uncovers as existing in a primary relation to modernity. Indeed, such a claim is often taken as necessary to avoid the specter of derivativeness that haunts the global modernism project. The post-war and contemporary writers and milieus that I consider in this book, however, are primarily concerned with their relationship to earlier iterations of modernism. They therefore constitute precisely the kind of second-order, derivative modernism that theorists of global modernism mostly repudiate. In this book, I investigate how a primarily European modernism has been constructed and deployed by scholars and writers who understood themselves to be writing *after* modernism, in all senses of the word.

For this reason, this book's understanding of modernism's role in post-war and contemporary writing has more in common with David James and Urmila Seshagiri's concept of metamodernism than with existing theories of global modernism. Like James and Seshagiri's twenty-first-century metamodernists, the late twentieth-century writers that I examine in Chapters 2–4 relate to modernism as "an era, an aesthetic, and an archive that originated in the late nineteenth and early twentieth centuries."[67] Modernism returns in this model not as a straightforward continuity of the past into the present, but as an imagined construction, a "mythos" that allows contemporary writers to work through new issues.[68] These writers make use of modernism, that is, as a kind of resource. As James has it in his book *Modernist Futures*, their "modes of working resonate with priorities that they don't

---

[65] Douglas Mao and Rebecca L. Walkowitz, "The New Modernist Studies," *PMLA* 123, no. 3 (2008): 737–48.

[66] Susan Stanford Friedman, "Periodizing Modernism: Postcolonial Modernities and the Space/Time Borders of Modernist Studies," *Modernism/Modernity* 13, no. 3 (2006): 432. Emphasis in original.

[67] David James and Urmila Seshagiri, "Metamodernism: Narratives of Continuity and Revolution," *PMLA* 129, no. 1 (2014): 88.

[68] Ibid., 87.

passively inherit from modernism, like period-souvenirs, but that revitalize modernist aesthetics for tackling a new spectrum of artistic, cultural, ethical and political demands."[69] The focus in this model is on the revitalization of modernist resources—what James calls "modernist aesthetics"—in new contexts. It foregrounds the ways in which modernism, returning *beyond* its historical moment, is recontextualized and redeployed, coming to reflect the concerns of the new moments in which it is taken up again.

With its focus on literature written between 1945 and 1990, *The Art of Hunger* is concerned with modernism's return in a slightly earlier period than many studies of modernism's contemporary revival. James and Seshagiri apply the term "metamodernist" to a primarily twenty-first-century body of work, which they see as reacting against an earlier postmodernism.[70] Similarly, writers including Nicholas Brown, and Michael D'Arcy and Mathias Nilges have claimed that contemporary literature represents a break with postmodernism and a return to modernism, including what D'Arcy and Nilges call "the modernist question of aesthetic autonomy."[71] *The Art of Hunger* is concerned, in contrast, with what intervenes in the period between modernism proper and this current juncture, and with how modernism and aesthetic autonomy survived the moments in the intervening period in which neither was securely in the cultural ascendant. In this sense, this book might be understood as an attempt to map the space between modernism and its contemporary returns, tracing out a more embattled history in the in-between periods, in which modernism and modernist ideas of aesthetic autonomy persisted in hostile environments. Understanding these lulls in modernism's popularity is important for a full sense of its influence on, and construction by, later writing, and, I suggest, it offers a new way of understanding its relationship to the literary developments of the latter half of the twentieth century. This book traces modernism's role in periods that we ordinarily think of as late modernist (Chapter 2), postmodern (Chapter 3), and postcolonial (Chapter 4). In each, it shows that these designations do not so much name a period or approach to the world that succeeds, surpasses, or displaces modernism, but rather one that engaged with and constructed its own particular modernist mythos, often in order to reject or problematize it. As I argue in relation to Paul Auster's postmodern writing in Chapter 3, this focus on the intervening periods and their

---

[69] David James, *Modernist Futures: Innovation and Inheritance in the Contemporary Novel* (Cambridge: Cambridge University Press, 2012), 29.

[70] James and Seshagiri, "Metamodernism," 93.

[71] Michael D'Arcy and Mathias Nilges, "Introduction: The Contemporaneity of Modernism," in *The Contemporaneity of Modernism: Literature, Media, Culture,* ed. Michael D'Arcy and Mathias Nilges (New York: Routledge, 2016), 2; Brown, "The Work of Art."

returns to a now déclassé modernism allows us to add nuance to the periodization on which recent studies of modernism's return are implicitly or explicitly based.

Modernism's importance to the literary and intellectual history of these intervening periods lies to a significant extent in the way in which it came to be identified with the concept of aesthetic autonomy. For much of the period under discussion in this study, a writer's or thinker's relationship to modernism was a way of signaling his or her relationship to aesthetic autonomy. Conversely, debates about aesthetic autonomy inevitably found themselves grappling with modernism's legacies and influences. What is important about modernism for the late twentieth-century literary fields I examine, in other words, is its association with a specific aesthetics. By "aesthetics," I mean a set of theories and ideas about art, sometimes deriving from a philosophical tradition like the one outlined in Section 2 of this introduction, which seek to explain how we understand and experience art and art objects. This use of the term should be distinguished from the way in which it is sometimes used by literary scholars to refer more broadly to a text's formal qualities, or its "literariness." Aesthetics as I use it here is neither form nor style. The modernist legacies that I am interested in have less to do with the reprisal of formal techniques like stream-of-consciousness or collage, than with a theory about art's relationship to society that became widely associated with modernism in the late twentieth century. Similarly, the art of hunger describes not so much a shared set of formal resources—although the texts I consider tend, on the whole, to be rather on the slim and direct side—but the use of hunger as a way of dramatizing an unfree and embodied mode of aesthetic autonomy. The aesthetics of the art of hunger certainly has consequences for form, and I seek to draw these out in each chapter, considering how Beckett's fascination with permutation and rhythm, Auster's use of abstraction and metafiction, and Coetzee's negotiations with realism all derive from each writer's understanding of the aesthetics of the art of hunger. But these formal consequences are not necessarily shared among writers, and do not in the end lie at the heart of these writers' relationships to one another or to modernism. Instead, what binds them together is a shared figure—the figure of hunger—through which they dramatize a shared aesthetics.

5. A HUNDRED AND FIFTY YEARS OF THE ART OF HUNGER

This book follows the dissemination of the art of hunger over a period of 150 years and across three continents, showing how it was repeatedly taken up in new contexts in order to dramatize aesthetic autonomy's impossibility and art's unfreedom. Chapter 1 begins with modernism itself, mapping out the complex of ideas and aesthetic positions that are brought together under the banner of the art of hunger. In this chapter, I reconstruct the canon that forms the basis of later writers' deployment of the art of hunger, bringing together texts such as Melville's "Bartleby the Scrivener," Rimbaud's poetry, Hamsun's *Hunger*, and Kafka's "A Hunger Artist." Reading these texts and authors both in their own moments and as they have been read by later writers and scholars, it seeks to derive the theory of art that later writers engage with when they redeploy the art of hunger in new contexts.

Chapter 2 takes up this story in post-World War II France, where the aftermath of war produced fierce debates about the status of aesthetic autonomy, presided over by the field-shaping influence of Jean-Paul Sartre and his theory of intellectual *engagement*. In this context, Samuel Beckett emerges as a transitional figure in the art of hunger tradition: both its last modernist and its first standard-bearer in the post-war period beyond modernism. Situating Beckett's writing from the 1940s onwards within the post-war French debates about the status of aesthetic autonomy, this chapter follows Beckett's resistance to both *littérature engagée*, and defenses of autonomy that linked art to freedom. Hunger, tied in his writing of this period with obligation, unfreedom, and the collapse of collective and political communities, becomes the vehicle through which he develops this minority aesthetic position.

The debates about aesthetic autonomy and writerly responsibility that emerged in post-war France cast a long shadow over the later twentieth century. Chapters 3 and 4 follow the reverberations of these debates as they are taken up globally. Chapter 3 examines the questions raised about the role of art in the aftermath of the 1968 student protests in France and the US, as aesthetic autonomy was being absorbed into the university and the university itself was changing in response to the emergence of what in the US became known as "French theory." Paul Auster, who was a student at Columbia in 1968 and spent the early 1970s in Paris, moves between these two milieus, using his commitment to an art of hunger position to locate himself outside both. In the process, Auster reinvents the art of hunger in line with the preoccupations of his own historical moment, locating the beseiged author at the center of the tradition, and linking the art of hunger's old preoccupation with aesthetic autonomy to the new 1960s and 1970s quest for personal authenticity.

Finally in Chapter 4, Auster's near-contemporary, J. M. Coetzee, takes us to South Africa in the dying days of apartheid, where the call to political responsibility returns with a new urgency. Coetzee, however, breaks with this consensus, maintaining a commitment to aesthetic autonomy through his investment in a European modernist tradition that incorporates the art of hunger. In a context where hunger itself was highly politicized, Coetzee's 1983 novel *Life & Times of Michael K* produces an anti-politics of hunger, whose autonomy rests in the disjuncture between its white author and its Coloured protagonist. Updating the art of hunger's anxieties about art's unfreedom, Coetzee's novel responds to its social context by holding itself apart from it, constantly calling into question the potential of the novel to imagine Michael K's freedom.

Unlike much work in this field in recent years, this book is not intended as an argument either for or against aesthetic autonomy. Instead, I seek to show that debates about the role of aesthetic autonomy—and the parallel debates about the value of modernism—have been structural to how we thought about art and literature in the twentieth century. The art of hunger tradition occupies an important position within these debates, precisely because it dismantles so many of aesthetic autonomy's most convincing justifications, while nonetheless remaining committed to the concept. To imagine an art that does not have a secure social context and that cannot lead its writers or its readers to freedom requires that we develop new ways of understanding what the point of such art might be. This book suggests that art might be valuable for the way in which it investigates constraints, limitations, and forms of necessity, as much as for the way it opens onto new and better worlds or strives to liberate its readers or its writers from their bonds. It stages the sense that art is in crisis, and by making this aesthetic crisis something visceral and embodied, it makes it into a site for thinking through questions that exist at the cusp of politics and philosophy, where the unfree, suffering body collapses questions about the nature of being and questions about the nature of power. By not imagining that aesthetic autonomy provides a model for freedom, the art of hunger provides an occasion to think through the unpleasantness of different kinds of necessity and obligation. It ends by suggesting that an art that is in crisis, an aesthetic autonomy on the brink of collapse, is one that might teach us something important about the prospects for embodied autonomy beyond the realm of art.

1

The Modernist Art of Hunger

From the Lost Generation to surrealism, key figures of modernism imagine themselves as part of a growing constellation of starving artists, constructing a genealogy of hungry forebears into which they insert themselves. Henry Miller, for instance, imagines Arthur Rimbaud as an exemplary starving artist—"His energy is boundless, his will indomitable, his hunger insatiable.... How well I understand his mania!"—before launching into a long reverie on his own experiences of hunger.[1] "Sometimes," concludes the American, seeking to underscore the parallels between himself and Rimbaud, "I think I was born hungry."[2] For Miller, Rimbaud's anti-social hunger epitomizes his rakish independence from social norms and exigencies, and provides the link that binds Miller himself into the tradition of *poètes maudits*. Miller is far from alone among his generation of modernists in seeking to construct an aesthetic tradition that takes hunger as its defining experience. Ernest Hemingway, in his 1964 memoir of "Lost Generation" Paris, presents this milieu as perpetually short of food. Hunger binds his social world together, forming the basis on which he constructs artistic identifications: "I learned to understand Cézanne much better and to see truly how he made landscapes when I was hungry," he writes. "I used to wonder if he were hungry too when he painted; but I thought possibly it was only that he had forgotten to eat."[3] Similarly, André Breton calls on starvation to guarantee his innovation of automatic writing, observing parenthetically that, "Knut Hamsum [*sic*] ascribes this sort of revelation to which I had been subjected as deriving from hunger, and he may not be wrong. (The fact is I did not eat every day during that period of my life)."[4]

The proliferation of starving artists in modernism is part of the period's self-mythologization. Hunger offers a point of identification that allows

---

[1] Henry Miller, *The Time of the Assassins: A Study of Rimbaud* (New York: New Directions, 1956), 20–2.

[2] Ibid., 22.

[3] Ernest Hemingway, *A Moveable Feast* (London: Arrow Books, 2000), 39.

[4] André Breton, "Manifesto of Surrealism (1924)," in *Manifestoes of Surrealism*, trans. Richard Seaver and Helen R. Lane (Ann Arbor: University of Michigan Press, 1969), 33–4.

these writers to construct a tradition out of earlier writers' and artists' attempts to imagine a position outside the social order and, most importantly, outside the market. Their starvation and their refusal of productive or profitable labor are the natural consequences of one another; as Miller says of Rimbaud, "It was from the moment he began to earn a living that his real difficulties set in."[5] Hunger is the inevitable consequence of their refusal of the market structures that provide the only obvious way of feeding themselves as artists. Far from being an impediment to their art, however, hunger gives these writers access to a state of heightened aesthetic experience. Hemingway can finally understand Cézanne's artistry when he is hungry, and Breton speculates that hunger might have prompted his discovery of automatic writing, one of the major aesthetic breakthroughs of his career. Breton's Hamsun experiences aesthetic revelations, and Hemingway's Cézanne paints on an empty stomach. Rimbaud's entire existence, in Miller's account, is an aesthetic one, with hunger as one of its animating states. Miller himself, in *Tropic of Cancer*, records the experience of attending a concert on an "empty belly" as one of heightened aesthetic receptivity, "as though my skull had a thousand tiny mirrors inside it."[6] Placing them outside mass society and its market relations, hunger grants these writers access to an intensified form of aesthetic experience. The shared fact of their starvation makes them into artists, by giving them access to the sphere of the aesthetic.

These writers, in other words, use hunger to stake their claim to an autonomous art. In both the modernist period and the later twentieth-century mythos of modernism, aesthetic autonomy was understood first and foremost as art's autonomy from the market. This definition provides us with one of the most familiar narratives of modernism, which takes it as a product of art's anxiety about the growth of what Andreas Huyssen calls "an increasingly consuming and engulfing mass culture."[7] The impulse to read modernism as mass culture's other—an impulse that stretches in different forms from Huyssen to Adorno to Bourdieu and beyond—has done more than anything else to cement the association between modernism and aesthetic autonomy. It has also been central to many of those thinkers, from Adorno to Nicholas Brown, who seek to imagine (modernist) aesthetic autonomy as a route to freedom, by understanding it as a state of resistance to or exemption from the exigencies of capitalist cultural production. Hunger for Hemingway, Miller, and Breton, and for their

---

[5] Miller, *The Time of the Assassins*, 20.

[6] Henry Miller, *Tropic of Cancer* (New York: Grove Press, 1961), 74.

[7] Andreas Huyssen, *After the Great Divide: Modernism, Mass Culture, Postmodernism* (Bloomington, IN: Indiana University Press, 1986), vii.

versions of Rimbaud and Hamsun, dramatizes this anti-commercial, autonomous modernism. Placing them outside the market and mass culture in a way that gives them privileged access to the aesthetic, it becomes a shorthand for their status as autonomous modernist artists. In the hands of writers like Miller, Hemingway, and Breton, starvation becomes a mark of their refusal to bow to social and economic necessity. The prestige that it offers grants them a position within a restricted community of like-minded aesthetes, be that Breton's surrealist coterie or Hemingway and Miller's expatriate milieu. In this sense, the starving artist is the exemplary personality of what Pierre Bourdieu calls the "society of artists," that limited social world that "offers the most favorable and comprehensive welcome to the audacities and transgressions that artists and writers introduce, not only into their works, but also into their existence (itself conceived as work of art)."[8] To care so little for the approval of broader society that one is willing to starve is the most audacious, most transgressive of positions, and in its very extremity, it serves to dramatize their commitment to autonomy and to the social world in which that autonomy is prized. These writers fashion themselves as exemplars of what Bourdieu calls the "new social personality" from which "the invention of the pure aesthetic is inseparable."[9] This personality is "the great professional artist who combines, in a union as fragile as it is improbable, a sense of transgression and freedom from conformity with the rigor of an extremely strict discipline of living and of work."[10] Starvation, simultaneously dramatizing these writers' commitment and their transgression, is a privileged marker of this personality.

The value of this position, as Bourdieu affirms, is not only that it creates a social context for ostensibly anti-social art, but also that its social milieu is able "to be its own market."[11] In this sense, the paradox of the modernist starving artist is that their exclusion from the general economy and broader society—what Bourdieu calls the "sub-field of large-scale [cultural] production"—is precisely what grants them legitimacy and even certain limited kinds of financial success within the "sub-field of restricted production" of the society of artists.[12] Indeed, two decades of work on modernism's sociological and commercial aspects have dismantled the notion that modernist claims to autonomy can simply be taken at face value. Scholars such as Lawrence Rainey, Joyce Wexler, Aaron Jaffe,

---

[8] Pierre Bourdieu, *The Rules of Art: Genesis and Structure of the Literary Field*, trans. Susan Emanuel (Stanford: Stanford University Press, 1995), 58.
[9] Ibid., 111.   [10] Ibid.   [11] Ibid., 58.
[12] Pierre Bourdieu, "The Field of Cultural Production, or: The Economic World Reversed," *Poetics* 12 (1983): 333.

and Jonathan Goldman have shown that the binary division between modernism and mass culture belies the complex negotiations that modernists performed with the market.[13] As Rainey argues, modernism might be best understood, not so much as a straightforward form of resistance to mass culture, but rather as "a strategy whereby the work of art invites and solicits its own commodification," albeit seeking to become "a commodity of a special sort."[14] Rainey and Bourdieu, along with most of these other scholars of "material modernism," imagine the specialness of the commodified modernist art object to lie in its embrace of a posture of autonomy, and its production of what Andrew Goldstone, following Bourdieu, calls a "relative autonomy" from social and economic structures.[15]

Late modernists like Breton, Miller, and Hemingway therefore construct the starving artist as the persona that stages their commitment to relative autonomy. The stability of this position assumes, however, the existence of a society of artists who can provide "a form of social recognition for those who otherwise appear (that is, to other groups) as a challenge to common sense," as well as a market to financially support the starving artist and to keep his poverty from culminating in his death.[16] But while this sociable anti-socialness characterizes the later writers, it does not hold so straightforwardly for the earlier generation of hunger artists that they take as their models and from which they fashion their lineage of starving artists. For writers like Hamsun and Rimbaud, as well as other exemplary hunger artists like Kafka or Melville's Bartleby, hunger dramatizes the precariousness of the attempt to achieve autonomy in the absence of a society of artists. In these earlier manifestations, starvation is the sign and product of the contradiction that lies at the heart of aesthetic autonomy, and the mark of its impossibility. It makes visible that which most versions of modernist autonomy efface and which the later starving artists glamorize: the impossibility of survival that does not involve selling oneself. In transplanting the starving artist to a more secure social environment, writers like Hemingway, Miller, and Breton retain hunger's role as a figure for aesthetic autonomy, imagined as a form of social and

---

[13] Lawrence Rainey, *Institutions of Modernism: Literary Elites and Public Culture* (New Haven: Yale University Press, 1998); Joyce Piell Wexler, *Who Paid for Modernism? Art, Money, and the Fiction of Conrad, Joyce, and Lawrence* (Fayetteville, AR: University of Arkansas Press, 1997); Aaron Jaffe, *Modernism and the Culture of Celebrity* (Cambridge: Cambridge University Press, 2005); Jonathan Goldman, *Modernism Is the Literature of Celebrity* (Austin, TX: University of Texas Press, 2011).

[14] Rainey, *Institutions of Modernism*, 3.

[15] Andrew Goldstone, "Relative Autonomy: Pierre Bourdieu and Modernism," in *The Contemporaneity of Modernism: Literature, Media, Culture*, ed. Michael D'Arcy and Mathias Nilges (New York: Routledge, 2016), 65–79.

[16] Bourdieu, *The Rules of Art*, 58.

economic exclusion, but they dampen the attentiveness to aesthetic autonomy's internal contradictions.

I return in this chapter to the earlier writers of the art of hunger in order to excavate the complex relationship to aesthetic autonomy that underlies the more typified and stereotyped figure of the starving artist as imagined in surrealism, the Lost Generation, and other manifestations of coterie modernism. Although the works of these earlier writers are available for mythologization in ways that have been highly influential, the texts themselves barely envisage the intergenerational community or tradition that produces the mythos of the starving artist. Instead, they write from more avowedly marginal positions, and imagine hunger as a function of that marginality and social exclusion—an exclusion unredeemed by the emergence of a society of artists within which autonomy could become self-sustaining. As a result, these earlier writers more forcefully dramatize a principle that Bourdieu derives from his study of nineteenth-century France: that it is "money (inherited) that guarantees freedom with respect to money."[17] The hunger artists examined in this chapter, seeking to imagine an unprofitable art that is outside the market and without inherited wealth, end by imagining an art that cannot be free. In the figure of hunger, they trope the dilemma of aesthetic autonomy's impoverished unfreedom.

This chapter sketches the aesthetic framework of the art of hunger through four of its exemplary texts: Kafka's "A Hunger Artist," Knut Hamsun's *Hunger*, Melville's *Bartleby, the Scrivener*, and the poetry of Rimbaud. Through these texts, I draw out five principles that underlie this peculiar tradition. First, the art of hunger is an autonomous art without a society of artists and the market that this provides. As such, it dramatizes more directly and painfully than other accounts of modernist autonomy the tension between the aspiration to autonomy and the need to earn a living. Second, this exclusion from the market renders the artist a non-subject, a subject devoid of will, creating an opposition between aesthetic autonomy and the personal autonomy of the artist. Third, this unautonomous subjectivity is a gendered position, which entails a failed or marginalized masculinity. Fourth, the art of hunger, despite its position outside the market, does not produce a viable politics of resistance. Instead, its refusal breeds an anti-politics. Finally, the art of hunger refuses or disavows the freedom promised by transcendence. Instead, it aspires to become a literal art: an art of "absolute metaphor," of performance, and of

---

[17] Ibid., 84.

what Victor Schklovsky calls "trans-sensible language."[18] Running through these separate claims is a common thread that animates the tradition as a whole: the art of hunger imagines aesthetic autonomy as a form of social and economic exclusion, not in order to figure its freedom from social pressure, but to explore its unfreedom.

The chapter unfolds in a rough reverse chronological order, beginning with Kafka, who is located firmly within the modernist period, and working back through Hamsun, an early modernist, to Melville and Rimbaud, writers who are generally taken to predate modernism. The goal of this retrospective structure is to foreground the way in which the art of hunger emerges from a complex process of rereading and rewriting, which links the texts in multi-directional ways. On the one hand, earlier writers develop tropes that are then reprised, expanded, clarified, and reworked in later writing. But, as T. S. Eliot so famously reminds us in "Tradition and the Individual Talent," later writers also reshape the critical field, producing conditions that alter the reception of earlier texts and, in the cases of Rimbaud and Melville, allow them to be read as part of a tradition to which historically they do not necessarily belong. The starving artists with which I began this chapter are crucial to this bidirectional construction of a canon of hunger artists. They represent some of the first and most influential figures to construct a canon from these writers, by reading them alongside one another as part of their personal canons. But their readings are already rereadings, and they tend to operate by making the art of hunger more social, more heroic, and less unfree—repackaging it, effectively, as a kind of celebrity, available to be sold to a mass audience. This figure has been enormously influential—the starving artist remains a recognizable social personality to this day—and has made the art of hunger available as a figure both in the popular imagination, and in the private imaginaries of other writers, including those I examine in Chapters 2–4. This chapter seeks to understand the logic of the art of hunger, as distinct from the more market-oriented logic of the starving artist, by charting the constellation of ideas that emerge from the texts themselves, when read together as part of a tradition. To this end, it unfolds both retrospectively and accumulatively, mapping clusters of ideas that exfoliate out from the equation of aesthetic autonomy with unfreedom that lies at the heart of the tradition.

---

[18] Hugo Friedrich, *The Structure of Modern Poetry: From the Mid-Nineteenth to the Mid-Twentieth Century*, trans. Joachim Nergroschel (Evanston, IL: Northwestern University Press, 1974), 51; Viktor Shklovsky, "On Poetry and Trans-Sense Language," trans. Gerald Janecek and Peter Mayer, *October* 34 (Autumn 1985): 9.

1. AUTONOMOUS ART AND EXCLUSION FROM THE MARKET: KAFKA

Like later starving artists, the modernists at the center of this chapter understand hunger as a figure for aesthetic autonomy, using it to dramatize the experience of being excluded from the market. Kafka's 1922 short story "A Hunger Artist" (Ein Hungerkünstler) is the central text of this tradition, a parable of the art of hunger whose framing of the relationship between art and hunger has shaped both the writing of later texts and the reading of earlier ones. At the heart of Kafka's story is a deep anxiety about the relationship between art and the market, and a sustained interrogation of the possibility of autonomous art in a commercialized context. The eponymous hunger artist dramatizes this tension. As a professional faster, selling (via his impresario) the spectacle of his superhuman capacity to survive without food, he is a consummate figure of the changing cultural marketplace at the turn of the twentieth century. "Human skeletons" and hunger artists form part of the array of performers common at freak shows during the later years of the nineteenth century, and it is probable that this story derives from Kafka's knowledge of such figures.[19] As Agustí Nieto-Galan has noted, the emergence of such figures signals a shift in the cultural function of self-starvation. No longer a sign of religious or mystical election, it "progressively became a commodity in the urban marketplace which could be exploited for both amusement and profit."[20] Kafka's protagonist belongs self-consciously (if, as we shall see, uncomfortably) to this world of commercialized self-starvation. From its first lines, the story positions the hunger artist's popularity and profitability at the center of the tale, opening: "During these last decades the interest in professional fasting has markedly diminished. It used to pay very well to stage such great performances under one's own management, but today that is quite impossible."[21] From the outset, the hunger artist is framed as a creature of the commercialized public sphere, whose position within this cultural marketplace is rapidly declining.

---

[19] Breon Mitchell, "Kafka and the Hunger Artists," in *Kafka and the Contemporary Critical Performance: Centenary Readings*, ed. Alan Udoff (Bloomington, IN: Indiana University Press, 1987), 236–55.

[20] Agustí Nieto-Galan, "Mr Giovanni Succi Meets Dr Luigi Luciani in Florence: Hunger Artists and Experimental Physiology in the Late Nineteenth Century," *Social History of Medicine* 28, no. 1 (2014): 64.

[21] Franz Kafka, "A Hunger Artist," in *The Complete Short Stories of Franz Kafka*, ed. Nahum N. Glatzer, trans. Willa Muir and Edwin Muir (London: Vintage, 2005), 268.

Seen from this angle, hunger art is a form of mass culture, sustained and produced by the attention of the masses. But the fascination of the masses imposes a number of unacceptable constraints on the hunger artist's art. Chafing against these limitations, he seems to dream of an autonomous art, an art that he could practice without being forced to submit to the whims of the masses. Above all, he rages against the way that public attention dictates the duration of his fast, which his impresario limits to forty days, because "after that the town began to lose interest, sympathetic support began notably to fall off."[22] This limitation outrages the hunger artist, who "felt that there were no limits to his capacity for fasting," and who dreams of the perfect fast he could perform were he not limited by public taste. Faced with the indignity of this limitation, and the humiliations of the rituals that surround the breaking of the fast, the hunger artist laments the "whole world of non-understanding" that confronts him in the uncomprehending masses and in the impresario's framing of his art for the public.[23] The hunger artist, in this reading, dramatizes the contradiction between an absolutely autonomous art, unconstrained by the attitudes of the masses, and the need to sell art for an audience—the tension, that is, between high art and mass culture—that is so often taken to define modernism.

Where high art and aesthetic autonomy are conventionally linked to an all-consuming commitment to art, to the exclusion of any concern with audience, however, the hunger artist remains deeply anxious about his reception. His frustration with the masses is as much about the lack of recognition that they grant him as about the limitations they place on the purity of his art. His complaint against his forestalled fast turns on its denial of the glory to which he imagines himself entitled: "Why should he be cheated of the fame he would get for fasting longer, for being not only the record hunger artist of all time, which presumably he was already, but for beating his own record by a performance beyond human imagination?"[24] If the hunger artist fails to find satisfaction in making art for the masses, he finds even less in the years after public interest declines, where, relegated to a circus sideshow, he is able to fast without constraints. Here, free from the dictates of a market that has now abandoned him, he finds himself still dissatisfied: "the artist simply fasted on and on, as he had once dreamed of doing, and it was no trouble to him, just as he had always

---

[22] Ibid., 270.   [23] Ibid., 273.   [24] Kafka, "A Hunger Artist," 271.

foretold, but no one counted the days, no one, not even the artist himself, knew what records he was already breaking, and his heart grew heavy."[25] The purity of his art requires a form of recognition that is as unavailable to art that is fully autonomous from the market as it is to art that submits wholeheartedly to it.

In this sense, the hunger artist's dream of autonomy is best understood on Bourdieu's model: he aspires to the kind of autonomy guaranteed by a society of artists, a group who would provide both a market and a form of social recognition for his art, while allowing him to retain his distance from the masses. Early in the story, the narrator tells us that the practice of providing a coterie of watchers who would ensure that the hunger artist did not eat during his fast "was nothing but a formality, instituted to reassure the masses, for the initiates knew well enough that during his fast the artist would never in any circumstances, not even under forcible compulsion, swallow the smallest morsel of food; the honor of his profession [Kunst] forbade it."[26] The opposition between the masses, who demand an inauthentic spectacle of rigor and artistic honor, and the initiates, who, the hunger artist believes, truly understand the nature of the hunger artist's art, mirrors Bourdieu's opposition between the subfields of large-scale and restricted cultural production. But the tragedy of "A Hunger Artist" is that the story's protagonist, who we later learn is "the sole completely satisfied spectator of his own fast," never finds this audience of initiates. The watchers, either overly suspicious or resigned to his deceit, cannot understand or truly admire the hunger artist's art. Nor can the impresario or the circus overseer, who both relate to his feats not on their own terms but simply as a more or less profitable commodity to sell on to the uncomprehending masses. Without a knowing coterie of initiates, the hunger artist's autonomous art becomes a solipsistic, unrewarded, and ultimately fatal exercise. "A Hunger Artist" thus dramatizes the impossibility of an autonomous art that lacks the social context—the society of artists or the audience of initiates—to sustain its autonomy.

Readers of Kafka are likely to recognize this collapse of social context as part of the story that accompanies the reception of Kafka himself. As a German-speaking Czech Jew, Kafka's ethnic, linguistic, and national marginality has been central to the way he has been read. Deleuze and Guattari's reading of Kafka's writing as an exemplary minor literature—"that which a minority constructs within a major language" and in which "language is affected with a high coefficient of deterritorialization"—reflects his broader

---

[25] Ibid., 276.
[26] Ibid., 268–9; Franz Kafka, *Die Erzählungen*, ed. Roger Hermes (Frankfurt am Main: Fischer, 2008), 393.

reception as an idiosyncratic, isolated, and marginal writer.[27] Kafka writes from a country whose literary community had, since the late nineteenth century, been reorienting itself towards Europe. As Katherine David Fox has argued, by "looking beyond the city's traditional place at the centre of a Czech cultural system, [late nineteenth-century writers] relocated it to the periphery of a European one."[28] As the twentieth century dawned, the German-speaking Jews of this Czech outpost found themselves, as Scott Spector has shown, to be "decentred," squeezed between "a burgeoning racialist *völkisch* ideology on the one side, and a Czech nationalism that was as antisemitic as it was anti-German on the other."[29] In fact, the common view of Kafka as marginal and without an immediate context for his writing is not entirely accurate. As Spector's book shows, German-speaking Czech Jews did not belong to a straightforwardly minority culture and in fact had access to vibrant cultural and artistic circles. But whatever the truth of Kafka's historical circumstances, his reception as part of world literature has detached him from his initial historical and social contexts, allowing him to circulate as a figure who, like his hunger artist, experiences the torments of an autonomous art that lacks a social context.

This sense of Kafka's marginality is amplified by his writing, which tends to both emphasize and perform social exclusion. While the inextricability of the hunger artist's art from the commercial context of its production is one reason for his failure to find an appropriate social context, the difficulty also lies in the nature of his art itself. By its nature, hunger makes an unsatisfying spectacle. Characterized only by an absence—by the refusal to eat over long periods of time—it is by definition unobservable. As the narrator informs us, suspicions like those of the watchers "were a necessary accompaniment to the profession of fasting."[30] Even the hunger artist's skeletal frame—the most visually interesting aspect of his performance—is not a reliable index of his hunger. On the contrary, the hunger artist speculates that it was "dissatisfaction with himself that had worn him down," his emaciation a product not directly of his starvation but instead of the fact that, "he alone knew, what no other initiate knew, how easy it was to fast."[31] The disjuncture between the spectacle and the experience of the hunger artist's starvation makes his performance into a paradoxically unobservable art, one whose most complete audience can only ever be the

---

[27] Gilles Deleuze and Félix Guattari, *Kafka: Towards a Minor Literature* (Minneapolis: University of Minnesota Press, 1986), 16.

[28] Katherine David-Fox, "Prague–Vienna, Prague–Berlin: The Hidden Geographies of Czech Modernism," *Slavic Review* 59, no. 4 (2000): 736.

[29] Scott Spector, *Prague Territories: National Conflict and Cultural Innovation in Franz Kafka's Fin de siècle* (Berkeley: University of California Press, 2000), 4.

[30] Kafka, "A Hunger Artist," 269.   [31] Ibid., 270.

performer himself. The autonomous art depicted by Kafka's story is therefore an impossible one, caught between autonomy's need for a social context and hunger's inherent resistance to an audience. The impossibility of Kafka's hunger art leads him to imagine the aspiration towards aesthetic autonomy as a spectacle of unfreedom. The setting of the story, which moves through a variety of cages as the hunger artist's fame declines, renders this spectacle literal: in order to perform his art, he must be literally imprisoned and, indeed, this imprisonment itself forms part of the spectacle and thus part of his art. What changes over the course of the story is not the fact of his imprisonment but its position in relation to an audience, and therefore the nature of the unfreedom to which he is subject. In the opening pages of the story, when public interest in his art remains strong, he finds himself intolerably subject to the dictates of the market, with all the limitations this imposes on his art. By the story's end, however, the public's lack of attention leaves him exposed to the opposite pole of necessity: his art's subjugation to the limitations of his own body. Although, as he insists, the hunger artist has an exceptional capacity to survive without food, his death at the story's end reveals that this capacity is not without its limits. Indeed, the fore-shortening of his fast in response to public demands early in the story creates an illusion of immortality or invincibility, an illusion that there are "no limits to his capacity for fasting."[32] The removal of the public's artificial limits on his fast, however, reveals an underlying natural limit in his own mortality. The hunger artist therefore stages his unfreedom as a movement between two poles of subjugation: his subjugation to the logic of the market, on the one hand; and his subjugation to the limits of his own body, on the other. Trapped between his body's need for sustenance as a horizon of necessity and the market as a horizon of coercion—trapped, that is, between a mass audience and no audience at all, with no possibility of the restricted audience necessary for a truly autonomous art—the hunger artist's art is structurally unfree.

The hunger artist's deathbed confession to the circus overseer renders this unfreedom as a question about personal autonomy. As he lies dying, the hunger artist confesses that his fast was unworthy of admiration, explaining that he only starves, "Because I have to fast [ich hungern muß], I can't help it [ich kann nicht anders] . . . Because I couldn't find the food I liked. If I had found it, believe me, I should have made no fuss and stuffed myself like you or anyone else."[33] With his final words, the hunger artist disavows responsibility for his fast, emphasizing that it is not a freely

---

[32] Ibid., 271.   [33] Ibid., 277; Kafka, *Die Erzählungen*, 403.

chosen enterprise but a form of compulsion or obligation. In a parodic rewriting of the Kantian aesthetic tradition's view of aesthetic autonomy as the renunciation of one's interest in food, his art's necessity is presented as a product of the hunger artist's lack of taste. The hunger artist suggests that insofar as his disinterest in eating is unchosen, it is not free ("ich hungern muß, ich kann nicht anders"). In contrast, the panther who replaces the hunger artist in the story's final paragraph is a model of self-contained freedom, whose "noble body, furnished almost to the burst point with all that it needed, seemed to carry freedom around with it too; somewhere in his jaws it seemed to lurk."[34] The animal conjoins freedom with public fascination in a combination that renders obsolete the hunger artist's emphasis on a specifically *aesthetic* autonomy—that is, an autonomy premised on the purity of art, recognized and authorized by an elite society of artists.

In this sense, "A Hunger Artist" suggests that the aesthetic autonomy that his hunger performs precludes the personal autonomy so central to the Kantian philosophical tradition more broadly, with its presumption of a freely choosing, rational, and autonomous subject. The opposition between aesthetic autonomy and individual autonomy staged by this story becomes one of the defining features of the art of hunger tradition. Autonomous art, in this tradition, is that which is not freely chosen: hunger that has no rational motivation, and that is therefore not an exercise of conscious discipline. But without this free choice, the artist is not autonomous—he is not an agent of freedom. The art of hunger, therefore, describes an art that is unfree by imagining aesthetic autonomy and the artist's personal autonomy to be mutually exclusive, at least in the context of an autonomous art for which there is no society of artists. It dramatizes aesthetic autonomy as a mode of unfreedom that lacks its proper social milieu.

2. HUNGER AND THE COLLAPSE OF THE AUTONOMOUS SUBJECT: HAMSUN

The art of hunger's tension between aesthetic autonomy and the self-possessed subjectivity associated with individual autonomy is more fully elaborated in Knut Hamsun's semi-autobiographical novel *Hunger* (*Sult*). First published in 1890, it is often credited as one of the first modernist

---

[34] Ibid., 277.

novels and specifically one of the earliest examples of modernist psychological narration. Although relatively neglected today, during his lifetime
Hamsun was a central figure in European modernism. Hailed as an
exemplary embodiment of modernist autonomy, he became one of the
most important influences on those who took up the mantle of writerly
starvation after him. In 1929, for his seventieth birthday, he was presented
with two *Festschriften* whose lists of contributors read like a roll-call of key
figures in European modernism: André Gide, Thomas Mann, Herman
Hesse, Robert Musil, Stefan Zweig, Maxim Gorky—even Albert Einstein.
As Hamsun's biographer records, "For the contributors he stands as the
great example of the unyielding and uncompromising artist, indifferent
to misunderstanding, one who sacrificed everything for his art, and won
the victory."[35]

If Hamsun was feted by his contemporaries and heirs as the living
embodiment of the modernist ideal of aesthetic autonomy, *Hunger* is in
many respects the key text of this reception. A kind of *Künstlerroman*,
Hunger follows its unnamed writer-protagonist through a period of
failure and poverty, as he finds himself caught, like Kafka's hunger artist,
in the contradiction between his art and the demands of the market.
Like the hunger artist, Hamsun's protagonist is a creature of the cultural
marketplace. Everything he writes, he writes in hope of selling, and, on
those occasions when he manages to produce something, he assesses it
like a commodity. "I weigh the piece in my hand," he says of one of his
stories, "and appraise it on the spot at five kroner, by a rough estimate."[36]
But like "A Hunger Artist," *Hunger* is the record of its protagonist's
inability to succeed in this marketplace, and the vicious circle of economic and aesthetic failure that results. As Paul Auster writes in an essay
on the novel (reprinted as its introduction in some editions), "he must eat
in order to write. But if he does not write, he will not eat. And if he cannot
eat, he cannot write. He cannot write."[37] The protagonist's starvation
produces a precipitous mental decline, preventing him from writing. In a
market where writing is transformed immediately into income, the protagonist's body therefore becomes the mediator between market forces and
aesthetic production, yoking them together in the devastating logic by
which no writing means no food but no food means no writing. In this
sense, *Hunger* dramatizes the fraught position of literature in a world of

---

[35] Robert Ferguson, *Enigma: The Life of Knut Hamsun* (London: Hutchinson,
1987), 300.
[36] Knut Hamsun, *Hunger* (Melbourne: Text Publishing, 2006), 34–5.
[37] Paul Auster, "Introduction: The Art of Hunger," in *Hunger*, by Knut Hamsun
(Melbourne: Text Publishing, 2006), viii.

embodied subjects who depend upon income from writing for survival. In its recalcitrant, stubborn protagonist, it provides a model for later starving artists and a figure of "the unyielding and uncompromising artist" with which Hamsun himself would come to be identified by his modernist peers. In this sense, *Hunger*, like "A Hunger Artist," dramatizes aesthetic autonomy as a form of exclusion from the market.

Often cited as one of the earliest examples of stream-of-consciousness narration, *Hunger* charts the protagonist's mental state through the tumult of semi-starvation, as his subjectivity loses its coherence in a series of self-contradictory gestures, thoughts, and actions marked only by their apparent lack of motivation.[38] He loses track of himself from moment to moment, becoming at points so absorbed in a simple question that "I forget where I am and stand like a solitary buoy in the middle of the ocean, surrounded on all sides by surging roaring waves."[39] His thoughts compete with each other without resolving into focus or action; his actions occur without apparent thought, animated by, as Nicholas Royle writes, "a ghostly irony that is a power of interruption, discontinuity, non-presence."[40] Interspersed with these unmotivated actions and the tumults of thought that accompany them are various intensely observed sense-impressions, the constant pains and distractions of a body dying of starvation and exhaustion, as well as periods of complete dissociation, intense lethargy, or dazed stupor. This succession substitutes for both plot and character, producing what Sverre Lyngstad calls a "kaleidoscopic literary texture" that follows the randomly shifting attention of the narrator-author.[41]

With his discontinuous, ungovernable consciousness, Hamsun's protagonist is far from the rational autonomous subject on whom modern theories of freedom frequently rely. His actions are either reactive or unmotivated, his motivations impenetrable even to himself. At one point, he is suddenly "seized by a strange desire" to follow two sisters whom he encounters on the street, taunting them with nonsensical questions.[42] He repeatedly lies "without any ulterior motive," simply because, "My thoughts fluttered about in disarray and gave me more fanciful notions than I could handle."[43] With such limited capacity to

---

[38] For an extensive discussion of *Hunger*'s relation to stream-of-consciousness narration and to modernist narrative techniques more generally, see Martin Humpál, *The Roots of Modernist Narrative: Knut Hamsun's Novels* (Oslo: Solum Forlag, 1998).

[39] Hamsun, *Hunger*, 43.

[40] Nicholas Royle, *The Uncanny* (Manchester: Manchester University Press, 2003), 216.

[41] Sverre Lyngstad, *Knut Hamsun, Novelist: A Critical Assessment* (New York: Peter Lang, 2005), 7.

[42] Hamsun, *Hunger*, 13.   [43] Ibid., 72.

understand or control his actions, he is unable to make free choices and unable to function as an autonomous, self-governing subject. In this sense, he fleshes out the unfree subjectivity of Kafka's hunger artist, offering a portrait of an artist driven not by freedom but by fleeting obsessions, unwilled compulsions, and unmotivated whims.

Starvation is both the cause and the effect of the *Hunger* protagonist's disintegrating subjectivity. Where theories of personal autonomy are conventionally premised on the mind/body dualism, his hunger dissolves the autonomous mind by rendering it subject to the materiality and unfreedom of his starving body. As Sverre Lyngstad argues, "what holds the hero together is nothing but his emaciated body, which to a large extent determines the behavior of his mind."[44] The body's centrality governs not just the protagonist's experience of the world, but the structure of the text itself, for the limits of the novel are identical with the periods in which the protagonist is starving. Times during which the protagonist is relatively well fed are excised from the text, their absences marked by the section breaks that divide the novel into four parts. The shape of this proto-stream-of-consciousness text, in other words, is determined by the state of its protagonist's body. Consciousness and starvation, mind and body, therefore become inextricable in *Hunger*'s narration, producing an art that is fully coextensive with hunger. In the process, the protagonist is rendered unfree, his personal autonomy sacrificed before the unfreedom of his disintegrating body.

In its attempt to trace the development of its young protagonist's writerly self, *Hunger* is a kind of *Bildungsroman*, but one that, uncharacteristically for the genre, foregrounds its protagonist's unfreedom. As Franco Moretti has argued, the classic *Bildungsroman* stages "the clash between individual autonomy and social integration," in order to dramatize the formation of bourgeois subjectivity.[45] But with a protagonist who is neither autonomous nor socially integrated and who becomes less so as the novel progresses, *Hunger* imagines this kind of formation as a frankly impossible task, at least for the impoverished artist. The novel's strangely shifting tenses compound this effect. Told in the first person throughout, the narrative voice shifts almost at random—sometimes even within a single sentence—between present and past tense. As several critics have noted, the effect of this technique is to reduce the narrator to "only an abstract narrative function," and thereby to render "neutral(ized)" the

[44] Lyngstad, *Hamsun, Novelist*, 19.
[45] Franco Moretti, *The Way of the World: The* Bildungsroman *in European Culture*, trans. Albert Sbragia (London: Verso, 2000), 67.

relationship between narrating self and experiencing self.[46] We therefore lose the retrospectivity of the narration, the point beyond the text from which the text is produced. In the process, we also lose the sense of distance and closure inherent in the *Bildungsroman*, which is conventionally granted by the fact that, as Kristin Ross has argued, "The novel of youth... is ventriloquized out of the mouths of the aged."[47] *Hunger*'s errant narrative voice, which grants us neither the immediacy of the subject-in-formation nor the reflective distance of the fully formed subject, constantly underscores the protagonist's failure to emerge as an autonomous subject.

Instead, the narrator constantly merges with—and then separates himself out from—the all-encompassing experience of the starving body. Staging the instability of the subject as an instability in narrative form, *Hunger* reflects the modernist claim that, as Samuel Beckett wrote of James Joyce's *Work in Progress*, "form *is* content, content *is* form... His writing is not *about* something; *it is that something itself*."[48] Such claims have historically served as a variation on claims to aesthetic autonomy: by assimilating content to form, they privilege the text's internal aesthetic features over its connection to the world beyond the text, imagining the literary text as a special kind of autonomous and internally coherent artefact that only appears to refer beyond itself. In this sense, Hamsun's partial identification of body with text creates the impression of an autonomous and self-referential aesthetic product. As a result, it produces a text that, like Kafka's "A Hunger Artist," seeks to imagine aesthetic autonomy without individual autonomy.

Moreover, because the starving body is a product of the pressures of a commercialized literary marketplace, the analogy between body and text has the effect of inserting the text, with its claims to aesthetic autonomy, back into the realm of commerce. The autonomy of *Hunger*, that is, lies not in its ability to hold itself apart from the literary marketplace, but precisely in its failure to thrive in this commercial world—a failure that produces the hunger that in turn generates the autonomous, self-referential text of the novel. The protagonist's failure as a commercially successful writer—his failure within a capitalist system premised on the autonomous bourgeois

[46] Humpál, *Modernist Narrative*, 57–8; see also Alber et al.'s claim that "the narrating and narrative parts of the consciousness are conflated": Jan Alber et al., "Unnatural Narrative, Unnatural Narratology: Beyond Mimetic Models," *Narrative* 18, no. 2 (May 2010): 123.

[47] Kristin Ross, "Rimbaud and the Resistance to Work," *Representations* 19 (1987): 63.

[48] Samuel Beckett, *Disjecta: Miscellaneous Writings and a Dramatic Fragment*, ed. Ruby Cohn (New York: Grove Press, 1984), 27.

subject—simultaneously renders him a failed autonomous subject, and his text an exemplary work of literary autonomy. Like "A Hunger Artist," *Hunger* imagines the contradiction between aesthetic and individual autonomy as taking place against the backdrop of a collapsing social context. Hamsun himself vacillated over the question of *Hunger*'s intended audience, following the familiar modernist hesitation between a broad public and an elite readership. If in 1888 he hoped to write, as he records in a letter, "for *people* wherever they found themselves," by the time he completed the novel in 1890, he was intending instead to write for something more like Bourdieu's society of artists, professing that "I absolutely cannot write for the masses," and preferring instead a "culturally sophisticated and select group of people" as his audience.[49] The reception of *Hunger* suggests that Hamsun's hopes for a select audience were borne out: in its immediate reception, the novel was well reviewed but sold poorly.[50]

Hamsun's reception, like Kafka's, is complicated by his marginality— both perceived and actual—in relation to a broader European modernism. As Timothy Wientzen has argued, in 1890, Norway was a rapidly modernizing but still self-consciously peripheral country, akin to what we might now call a "developing" economy.[51] In this context, according to Anna Westerståhl Stenport, "while modernity came quite late to Scandinavia, its accelerated aspects quickly brought a sense that fundamental social change needed to be matched by aesthetic changes," producing an early modernism in the context of a belated modernity.[52] These early Scandinavian modernists were positioned self-consciously on the margins of Europe but sought, like Kafka's Prague circle, a transnationalism that would allow them to position themselves within a cosmopolitan European literary sphere and "to write Scandinavia out of perceived marginality."[53] Moreover, within this small circle of Scandinavian letters, Hamsun sought, in a series of lectures that coincides with the publication of *Hunger*, to position himself aggressively in opposition to the earlier innovations of Henrik Ibsen and other major figures of early modernist Norwegian writing. The "largely hostile public reaction" that his polemics generated

---

[49] Quoted in Peter Sjølsyt-Jackson, *Troubling Legacies: Migration, Modernism and Fascism in the Case of Knut Hamsun* (London: Continuum, 2010), 27.

[50] Lyngstad, *Hamsun, Novelist*, 21.

[51] Timothy Wientzen, "The Aesthetics of Hunger: Knut Hamsun, Modernism, and Starvation's Global Frame," *Novel* 48, no. 2 (2015): 210.

[52] Anna Westerståhl Stenport, "Scandinavian Modernism: Stories of the Transnational and the Discontinuous," in *The Oxford Handbook of Global Modernisms*, ed. Mark Wollaeger (Oxford: Oxford University Press, 2012), 480–1.

[53] Ibid., 485; see also Leonardo F. Lisi, *Marginal Modernity: The Aesthetics of Dependency from Kierkegaard to Joyce* (New York: Fordham University Press, 2013).

is a classic instance of what Bourdieu would describe as position-taking within a literary field. But while it therefore marks Hamsun as part of a Bourdieusian literary field, it also threatened to confine him, as a young writer, to the margins of his own, already marginal, field. Moreover, as Hamsun's writing has circulated through European modernism and beyond, it—like Kafka's writing—has become decontextualized from its original literary field. Reread in new contexts, the peripherality of Scandinavian modernism confers a sense of eccentricity and idiosyncrasy on both text and author, exaggerating Hamsun's actual social isolation in 1890s Norway.

This sense of Hamsun's extra-social position is amplified by the text itself, which dramatizes the protagonist's radical exclusion from the social. Hamsun's hesitation between a mass art produced for a large audience and an autonomous art aimed at the restricted sub-field is not available to his protagonist, who, like Kafka's dying hunger artist, finds himself with no audience at all. In this sense, *Hunger*, like "A Hunger Artist," dramatizes the experience of producing an autonomous art without a social field. Stripped of this social context, the protagonist rages against the uncomprehending masses who refuse to become his proper audience. He constantly measures himself against social and moral standards, but systematically reneges on the conventions that underpin the social cohesion to which he seems to aspire, lying gratuitously, stealing, and refusing even to acknowledge the shared meaning of words. Like Kafka's hunger artist, he jealously guards the autonomy of his own inventiveness, even as he laments its lack of an audience. Having lied outrageously to a stranger in the street, for instance, he recalls furiously, "His composure bored me. How did this disgusting, blind old fool dare play around with the foreign name I had invented, as if it was just an ordinary name you could see on any huckster's sign in town!"[54] The characteristically modernist fear that the uncomprehending masses will reduce his linguistic experimentation to the commercialized banality of "any huckster's sign" is amplified by an awareness that, unlike most modernists, this writer lacks an audience who can understand and appreciate his creativity. Like Kafka's hunger artist, he suffers in the knowledge that he is "the sole completely satisfied spectator of his own fast."

The furious, antagonistic confrontations that *Hunger*'s protagonist has with the public are, on the one hand, the product of his lack of control over his own reactions—the product, that is, of his unautonomous subjectivity—and, on the other, constitutive of his claim to aesthetic

---

[54] Hamsun, *Hunger*, 28.

autonomy. His confrontations with social censure allow his self-constitution through and against the external perspective of the "man on the street." If hunger produces a formal narrative that disintegrates, only to be reconstituted in and through the lived experience of the starving body, the inverse is also true: the starving body coalesces into an incoherent subject through the experiences of rage and shame that are engendered by his confrontation with an audience. This incoherent subjectivity arises not as an autogenetic principle of autonomy but out of the simple *assertion* of autonomy in the face of a skeptical, indifferent, mocking, or outraged public. In the absence of a social milieu that can provide an audience for his autonomous hunger art, *Hunger* nonetheless continues to imagine aesthetic autonomy as a social phenomenon. Its sociality, however, becomes more straightforwardly antagonistic, a performance of dissidence and exclusion whose most visible sign is the protagonist's wasted frame and haggard appearance. In the pressures and antagonisms provoked by the starving body's display before a public, *Hunger*'s protagonist performs aesthetic autonomy without a social context as a traumatic experience of unfreedom and a spectacular collapse of the writer's personal autonomy.

3. MARGINALIZED MASCULINITIES: HAMSUN–RIMBAUD–KAFKA

The fraying of the autonomous subject that both Hamsun and Kafka describe as one of the chief effects of the art of hunger presents significant complications for the gender position of its artists. Such complications might be expected, given that the autonomous subject has historically been a gendered position. The personal autonomy granted to the individualist, rationalistic subject is widely regarded by feminist philosophers as "inherently bound up with masculine character ideals," even as some contemporary philosophers seek to redefine autonomy in the light of these feminist critiques.[55] If individualist, rationalistic forms of autonomy have historically presumed a male subject, then the collapse of the autonomous, presumptively or stereotypically masculine subject has significant consequences for the gendering of the non-subjects or unautonomous selves that are left in its wake.

Hamsun and Kafka both suggest that the art of hunger presupposes and creates a failed or marginalized masculinity. Its gendered nature is already

[55] Catriona Mackenzie and Natalie Stoljar, "Introduction: Autonomy Refigured," in *Relational Autonomy: Feminist Perspectives on Autonomy, Agency, and the Social Self*, ed. Catriona Mackenzie and Natalie Stoljar (New York: Oxford University Press, 2000), 3.

suggested by the fact that the texts assembled in this book constitute a canon exclusively by and about men. Moreover, most of these texts either strip their male heroes of all social relation, as in *Hunger*, or place them within primarily or exclusively male milieus into which the protagonists fail to integrate, such as the commercialized show business of "A Hunger Artist," or the law firm depicted in Herman Melville's *Bartleby*. The art of hunger, in other words, is an art that is produced by solitary male writers. This gender position is consistent with the way in which the tension between modernism and mass culture has been figured by writers and scholars since the nineteenth century. As Andreas Huyssen has argued, modernist autonomy is premised on a gendering of culture, whereby "mass culture is somehow associated with woman while real, authentic culture remains the prerogative of men."[56] The commitment to an art of hunger is a commitment to "real, authentic culture" and its autonomous art, and it is therefore a presumptively masculine position. But, as I argue in Sections 1 and 2, these writers dramatize the disjuncture between different kinds of autonomy: between aesthetic autonomy, to which they remain committed, and personal autonomy, now rendered impossible. Because both of these forms of autonomy are linked in the discourse of their day to masculinity, the art of hunger ends by positioning its writers as failed, failing, or marginalized men: masculine in their aesthetic autonomy, but feminized through their lack of personal autonomy.

The art of hunger, in this sense, represents a special case of what Rita Felski calls the "feminized male," an influential gender position in the modernist period, whereby "an imaginary identification with the feminine emerged as a key stratagem in the literary avant-garde's subversion of sexual and textual norms."[57] For the writers I examine here, hunger itself underlies this cross-gender identification. As Walter Vandereycken and Ron van Deth have shown, hunger and self-starvation have been associated with women since at least the medieval period.[58] This gendering of hunger achieved a particularly influential formulation in the nineteenth century where, as Anna Krugovoy Silver has argued, middle-class femininity came to be identified with an "anorexic logic" that valued slenderness and a renunciation of appetite.[59] As men who starve, the hunger artists of

---

[56] Andreas Huyssen, *After the Great Divide: Modernism, Mass Culture, Postmodernism* (Bloomington, IN: Indiana University Press, 1986), 47.

[57] Rita Felski, *The Gender of Modernity* (Cambridge, MA: Harvard University Press, 1995), 94, 91.

[58] Walter Vandereycken and Ron van Deth, *From Fasting Saints to Anorexic Girls: The History of Self-Starvation* (London: Athlone Press, 1994).

[59] Anna Krugovoy Silver, *Victorian Literature and the Anorexic Body* (Cambridge: Cambridge University Press, 2002), 27.

this book therefore adopted a feminized position. Moreover, they repeatedly associate hunger with attitudes and traits that are themselves feminized, from Kafka's hunger artist's link to mass culture, to Hamsun's emphasis on hunger as an irrational, embodied state. If hunger stages a kind of radical autonomy, it understands this autonomy not as a position of exemplary masculinity, but as the instantiation of a feminized masculinity—a masculinity from the margins.

Hunger in these texts poses a problem for gender difference. While starvation lessens the inhibitions and self-control of a character like *Hunger*'s protagonist, it also greatly reduces his sex drive. To the extent that gender difference was understood in this period as premised on heterosexuality, hunger is therefore represented as bringing about a loosening of gender roles. Refusing a proposition from a prostitute, for instance, the protagonist of *Hunger* laments, "Alas I had no real bounce in me these days. Women had become almost like men to me. Want had dried me up."[60] In the absence of sexual interest, whose decline he links explicitly to hunger, he imagines gender as dissolving into indifference, women into men. But while the texts of the art of hunger do suggest that hunger troubles gender identities, the dissolution of gender anticipated by the protagonist in this scene is not complete: women are only *almost* like men and the distinction still somehow tenuously holds. Gender is troubled and undone—but not surpassed—by hunger.

In *Hunger*, the compromised heterosexual masculinity of the text's protagonist is central to one of his most sustained encounters with a member of the public: his strange, abortive romance with a woman he names Ylajali (we never learn her real name). Their "relationship" begins with him following her through the streets of Kristiania (now Oslo) in the novel's opening pages and culminates in her refusal of his sexual advances at the end of Part Three. In its climactic scene, Ylajali induces the protagonist to "go on and tell me" the details of how he had been living, assuming him to be leading a dissolute, self-destructive, and alcoholic existence. What he tells her instead—something akin, we assume, to the story we ourselves have been reading up to this point—horrifies and repulses her, and she immediately recoils from their flirtation. The protagonist is dismayed: "Was I less worthy now, in her eyes, than if I had only myself to blame for my hair falling out, because of unbridled living? Would she have thought better of me if I had turned myself into a roué?"[61] The answer to both these questions seems to be "yes." Ylajali has, in effect,

[60] Hamsun, *Hunger*, 119–20.　　[61] Ibid., 169.

misrecognized the novel's protagonist as a starving artist, assuming him
to be performing a kind of rakish, transgressive masculinity. This masculinity's attractiveness is premised on its intentionality and its autonomy:
she hopes he would have "only myself to blame" for his actions and that
his persona would be something that he had "turned myself into." Her
disappointment arises not from his physical state, but from the realization that this state is not an index of his exemplary individual autonomy, but simply of his subjugation to circumstances, his exclusion from
the market, his myriad failures rather than his triumphant renunciation.
The starving artist—a figure like Hemingway or Breton or Miller—makes
the hunger artist socially intelligible by casting him as an autonomous and
therefore properly masculine subject. In contrast, the hunger artist—of
which the protagonist of *Hunger* is a chief example—is a failed autonomous
subject, a feminized and therefore sexually uninteresting (even sexually
repulsive) man.

Like Felski's feminized male avant-gardists, the protagonist of *Hunger*
finds the germ of aesthetic self-consciousness in the experience of failed
masculinity. Bridling at Ylajali's sudden withdrawal of intimacy, he defen-
sively formulates a theory of poverty's aesthetic virtues: "The intelligent poor
individual was a much finer observer than the intelligent rich one.... He is
alert and sensitive, he is experienced, his soul has been burned."[62] His
hunger, he suggests, makes him unusually receptive. This receptivity—
itself a paradigmatically feminized position—does nothing to bolster his
masculine sexual prowess, but it recasts both his unchosen poverty and his
compromised masculinity as the foundation of an aesthetic sensibility.
It imagines poverty not as the site of heroic, transgressive masculinity, but
rather as a state whose feminized masculinity makes the protagonist an
exemplary figure of aesthetic response.

The link between a feminized masculinity and the position of the writer
is elaborated in more detail in the work of Arthur Rimbaud, whose 1873
farewell to poetry, *A Season in Hell* (*Une saison en enfer*), pairs his sections
describing his love affair with fellow poet Paul Verlaine and his experiments in poetic invention as his two "Deliriums." Like Kafka and Hamsun,
Rimbaud imagines hunger as a figure for writing as such. *A Season in Hell*
opens by figuring the tumultuous few years in which he wrote poetry as
the period of his exclusion from a banquet. His turn away from poetry, he
explains in the poem's opening, is provoked by a desire to abandon the
hunger of writing and return to normal appetites: "on the verge of giving
my last *croak*, I thought of looking for the key to the ancient banquet

where I might possibly recover my appetite."[63] Rimbaud's exclusion from the banquet links his writing to an exclusion from the social life of the community. "Now," he writes, "I am an outcast [maudit]. I loathe my country."[64] The banquet figures the integrated social life that would have situated the young Rimbaud within a national and social context, giving him friends and identity. Imagining his exclusion from it, he imagines his starvation as a form of social isolation.

Rimbaud figures this exclusion from society as a failure to conform to the norms of contemporary masculinity. His exclusion from the banquet is prompted by his disillusionment with Beauty, figured as a women whom he "pulled...down on my knees.—I found her embittered and I cursed her."[65] Once outside the banquet, "debauchery and the companionship of women were denied me."[66] He takes up with a demon— presumably his lover, Verlaine—who "do[es] not like women" on the grounds of their contemptible conformity to social norms: "All they want now is a secure position. When security is reached, their hearts and their beauty are set aside. Only cold scorn is left, the food of marriage today."[67] Rimbaud implicitly figures his tumultuous relationship with Verlaine as a conscientious abstention from the unsatisfying food of contemporary marriage. Like Hamsun, he figures his social exclusion through his exclusion from heterosexuality and with it the codified forms of masculinity that attend the bourgeois marriage. But outside these strictures, Rimbaud finds himself in the feminized position of the outlaw woman, "dancing the witches' sabbath in a red clearing with old women and children."[68]

Exiling himself from women (at least, women in their roles as wives) and the reproductive institutions with which they are associated, Rimbaud disavows the possibility of genealogy. In his 1872 poem "Comedy of Thirst" ("Comédie de la soif"), he explicitly imagines thirst as the refusal of inheritance. He rejects in turn the comforting country drinks—dry wine, cider, milk, tea, and coffee—of his parents and grandparents; the "pure drinks | These water flowers for glasses" of stock poetic diction offered to him by the Spirit; and the fashionable absinthes and wines of his friends.[69] At each juncture, Rimbaud's devotion to his thirst is a rejection of a social context that would position his poetry in a lineage and grant it a social meaning.

In assuming a feminized position that excludes actual women, Rimbaud disrupts not just genealogical models of filiation and literary sociality, but

---

[63] Arthur Rimbaud, *Complete Works, Selected Letters: A Bilingual Edition*, trans. Wallace Fowlie (Chicago: University of Chicago Press, 2005), 265.

[64] Ibid., 269.   [65] Ibid., 265.   [66] Ibid., 271.   [67] Ibid., 281.

[68] Ibid., 267.   [69] Ibid., 175, 177.

also the prospect of active, masculine labor. As Rónán McDonald reminds us in relation to Ireland, the sustaining of the *patrie* is often understood in this period as relying on active, masculine citizenship.[70] Rimbaud, who proudly proclaims, "I loathe my country [patrie]," actively resiles from this model of masculine citizenship, declaring himself "lazy and brutal."[71] Like the Irish modernists that McDonald discusses, Rimbaud develops a model of "male inactivity."[72] Refusing work, Rimbaud rejects the growing professionalization of writing in the nineteenth and twentieth centuries, insisting on the aesthetic as a domain that is excluded from the capitalist demand to sell one's labor. But as Kristin Ross has shown, Rimbaud's refusal of work—like that of other writers in this tradition—also distinguishes itself from the aristocratic refusal of labor more typically associated with aesthetic autonomy, through Rimbaud's willing "embrace of inferiority."[73] The art of hunger stages precisely this "inferior" aesthetic autonomy. Hunger dramatizes the stakes of the refusal of labor and professionalization for those who are not aristocratic, and reimagines autonomy not as a heroic freedom from social norms but as a feminized exclusion from them.

In the *Letter to his Father* (1919), Kafka develops Rimbaud's espousal of a marginal masculinity, opposed to both genealogy and labor, in the context of the family dinner table. Written to and against his domineering father, the letter repeatedly figures his father's hearty appetite as part of a constellation of traits associated with his hegemonic masculinity, while underscoring the son's distance from this masculine ideal. "I did not, for instance, have your strength, your appetite, your skill," Kafka writes, drawing a firm distinction between his father's appetitive masculinity and his own disinterest in food.[74] Against this backdrop, the fasting of a character like the hunger artist gestures towards an alternate model of masculinity, one premised not on appetite but on the feminized renunciation of food. As Heather Merle Benbow argues, "Adopting a marginalized, feminized status, Kafka's male figures employ an oppositional eating practice that challenges hegemonic masculinity."[75] By renouncing food

[70] Rónán McDonald, "Nothing to Be Done: Masculinity and the Emergence of Irish Modernism," in *Modernism and Masculinity*, ed. Natalya Lusty and Julian Murphet (Cambridge: Cambridge University Press, 2014), 71–86.

[71] Rimbaud, *Complete Works*, 269.

[72] McDonald, "Nothing to Be Done," 72; see also Miller, *The Time of the Assassins*, 21–2.

[73] Ross, "Rimbaud and the Resistance to Work," 78.

[74] Franz Kafka, *Letter to his Father/Brief an den Vater*, trans. Ernst Kaiser (New York: Schocken Books, 2015), 25.

[75] Heather Merle Benbow, " 'Was Auf Dem Tisch Kam, Mußte Aufgegessen . . . Werden': Food, Gender, and Power in Kafka's Letters and Stories," *The German Quarterly* 79, no. 3 (2006): 347.

altogether, the hunger artist rejects the affirmative masculinity associated with Kafka's father, in favor of a performance of indifference and weakened appetite.

What is at stake in these competing forms of masculinity is, for Kafka, a question of power and freedom, of control and constraint. In the *Letter*, he makes the dinner table the principal site of his relationship with his father, the latter's teaching equated with "the teaching of proper behavior at a table."[76] This dinner table teaching is bound up in an oppressive system of power relations. Kafka imagines himself as "a slave" who "lived under laws invented only for me," in contrast to both his father, who lived in a world "concerned with government, with the issuing of orders and with the annoyance about their not being obeyed," and to the rest of the world, who "lived happily and free from order and from having to obey."[77] The practices and rituals of eating become for Kafka the source of his oppression, in contrast to both the tyranny of his father and the freedom of everyone else. The power dynamics of the family dinner table, in other words, translate the relations between dominant and subordinate masculinities into systems of oppression and exclusion, in which Kafka imagines himself, a picky eater and a vegetarian, in the oppressed position.

In this context, the hunger artist's unfreedom comes into sharper focus. Like the Kafka of the *Letter*, the hunger artist suffers from a lack of appetite, which places him outside the hegemonic regime of dominant masculinity. His hunger might therefore be understood as the full expression of the subordinated masculinity—weak, subjugated, hungry—that Kafka develops in the *Letter*. But whereas Kafka imagines his dietary habits through and against the hegemonic masculinity of his father, the hunger artist's performance of a weakened, hungry, and marginalized masculinity is not obviously defined in contradistinction to its successful or ideal form. The difference, in essence, lies in the distinction between oppression and unfreedom. In the *Letter to his Father*, Kafka imagines himself oppressed, reading the negotiation between different masculinities as an overt exercise of power by the father, which leaves the son in a position of subservience. His idiosyncratic dietary habits provide the territory on which this war is waged, the setting for the operation of his father's power. In "A Hunger Artist," in contrast, the eponymous figure is not persecuted on account of his refusal to eat. Instead, his hunger brings him up against different limitations to his autonomy and his freedom: the demands of the market, the mortality of his body, and his own lack of taste. He feels himself to be unfree, but not directly oppressed. His marginalized masculinity is not a

---

[76] Kafka, *Letter to his Father*, 23. [77] Ibid., 25.

directly oppositional position. Indeed, it barely comes into contact with the coercive operations of hegemonic masculinity. Unfree but not necessarily oppressed, the hunger artist—like the protagonist of *Hunger*—stands at the head of a tradition that imagines aesthetic autonomy as a position of feminized—and thus, unfree—masculinity.

4. THE ANTI-POLITICS OF REFUSAL: KAFKA–HAMSUN–MELVILLE

While the art of hunger carves out an alternate form of masculinity, its refusal of dominant gender roles does not necessarily entail a direct political challenge to them. As Felski suggests, "to assume that male identification with the feminine is *necessarily* subversive of patriarchal privilege may be to assume too much."[78] While the Kafka of the *Letter* is hyper-alert to the power dynamics inherent in the gendering of eating, the performance of masculinity in "A Hunger Artist" is considerably less interested in challenging or even identifying patriarchal systems of power. Moreover, as Benbow acknowledges, despite his critique of hegemonic masculinity, Kafka cannot easily be understood as a feminist writer.[79] These texts depict a struggle between different forms of masculinity, rather than one that specifically valorizes women or acknowledges their more substantial oppression within the gendered power dynamics around food. More dramatically, Rimbaud's attitude towards women is openly misogynistic, while Hamsun's protagonist's relationship with Ylajali begins with him stalking her and ends with him only barely refraining from raping her. Both reveal the extent to which failed or feminized masculinities may remain as bound up with misogyny and sexual violence as more successful or conventional masculine gender performances.

The ambivalence over the politics of the hunger artists' gender performances points to a larger ambivalence over politics more generally in the art of hunger. Given their marginal position and their refusal of social norms, critics have often read writers in this tradition as heroic figures of critique, or as agents of political resistance. As Fredric Jameson notes, the received ways of reading Kafka see him as staging the trauma of "authority now staged as the father, the state, or God himself."[80] As the master critic of modern bureaucracy in a work like *The Trial*, or as a fabulist of the real

---

[78] Felski, *The Gender of Modernity*, 93.
[79] Benbow, "Was Auf Dem Tisch Kam," 348.
[80] Fredric Jameson, *The Modernist Papers* (London: Verso, 2007), 96.

in his short stories, Kafka is understood as performing the political work of exposing the operations of authority, writing against the violence of the status quo. That Kafka shares a position at the head of this tradition with Knut Hamsun, however, might already give us pause. Hamsun's reputation continues to suffer from his enthusiastic embrace of Nazism in the 1930s and 1940s, which induced him to offer his vigorous support to the Nazi invasion of Norway during World War II and, incredibly, to send his Nobel Prize medal as a gift to Joseph Goebbels in 1943.[81] Leo Löwenthal, a member of the Frankfurt School, offered one of the most influential condemnations of Hamsun's politics in his 1957 study *Literature and the Image of Man*, which argues that the roots of Hamsun's fascism are evident throughout his writing and as far back as the 1890 text *Hunger*. Löwenthal points to a number of themes in *Hunger* that he finds to be proto-fascist: "the abandonment of any participation in public life, submission to the stream of incomprehensible and incalculable forces, distrust of the intellect, flight from the city and escape to nature."[82] But these themes are also detectable in the writing of Kafka, Rimbaud, and many of the other hunger artists of this study—and particularly in those aspects of their writing that are commonly read as subversive, critical, or antagonistic to the political status quo.

My point is not that Löwenthal is right to find the traces of fascism in texts that predate the existence of the ideology by several decades, and still less that the similarity between Kafka or Rimbaud and Hamsun on these points ought to encourage us to think of the art of hunger as itself a fascist tradition. Instead, I want to suggest that the conditions that allow Hamsun, Rimbaud, and Kafka to be read together as exemplars of a single tradition might encourage us to rethink the political function of these texts. The art of hunger's exploration of unfreedom is less a form of critique than the basis for an anti-politics, an attempt to resile from political commitment and to explore the ways in which we are unfree, above and beyond the ways in which we might be oppressed by specific political systems. Hunger itself provides the conditions that allow these writers to imagine unfreedom outside the terms of oppression, and therefore to imagine it in terms other than those that would generate political critique.

The clearest example of the way that hunger distorts the force of political critique in these texts comes in Herman Melville's 1853 story

---

[81] Monika Zagar, *Knut Hamsun: The Dark Side of Literary Brilliance* (Seattle: University of Washington Press, 2011), 196.

[82] Leo Löwenthal, *Literature and the Image of Man: Sociological Studies of the European Drama and Novel, 1600–1900* (Boston : The Beacon Press, 1957), 194.

Bartleby, the Scrivener. This story turns principally around the refusals of the eponymous character, a law-copyist or scrivener, as recounted by his employer. With a mounting absolutism, Bartleby refuses to do as instructed: he refuses to compare documents, to run errands, to answer questions about himself, and finally to copy at all, each time responding to requests with the opaque but immovable formula: "I would prefer not to." Finally, he refuses to be fired, and refuses to leave the lawyer's office, even after the lawyer himself moves out in desperation. He is eventually taken to prison, where his final words—"I would prefer not to dine today.... It would disagree with me; I am unused to dinners"—foreshadow his apparent death from starvation some days later.[83]

As a commercial writer who refuses to submit to the demand for productivity levied on workers in the capitalist system, Bartleby epitomizes the anti-market, anti-work mode of aesthetic autonomy. Accordingly, Bartleby has often been read as a figure for his creator: "a parable," as Leo Marx has influentially argued, "having to do with Melville's own fate as a writer."[84] As both an alter ego for the literary Melville and a commercial writer with no aesthetic aspirations, Bartleby is suspended in the conceptual abyss then emerging between the aesthetic and the commercial, and his doomed refusal acquires its hopelessness from his attempt to pull away from the commercial structures towards something more autonomous, more aesthetic. In this sense, starvation functions for Bartleby, as for Kafka, Rimbaud, and Hamsun, as the mark of the irreconcilability of aesthetics and the market—that is, of the impossible espousal of aesthetic autonomy.

If Bartleby's immovable refusals make his life into a figure for aesthetic autonomy, they have also made him, for a certain tradition of political thinkers, an exemplary figure of resistance. Michael Hardt and Antonio Negri hold Bartleby up as "the beginning of a liberatory politics," although they go on to caution that "it is only the beginning. Their refusal itself is empty.... Beyond simple refusal, or as part of that refusal, we need also to construct a new mode of life and above all a new community."[85] Slavoj Žižek radicalizes this position, arguing that Bartleby represents not a preliminary refusal, but the whole goal of political activity. He is "a kind of *arche*, the underlying principle that sustains the entire movement; far from 'overcoming' it, the subsequent work of construction, rather, gives

[83] Herman Melville, *Bartleby, the Scrivener: A Story of Wall Street* (Hoboken, NJ: Melville House Publishing, 2006), 61.

[84] Leo Marx, "Melville's Parable of the Walls," *Sewanee Review* 61, no. 4 (Autumn 1953): 603.

[85] Michael Hardt and Antonio Negri, *Empire* (Cambridge, MA: Harvard University Press, 2000), 204.

body to it."[86] Similarly, for Gilles Deleuze, "Bartleby is not the patient but the doctor of a sick America," a redemptive figure who embodies the full promise of the American revolution as a project for the realization of a "community of celibates."[87] Giorgio Agamben makes a similar claim, arguing that Bartleby is the "paradigm" for the "coming community."[88] For Agamben, Bartleby's paradigmatic political status derives from his embodiment of potentiality: "Bartleby is the extreme figure of the Nothing from which all creation derives; and at the same time, he constitutes the most implacable vindication of this Nothing as pure, absolute potentiality."[89] As such, Agamben's Bartleby creates a new ontology, on which his new politics will be founded. For all these thinkers, Bartleby promises a new system by his rejection of the status quo and of the actually existing political and economic arrangement. In this sense, these claims echo the most radical hopes for aesthetic autonomy in their commitment to understanding Bartleby's disinterest as producing a new order and a new mode of life.

These theorists' focus on Bartleby as the exemplary figure of a new political dispensation, however, relies on an emphasis on the political agency of what Deleuze calls Bartleby's "formula"—"I would prefer not to"—at the expense of his starving body. Despite Žižek's repeated calls for a politics that would "give body" to the formula "I would prefer not to," Bartleby already, quite literally, gives body to this formula—and that body starves to death. There is a tension therefore between the liberatory possibilities held out for the isolated and verbalized act of resistance, and the narrative trajectory in which the formula's repetition moves inexorably towards its speaker's solitary death. Bartleby's death not only suggests that resistance of this kind comes at significant personal cost. It also, more troublingly, forecloses the possibility of on-going political action, while leaving the social and political structures against which it is taken to act wholly untroubled.

A reading of *Bartleby* which foregrounds hunger therefore finds within the story less space for an affirmative politics, emphasizing instead the body as the horizon of necessity and unfreedom. Bartleby's narrativized

---

[86] Slavoj Žižek, *The Parallax View* (Cambridge, MA: MIT Press, 2006), 382.

[87] Gilles Deleuze, *Essays Critical and Clinical*, trans. Daniel W. Smith and Michael A. Greco (London: Verso, 1998), 89–90.

[88] Bartleby is discussed in a chapter of the same name in Agamben's *The Coming Community*: Giorgio Agamben, *The Coming Community*, trans. Michael Hardt (Minneapolis: University of Minnesota Press, 2007), 35–8; For an account of the status of these chapters as paradigms of the titular coming community, see Leland de la Durantaye, *Giorgio Agamben: A Critical Introduction* (Stanford, CA: Stanford University Press, 2009), 156–7.

[89] Giorgio Agamben, *Potentialities: Collected Essays in Philosophy*, ed. and trans. Daniel Heller Roazen (Stanford, CA: Stanford University Press, 1999), 253–4.

body, which starves to death in his cell, and the declamatory statement
("I would prefer not to") each have their own logics. The body offers a
kind of completion or perfection of the formula, which strips the latter of
its political efficacy at precisely the moment it reaches its most radical
form. Bartleby's politics, such as they are, therefore follow the same self-
foreclosing logic as the hunger artist's art. In this sense, Bartleby can be
read as both the champion and the failure of the aesthetics of those
theorists and philosophers, from Schiller to Rancière, who seek to stage
a rapprochement between politics and aesthetics by elaborating the political potential of aesthetic autonomy. Bartleby's role as an Ur-hunger artist
therefore highlights the difficulty of deriving a politics from this art of
unfreedom. It reveals the extent to which hunger in this tradition undoes
an affirmative politics grounded in either resistance or potentiality, by
bringing each up against the brute reality of a body that, by the nineteenth
century, was understood as marking the limits of human agency and
autonomy.

The fact that starvation functions in these texts to foreclose a politics of
resistance does not of course mean that hunger always voids a political
reading. On the contrary, the modernist period and the years that immediately preceded it saw some of the most important political deployments
of hunger in Western history. As James Vernon has shown, the late
nineteenth century was the period in which hunger was first constructed
as a humanitarian ill, a malady that demands restitution through political
and social response.[90] The early twentieth century meanwhile became the
period that saw the emergence of the hunger strike as a powerful form of
protest, from the hunger strikes of the suffragist movement, to the rise of
Irish hunger striking in the aftermath of the Easter Rising, to the internationally publicized fasts of Gandhi in India, which began in the 1910s
and continued until 1948. Emerging against this backdrop of diverse
forms of political and politicized hunger, the art of hunger shows not
that starvation cannot be political, but that it is not inherently so.

For hunger to become a vehicle for politics, two conditions must be
met. First, hunger must be made meaningful, the starving body induced
to "speak" in order to bear witness to some form of injustice. Second, this
meaning must be inscribed within a social field, so that the starving body
ceases to be exceptional and instead can be read as exemplary of larger
systems of power and broader social relations. It is this successful transformation of starvation into a political sign for collective suffering that
allowed hunger to become a humanitarian crisis in the nineteenth century,

---

[90] James Vernon, *Hunger: A Modern History* (Cambridge, MA; London: Harvard
University Press, 2007).

and hunger striking to emerge as a political response to other forms of injustice in the twentieth. The art of hunger, however, fails both conditions, being neither social nor meaningful. To the extent that it stages the collapse of a social context for aesthetic autonomy, it is a figure not for collective suffering but for the idiosyncratic exclusions of the individual artist. At the same time, as I argue in Section 5, the art of hunger insists on the literalness of the starving body, resisting (but never entirely preventing) its transformation into symbol, metaphor, or sign. As a result, the art of hunger produces not a model for a new politics, but an exploration of the unfreedom of embodiment that outlines instead an anti-politics of refusal.

5. ANTI-REFERENTIALITY AND EMPTY TRANSCENDENCE: HAMSUN– MELVILLE–KAFKA–RIMBAUD

The hunger artists of this study seek to write a stubbornly literal art, a form of literature that, tautologically, will be only what it is. This literal art aims for the radical form of autonomy that Andrew Goldstone calls "autonomy from reference," in which the text's self-containment, its refusal of reference to the outside world, becomes the mark of its autonomy.[91] The hunger artists, however, carry this anti-referential art in a more anti-social direction than the authors that Goldstone examines. Where Goldstone argues that writers like Wallace Stevens "understand that self-referential poetic as having a communal basis and a communal function," the art of hunger instead denies reference precisely as part of a broader reservation about shared or collective meaning—and ultimately about hermeneutics as such.[92] The emphasis on the literal that mobilizes this anti-hermeneutic art takes a range of forms, from a focus on the body and its performance of starvation, to an exploration of the rigorous and logical unfolding of a set of conditions, to an emphasis on the materiality of language at the expense of meaning. What these diverse formal manifestations share is a commitment to the literal in art. The literalism of the art of hunger imagines autonomous art as resting in an anti-social incommunicability that is also a refusal of transcendence and thus a tendency to remain at the level of language's and the body's materiality.

Hamsun's protagonist's invention of the word "*Kuboaa*" as he sits starving in a jail cell overnight typifies the attempt to free language from

[91] Andrew Goldstone, *Fictions of Autonomy: Modernism from Wilde to de Man* (Oxford: Oxford University Press, 2013), 149.
[92] Ibid., 151.

meaning. Running through a range of possible meanings for this word without committing to any, he concludes counter-intuitively, "It wasn't difficult to make sense of such a word."[93] Viktor Shklovsky has argued that this passage is an example of "trans-sensible language," a "'word' without concept and content that serve[s] to express pure emotion."[94] In this sense, Hamsun's invented word embodies a specific and radical form of aesthetic autonomy, one in which reference itself is understood as compromising autonomy, and which therefore locates literary autonomy at the level of the word's materiality. For Hamsun, this anti-hermeneutic quality allows him to assert his autonomy as a rejection of meaning's social function. His deliberation over the word's meaning is interrupted by his paranoia that meaning is being forced upon it from without: "Then it seems to me that someone was speaking, sticking his nose into my chat.... I had invented the word myself, and I was perfectly within my rights in having it mean anything whatsoever."[95] Creating an imaginary interlocutor, Hamsun's protagonist imagines the autonomy of his word—like the autonomy of his experience more generally—as social only in an aggressively oppositional way. In this sense, his version of autonomy from reference is significantly different to the more collective version that Goldstone identifies. Where Goldstone argues that Stevens's use of tautology relies on shared meanings and understandings to give it sense, Hamsun's new word violently refuses the imposition of shared meaning in order to preserve its irreducibly private meaning—and ends by producing no fixed meaning at all. Moving beyond the merely anti-referential, Hamsun's invention of words becomes anti-communal and anti-hermeneutic.

The mutual reinforcement of the resistance to meaning and the refusal of the social is a common theme throughout the art of hunger, which searches for its autonomy in the negation of community. But while Hamsun pursues this through an unbounded inventiveness, for other writers in the art of hunger tradition anti-referentiality arises instead from an attempt to reimagine art as uninventive and uncreative. Bartleby's "I would prefer not to," for instance, is an exemplarily literal verbal correlate to his behavior, rigorously translating his stated preference into inaction. When Deleuze calls this statement a formula, he is gesturing towards its specific kind literalness: its ability to unfold predictably and with a minimum of flourish the consequences of a stated preference.[96] This vision of literature as the predictable unfolding of all available options

[93] Hamsun, *Hunger*, 75.
[94] Shklovsky, "On Poetry and Trans-Sense Language," 9.
[95] Hamsun, *Hunger*, 76.　　[96] Deleuze, *Essays Critical and Clinical*, 68.

is what Jameson finds so distinctive in Kafka's work, and becomes, as I argue in Chapter 2, the formal principle of Beckett's late work, whose unfolding is driven by a permutative compulsion.[97] This emphasis on the rigorously logical and literal unfolding of consequences is, as Jameson argues of Kafka, "quite the opposite of inventiveness."[98] Its literalness undoes the possibility of an art founded on the autonomous individuality of the artist, making the writer instead into an amanuensis for the physical laws of body, causality, and mathematical or logical progression. This version of the literal as the rigorous and uninventive unfolding of possibilities differs formally and aesthetically from Hamsun's invention of new words. Whereas Hamsun seeks a radical form of creativity, Kafka, Melville, and Beckett instead privilege the uncreative. Nonetheless, in pushing their respective positions to the limit of non-sense, they each end in a repudiation of hermeneutics and meaning's social function.

Taking starvation as the source of this anti-social, anti-referential art, both these positions disrupt hunger's potential to be politically efficacious. Nonetheless, this resistance to the literal produces a kind of leaky availability for interpretation, as Hamsun's narrator finds in the proliferation of possible meanings that his word produces, or as we see in the obsessive attention accorded to Bartleby's "I would prefer not to" by generations of critics. By not being a sign for anything obvious, these texts are open to critics searching for unobvious meanings. As a result, they retain the faint prospect of political recuperation. By insisting on the literal unfreedom of their characters' experience, they tempt critics to seek out the promise of freedom—or at least the force of critique—hovering at the text's margins. A literature of unfreedom can therefore slip easily into a literature of critique, as unfreedom is read as a critical gesture. At the same time, the process of translating the starving body into language inevitably brings hunger into the orbit of interpretation. The presumptive interpretability of language makes the opacity of Bartleby's formula into an invitation to interpretation, while the opacity of his starving body becomes simply a mark of its critical disposability. As a result, the art of hunger's resistance to interpretation and its consequent refusal of hunger's political uses is always at risk of producing a proliferation of interpretation and political meaning despite itself.

The art of hunger is therefore always at risk of failure. Indeed, in a diary entry from December 6, 1921—just months before he began writing "A Hunger Artist"—Kafka suggests that this failure is inherent in the nature of writing itself:

---

[97] Jameson, *The Modernist Papers*, 96–112.   [98] Ibid., 101.

From a letter: "During this dreary winter I warm myself by it." Metaphors are one among many things which makes me despair of writing. Writing's lack of independence of the world, its dependence on the maid who tends the fire, on the cat warming itself by the stove; it is even dependent on the poor old human being warming himself by the stove. All these are independent activities ruled by their own laws; only writing is helpless, cannot live in itself, is a joke and a despair.[99]

The irresistible conclusion of Kafka's lament is that writing cannot be autonomous insofar as it is referential; that its inevitable metaphoricity compromises both its independence and its ability to generate and be subject to its own laws. When critics of Kafka, from Adorno to Deleuze and Guattari to Fredric Jameson, follow Walter Benjamin's reading of Kafka's stories as parables without a doctrine, they suggest that his writing aspires to forestall this metaphoricity, and thereby to become literal.[100] But if dependence is, as Kafka suggests, in the nature of language itself, then such an aspiration will always fail.

"A Hunger Artist" dramatizes this dilemma. By theorizing his art not through writing or any other representational medium, but through the performance of starvation, Kafka imagines an art that does not generate a gap between what it is and what it means. The performance of starvation is, ideally, neither referential nor metaphorical. Its force and its significance inhere straightforwardly in the minimally mediated starving body. Merging together two different freak show acts—the living skeleton, famous for his extreme thinness, and the hunger artist, renowned for his ability to fast for extended periods of time—Kafka's hunger artist comes as close as possible to making the body and act coincide, turning them into such perfect signs for each other that they no longer truly signify. He therefore embodies what Deleuze and Guattari call Kafka's "skeleton of sense," in which the tautology of the literal undoes meaning: "Since things are as they are . . . he will abandon sense, render it no more than implicit."[101]

But as we have already seen, the hunger artist's performance is inherently unobservable. His skeletal frame is therefore never a perfect analogue for his acts of self-starvation, slipping inevitably back into the slipperiness of signs that are at once dependent on the world and never entirely

[99] Franz Kafka, *Diaries 1910–1923*, ed. Max Brod, trans. Joseph Kresh and Martin Greenberg (New York: Schocken Books, 1948), 397–8.

[100] Walter Benjamin, *Illuminations: Essays and Reflections*, ed. Hannah Arendt, trans. Harry Zohn (New York: Schocken Books, 1968), 122; Theodor Adorno, "Notes on Kafka," in *Prisms*, trans. Samuel Weber and Shierry Weber (Cambridge, MA: MIT Press, 1983), 246; Deleuze and Guattari, *Kafka*, 19–21; Jameson, *The Modernist Papers*, 101–2.

[101] Deleuze and Guattari, *Kafka*, 20–1.

themselves. Moreover, if the emphasis on performance is meant as the negation of writing's miserable dependence, then it already fails in the straightforward sense that Kafka's hunger artist is already written. As such, he is "dependent" on the world in ways that critics (myself included) cannot help but fall back on: he is tied to Kafka and thus to his diaries; to history and thus to historical figures like Giovanni Succi and other hunger artists on whom Kafka based his story; and to interpretation, and thus to just the kind of quasi-allegorical reading that allows us to take the hunger artist as a figure for the writer. Reading Kafka's aesthetics out of "A Hunger Artist," we are already plunged back into the problem of metaphor, forced to produce a metaphorical reading of a purportedly anti-metaphorical art. This dilemma replays Kafka's despair over language, underscoring the way in which art—both in itself, and wherever it comes into contact with language—is cursed to remain dependent on the world, and in this sense, cursed to be unfree.

Kafka's hunger artist reflects a paradox that inheres in the art of hunger more generally: he is unfree both in his attempt to be literal (because the literal would keep him confined to the materiality of his body, and prevent starvation's repurposing as liberation through political or other meanings), and in the failure of that attempt (because this failure itself reflects the ways in which his autonomy is incomplete, always bound to the world, without thereby moving him beyond it). Freedom, in this context, would seem to require a movement beyond the literal entirely, a leap into a transcendent realm in which neither bodies nor social relations were limiting factors. In fact, "The Hunger Artist"—whose protagonist's fast, like that of Moses, Elijah, and Jesus before him, lasts for forty days—alludes to a religious reading that would understand starvation in these terms, as an act of transcendence in the traditional ascetic mode. In this too, however, the hunger artist fails, producing only what Peter Sloterdijk calls a "beheaded asceticism, in which the supposed tensile strain from above proves to be an aversive tension from within."[102] Tracing his fast to a personal failure of taste, the hunger artist does away with the self-overcoming, self-transcendent movement of asceticism. For Kafka's hunger artist, for whom his hunger is his art, the aesthetic is located in a practice of autonomy that frustrates transcendence through its emphasis on the literal and the immediate. In this failure of transcendence, the hunger artist is thrown back onto the finite confines of his material body,

---

[102] Peter Sloterdijk, *You Must Change your Life: On Anthropotechnics*, trans. Wieland Hoban (Cambridge: Polity Press, 2013), 71.

his art unfree in the metaphysical sense that it allows no scope to move outside of these material limitations. Rimbaud develops Kafka's flirtation with an art of failed transcendence and empty religiosity. In a letter to Paul Demeny in 1871, he imagines himself as a *"seer [voyant]"* producing a new form of art "by a long, gigantic and rational *derangement* of *all the senses*."[103] The goal of this derangement is "reaching the unknown," as he writes to Georges Izambard around the same time.[104] In this sense, it is an aspiration for a kind of transcendence, a faith in poetry's capacity to open up hitherto unknown paths. But as Hugo Friedrich argues, Rimbaud ultimately finds only an "empty transcendence," in which a religious vocabulary is repurposed in the performance of the impossibility of transcendence.[105] Hunger, with its long-standing association with asceticism and mysticism, is the central site of this repurposing, as Friedrich notes: *"Hunger* and *thirst* are frequent in Rimbaud's diction. These are the same words that the mystics and Dante used, in keeping with biblical language, to denote sacred yearning. In Rimbaud, however, such passages point toward the unquenchable."[106]

Rimbaud's 1872 poem "Fêtes de la faim" (Feasts of Hunger) exemplifies the empty transcendence of his use of hunger. The poem's first four-line stanza opens:

> Si j'ai du *goût* ce n'est guères
> Que pour la terre et les pierres
> Dinn! dinn! dinn! dinn! Mangeons l'air,
> Le roc, le charbon, le fer

> If I have any *taste*, it is for hardly
> Anything but rocks and stone
> Dinn! dinn! dinn! dinn! Let us eat air
> Rock, coal, iron[107]

Repudiating both the normal appetites that he elsewhere associates with integration into society, and the yearning for a truly incorporeal food—the body of the lord, manna from heaven—that we associate with religious fasting, Rimbaud's desire to eat stones produces an empty transcendence. Preferring to eat rocks, he simultaneously disavows his bodily need for food, and intensifies his affiliation with the material world. Even when his hunger turns its attention in a later stanza to religious artefacts—"Les vieilles pierres d'églises | Les galets, fils de déluges" (The old stones of

---

[103] Rimbaud, *Complete Works*, 377.   [104] Ibid., 371.
[105] Friedrich, *Structure of Modern Poetry*, 42.   [106] Ibid., 50.
[107] Rimbaud, *Complete Works*, 194–5.

churches | The pebbles, sons of floods)—he can engage them only in their most brutally material forms, seeking transcendence, again and again, through the untranscendable stone. The hunger for stones will return in Beckett's *Molloy*, who takes great delight in sucking pebbles (Chapter 2), and in Auster's poetry, where the stone is a repeated motif for the indigestible (Chapter 3). In each case, it marks a limit of transcendence, and thus signifies the impossibility of turning hunger into asceticism, of reimagining privation as a route to spiritual freedom.

"Fêtes de la faim" is reprinted in a revised form in the "Alchimie du verbe" (Alchemy of the Word) section of *A Season in Hell*. In this later version, the summons to eat the inedible—"Dinn! dinn! dinn! dinn! Let us eat air | Rock, coal, iron"—is revised to suggest that the impossible meal is already and perpetually under way: "Je déjeune toujours d'air | De roc, de charbons, de fer" (I always feed on air, | Rock, coal and iron).[108] This new version produces the speaker of the poem as a product of what Friedrich calls "absolute metaphor," a figure in which "metaphor, no longer a mere figure of comparison, now creates an identity."[109] The speaker of "Fêtes de la faim" *is* (and is not merely *like*) the kind of (impossible, unimaginable) person who can find nourishment in air and minerals. He is the product of a species of language that, as Kristin Ross suggests, seeks "to verge *beyond* representation, to function as a machine to produce, not reproduce, the real."[110] In this sense, Rimbaud's rock-eating speaker seeks to solve the same problem with metaphor that Kafka laments in his diaries: the problem of metaphor's (and language's) representational reliance on the world. The method of "absolute metaphor" strives towards a kind of language that is no longer bound to the world—a kind of language that is autonomous in Kafka's radical and anti-referential sense.

The autonomy of this anti-referential projection of an alternate reality is heightened in Rimbaud by his poetry's autopoetic tendency, in which the poem generates itself from its own internal logic. The lines that open the 1872 version of the poem, for instance, verge on the nonsensical on the level of pure meaning: "Ma faim, Anne, Anne | Fuis sur ton âne" (My hunger, Anne, Anne, | Flee on your donkey).[111] They make sense only on a strictly aural level, where they can be understood as arising from the progression of sounds: its half-rhyme with "faim" summoning "Anne"; the homonym of "Anne" and "âne" producing the donkey. Like Hamsun's invented words and like the art of hunger's inclination towards an anti-referential art more generally, this autopoetic impulse locates the

---

[108] Ibid., 290–1.   [109] Friedrich, *Structure of Modern Poetry*, 51.
[110] Ross, "Rimbaud and the Resistance to Work," 79.
[111] Rimbaud, *Complete Works*, 194–5.

autonomy of Rimbaud's poem in its capacity to produce a self-contained language that does not rely on reference to the outside world. Indeed, Rimbaud's speaker's hunger is nurtured by his desire to feast not only on rocks, but also on "le pré des sons," which Wallace Fowley translates as "the meadow of bran" but which could just as easily be "the meadow of sounds" (*son* meaning both "bran" and "sound" in French).[112] This pun imagines language as an alternate food, taking its material aspects—its sound rather than its meaning—as the source of its capacity to nourish. It reflects an extreme form of aesthetic autonomy, one analogous to Shklovsky's trans-sensible language, which develops the anti-referential desire for a literal art into a theory of art as the generator of self-contained worlds.

Seeking in poetry an alternate, self-generating world, Rimbaud's writing rejects both the social and the referential. He seeks autonomy in a liberation from the tyranny of the world as it is, from the rule of a world in which one only eats food and transcendence involves a leap into the immaterial. This approach inevitably fails, running headlong into the inevitable disappointments of empty transcendence and the flight back to the materiality of language and stones. In this sense, as writers have repeatedly affirmed, Rimbaud writes an art of the impossible. As Henry Miller writes, "The future is all his, even though there be no future."[113] Or as Yves Bonnefoy puts it, in a study that puts impossibility at the center of Rimbaud's writing: "So Rimbaud made himself collide with the impossible, without resolving anything, without any miracle taking place."[114] For both Bonnefoy and Miller, Rimbaud's status as a precursor for their respective literary projects is grounded in his necessarily failed confrontation with the impossible.

Bonnefoy seeks to redeem this Rimbaudian impossibility as a route to freedom. It is, he argues, a "tragic confrontation with the absolute" that leads Rimbaud to write, "the most liberating [poetry] . . . in the history of our language."[115] As he writes in the concluding line of his study: "the Phoenix of freedom, which makes its body out of burnt hopes, comes to beat the air here with its new wings."[116] If Rimbaud's poetry were liberating, however, it would be so only in the sense that he has left society and its understanding of reality behind in a definitive way, launching

---

[112] Ibid., 194–5.　　[113] Miller, *The Time of the Assassins*, xi.

[114] "Rimbaud n'a donc fait que se heurter contre l'impossible, sans rien résoudre, sans qu'aucun miracle ait eu lieu": Yves Bonnefoy, *Rimbaud par lui-même* (Paris: Éditions du Seuil, 1951), 177.

[115] "l'affrontement tragique de l'absolu . . . sa poésie est la plus libératrice . . . de l'histoire de notre langue": Ibid., 178.

[116] "le Phénix de la liberté, celui qui fait son corps des espérances brûlées, vient battre l'air ici de ses ailes neuves": Ibid., 178.

himself into a confrontation with the absolute that can only be undertaken alone. But as Miller argues, to the extent that "the liberty he demanded was freedom for his ego to assert itself unrestrained," then, "that is not freedom."[117] And even this unsatisfactory egotistical freedom fails. In the image of eating rocks, Rimbaud runs up against the hard materiality of a world that, even in his imagination, remains stony and resistant. His empty transcendence refers itself back to the material world, and his attempt to find autonomy through the absolute metaphor or the autopoetic poem leads him not to transcend the known but, as he writes in the *Season in Hell* version of "Fêtes de la faim," to "consume myself."[118] As a result, Rimbaud's quest for freedom is always deferred, until, in the final line of *A Season in Hell*, this deferral points beyond poetry itself, to a future free from the disorder of his writerly life, in which "I shall be free *to possess truth in one body and soul.*"[119] Like Hamsun, Rimbaud locates freedom in an imagined future beyond the constraints of writing and hunger. He thus relegates writing to a period of unfreedom, associated with hunger, his divorce from truth, and his immersion in the blind impulses of the body. Regaining his appetite and attaining freedom become the same ambition—one that can only be realized by abandoning his vocation as a poet.

Read together, as they have often been by later critics and authors, Rimbaud, Melville, Hamsun, and Kafka elaborate a theory of hunger's relationship to literature. They posit hunger as a figure for a form of aesthetic autonomy that is both unfree and at risk of losing its social context. Outside the market and its systems of labor, outside masculinity and its models of genealogy and activity, outside liberal subjectivity and its assumptions about free will and free choice, the art of hunger sees aesthetic autonomy as a form of rebellion against society and its structures. But because it refuses all forms of community, it does not produce freedom or the impetus for political change. Instead, it traces an art of unfreedom that takes the starving body and the material, sonorous text as both the limit of its authors' freedom and the site of their art. The unfree, anti-social writing of the art of hunger provides the groundwork for the writers of surrealism and the Lost Generation, with whom this chapter began, and through them for a vernacular tradition of the starving artist. While for these writers, this reprisal of starvation helps to mark their position within a literary milieu, for another set of late twentieth-century writers

---

[117] Miller, *The Time of the Assassins*, 49.   [118] Rimbaud, *Complete Works*, 291.
[119] "il me sera loisible de *posséder la vérité dans une âme et un corps*": Ibid., 304–5.

the art of hunger instead serves as a way of figuring aesthetic autonomy in places where their milieu no longer embraces autonomy. For these later writers, like their modernist and proto-modernist forebears, the collapse of aesthetic autonomy's social context produces an art that can no longer imagine itself as free. The fate of this unfree aesthetic autonomy as it mediates modernism's role in the later twentieth century is the subject of Chapters 2–4 of this book.

2

Hunger in a Closed System

Samuel Beckett in Post-war France

"Between a Gozzoli as such and a Gozzoli from our exploded categories, I would die of starvation": so Beckett proclaims in a letter to his close friend and frequent correspondent Georges Duthuit in May 1949.[1] Given, that is, the choice between Italian representational art of the kind Duthuit loathed, and modern abstract art of the kind he favored, Beckett prefers to starve. His espousal of starvation refuses not just Duthuit's specific aesthetic position, but the very terms of the debate in which Duthuit is engaged, implying that even "our exploded categories" are determined by the figurative tradition to which they are ostensibly opposed. The debate against which he is positioning himself—the "bataille réalisme–abstraction"—dominated French art criticism in the post-war period. By proclaiming that he would rather die of starvation than engage its terms, Beckett places himself outside the oppositions on which the post-war French aesthetic field was founded. Like the modernist hunger artists discussed in Chapter 1, his espousal of an aesthetic position identified with hunger allows him to figure the collapse of a social context for his aesthetics.

Beckett's rejection of the terms of the post-war aesthetic debate are grounded in his skepticism of two of its axioms. First, Beckett rejects the call to make art political, which dominated thinking about art and literature in France in the 1940s. In this, he is part of a late modernist shift that understands aesthetic autonomy as entailing autonomy not just from the market, but also from politics. While for the early modernists discussed in Chapter 1 of this book, aesthetic autonomy was above all an attempt to exempt art from commercial considerations, by the 1930s, as Tyrus Miller has argued, the question of art's relationship to politics had

---

[1] Samuel Beckett, *The Letters of Samuel Beckett: Volume 2, 1941–1956*, ed. George Craig et al. (Cambridge: Cambridge University Press, 2011), 156.

become central to aesthetic debate.[2] In response, the controversy around aesthetic autonomy shifted to encompass the question of whether art should be political. In France in the aftermath of World War II, the answer to this question very often seemed to be an unequivocal yes. The lingering politicization of the aesthetic realm following the German Occupation of France meant that the most influential theories of art in the post-war period, from Communist social realism to Sartrean *littérature engagée*, reflected a growing consensus that aesthetic autonomy was politically irresponsible. In this context, even the apparently formalist distinction between realism and abstraction that Beckett alludes to in his distinction between the two Gozzolis implies a political choice between the Communist embrace of realism, on the one hand, and the emergent association between liberalism and post-war modernist abstraction, on the other. In this context, Beckett's suggestion that he would prefer to die of starvation suggests a shift in the art of hunger. Starvation in this new context begins to function as a dramatization not primarily of the tensions entailed by aesthetic autonomy's production of artistic poverty. Instead, it dramatizes the impossibility of an a- or anti-political aesthetic autonomy in a context that produces the politicization of art in all its forms.

A minority of thinkers in the post-war period shared Beckett's skepticism of the compulsory politicization of art, preferring aesthetic autonomy over the prevailing alternatives of social realism, or *littérature engagée*. Even those committed to some version of aesthetic autonomy, however, overwhelmingly subscribed to a more fundamental axiom, which was shared across the ideological and aesthetic positions of the post-war literary and artistic fields. This axiom held that art and literature provided a path to freedom. It underpinned both the defenses of and attacks on art's political uses, and became a surprisingly widespread point of consensus, cutting across the highly charged debates that characterized the French aesthetic field in the late 1940s. Given that both realism and abstraction were linked to this rhetoric of freedom, Beckett's proclamation that he would rather die of starvation than follow either path represents his break with this consensus, reflecting his preference for an art that is divorced not only from politics, but from the possibility of freedom itself. Like earlier hunger artists, Beckett uses starvation to dramatize his commitment to an art that is both autonomous and unfree, imagined as a fatal confrontation with the physical limits of his mortal body.

Beckett's art of hunger is a response to a field in which aesthetic autonomy is discredited and in crisis, where the social consensus on

---

[2] Tyrus Miller, *Late Modernism: Politics, Fiction, and the Arts Between the World Wars* (Berkeley: University of California Press, 1999), 32.

which modernist autonomy was built has fractured and disintegrated. In this context, it represents a crucial turn in the history of the art of hunger. The problem of producing autonomous art without a literary field organized around autonomy—the problem that I traced through modernist hunger artists in Chapter 1—returns in post-war France as the collapse of the viability of aesthetic autonomy not just (or primarily) as a way of organizing the literary field, but also as a philosophical concept. As the debate about art's relationship to politics comes to dominate philosophical discussions about aesthetic autonomy, the art of hunger's tendency to imagine art as unfree and anti-political acquires a new set of meanings. This chapter places Beckett's development of an aesthetics of starvation within the context of post-war French literary and artistic debates, arguing that the art of hunger develops in his writing as part of a larger shift towards an unfree, anti-political art. Writing against both the association between art and freedom that runs throughout the post-war French literary field and the politicization of hunger that pervades French and Irish national discourse at this time, Beckett's art of hunger theorizes an unfree art through the falling away of political and aesthetic communities.

The second half of this chapter argues that the theory of art that Beckett develops in reaction to post-war French aesthetic debates finds expression in the form of Beckett's late prose. The unfreedom of Beckett's autonomous art culminates in the formal subjugation of body and affect to abstract, logical form, in a process that develops from the sucking stones episode of *Molloy* in the post-war period, to its full realization in the late prose of the 1960s through to the 1980s. The aesthetic positions entailed by the art of hunger are realized in Beckett as a set of formal processes that act on both reader and character. They produce an embodied aesthetics, where embodiment becomes the site of the body's unfreedom, its subjection to the pattern and permutation that constitutes the internal logic of the text itself in the late prose. This process reconceives aesthetic autonomy as a formal strategy and not simply an aesthetic concept, in which texts develop as closed systems that generate their own idiosyncratic laws. Read this way, I argue that Beckett's late prose as a whole can be understood as an extrapolation of the art of hunger into a question of textual form.

1. AUTONOMY, ENGAGEMENT, AND *ÉPURATION*

Debates over the relationship of art to politics, and the viability of aesthetic autonomy in a newly politically charged context dominate the post-war French literary field. The problem of literary commitment became a particularly urgent one in post-war France, where the cultural prestige of French writers was put under pressure by attempts to come to terms with the fraught moral and political legacies of the Occupation. As Gisèle Sapiro argues, this period of French history poses particularly stark challenges for aesthetic autonomy, asking us to consider, "What happens to literary autonomy in a period of crisis," particularly one in which "the literary field witnessed the abolition of those conditions that had assured its relative independence."[3] The attempt to answer this question presents the first sustained post-war crisis for aesthetic autonomy, and produces a body of philosophical and theoretical thought that, from Sartre's *What is Literature?* to Blanchot's post-war writings and Barthes's *Writing Degree Zero*, set the terms of subsequent debates about the nature of literature and its relationship to politics.

The foundations for these debates were laid during the German Occupation of France (1940–4) and in the purge of writers and intellectuals that immediately followed the Liberation in 1944. For the French literary field, the Occupation seemed to mark the end of an autonomous literary or cultural sphere, mobilizing and polarizing French intellectuals and writers around political questions to an unprecedented degree. Many of France's leading inter-war intellectuals emerged during the war as Nazi sympathizers or collaborators, with influential writers such as Charles Maurras and Robert Brasillach writing in support of the Vichy regime. Meanwhile, the Resistance also mobilized intellectuals in opposition to the Occupation, and in 1941 the Comité National des Écrivains (CNE) was formed as the writer's branch of the Resistance, under the auspices of the Communist Party. The CNE's clandestine publication, *Les Lettres françaises*—which was run by Jean Paulhan and Jacques Decour, and carried unsigned work by writers such as Louis Aragon, Paul Éluard, François Mauriac, Raymond Queneau, and Jean-Paul Sartre—insisted from the outset on the political responsibility of writers and intellectuals, aggressively denouncing those they suspected of collaboration.

Even for those writers who sought to retain an autonomous position, the totalitarian nature of the Occupation made this impossible. The hyper-politicized environment of the war years colored all aspects of life, from the most literary to the most quotidian. The German occupiers in the north and the collaborationist Vichy regime in the south both took over periodicals, presses, and broadcasters, heavily censoring and controlling what was published and broadcast. Writers who wished to publish were forced to choose between venues that, by virtue of their continuing

---

[3] Gisèle Sapiro, *The French Writers' War, 1940–1953*, trans. Vanessa Doriott Anderson and Dorrit Cohn (Durham, NC: Duke University Press, 2014), 3.

existence, operated to varying degrees with the sanction of the governing regime, or those that, operating clandestinely, declared their opposition to Vichy and the Nazi occupiers. Under such conditions, the space for aesthetic autonomy radically contracted, and, as Sapiro argues, the very question of "whether or not to publish in these conditions became a political issue. The most apolitical attitudes thus took on a political significance."[4]

The politicization of writing that characterized the war years continued to shape the French intellectual environment in the immediate aftermath of the war. The CNE's wartime denunciations set the tone for a flurry of prosecutions and ostracisms of collaborationist writers in the immediate aftermath of the Liberation. *L'épuration*—the juridical and extra-juridical purge of collaborators in the immediate aftermath of the Liberation—was a society-wide affair, but trials and denunciations of writers and intellectuals often assumed an out-sized symbolic importance. Brasillach was charged with treason for his wartime writings and executed; others were sentenced to prison terms of varying lengths. Some, like Céline, who had fled France as the Allies retook the country, were tried and sentenced in absentia. Many others were never tried by the courts, but were placed on blacklists by the CNE, which sought to exclude them wholesale from the post-war French literary field.

The intellectual response to *l'épuration* revealed the extent to which ambivalence about the merits of aesthetic autonomy structured the post-war French intellectual scene. On the one hand, charges levelled against collaborators and suspected collaborators frequently accused them of literally selling out to the Germans, sacrificing political and ethical principles in exchange for (often fictive) material gain. The old claim that the "pure writer" was one who "remained poor" is repurposed here as a guarantee not just of aesthetic autonomy but also of political virtue.[5] On the other hand, the suggestion that literature was autonomous from politics, rather than just from the market, came to be associated with the position of the collaborationist writers. During the purge trials, accused writers and their lawyers often appealed to the claim that literature was inherently autonomous, arguing that their writing's formal qualities held it outside the realm of the merely political.[6] The resulting association between aesthetic autonomy and collaboration lent weight to the CNE's wartime insistence on literature as an "instrument" and its disdain for

[4] Ibid., 14.
[5] Philip Watts, *Allegories of the Purge: How Literature Responded to the Postwar Trials of Writers and Intellectuals* (Stanford, CA: Stanford University Press, 1998), 28.
[6] Ibid., 54–6.

writers who, in professing fidelity to pure art, became (to the CNE's eyes) complicit in Nazi crimes.[7] Thus, while art's autonomy from the market remained a broadly accepted ideal in the post-war period, its autonomy from politics was discredited by its association with collaborationist writers.

In this context, the great debate that structured the French literary field at the end of the war was not initially between autonomous and non-autonomous art (the former being discredited in advance), but between the Communists' and the existentialists' different versions of a committed, political literature. In the immediate post-war years, the Communist Party assumed a position of "hegemony in the intellectual field," in part as a result of their central role within the Resistance.[8] They swept municipal and Constituent Assembly elections in 1945, strengthening their wartime claims to moral authority, and began to attract significant literary and cultural figures in large numbers, as long-time Communist Louis Aragon was joined by other major writers and artists, including Paul Éluard, Pablo Picasso, and Fernand Léger. In this context, as Anna Boschetti has argued, "the question of the correct relationship to the Communist Party," and with it the correct relationship to the party's belief that art be subject to the demands of politics, "shows itself to be the obsession of an entire generation" of writers and intellectuals.[9]

Jean-Paul Sartre provided the most influential response to the Communist position, developing a political but not straightforwardly didactic theory of literature. In the process, he became the central figure of the post-war literary field, coming to hold, as Boschetti argues, "undivided sway over the entire realm of French intellectual life," and shaping the anti-autonomous position for decades to come.[10] His clearest statement of this position comes in his influential essay *What is Literature?*, which was published serially in his journal *Les Temps modernes* in 1947 and collected in a single volume in 1948. Revising the Kantian claim that the aesthetic is characterized by its "finality without end," Sartre insists that while "the book is not, like the tool, a means for any end whatever," it does find an end in "the reader's freedom."[11] The engaged writer is one who responds to this demand, aiming "to recover this world by giving it to be seen as it is, but as if it had its source in human freedom."[12] This version of committed art is not, like the social realism promoted by the Communists,

[7] Ibid., 34–5.   [8] Sapiro, *The French Writers' War*, 442.

[9] Anna Boschetti, *The Intellectual Enterprise: Sartre and* Les Temps modernes, trans. Richard C. McCleary (Evanston, IL: Northwestern University Press, 1988), 153.

[10] Ibid., 1.

[11] Jean-Paul Sartre, *What is Literature?*, trans. Bernard Frechtman (New York: Philosophical Library, 1949), 47.

[12] Ibid., 57.

simply a reflection of the world as it exists, but it nonetheless conceives of art as committed, heteronomous, and bound to the world. At the same time, as Suzanne Guerlac has argued, Sartre's position is more autonomous than is sometimes supposed.[13] In particular, he remains committed to literature's economic autonomy, arguing that "the writer is not paid; he is fed, well or badly, according to the period, for his activity is *useless*."[14] This uselessness grants literature its critical capacity, allowing it to exist outside of society's institutions and conventions, and thus to "give society a *guilty conscience*."[15] Sartre, in other words, follows the polemicists and accusers of the purge in distinguishing between art's autonomy from the market and its autonomy from politics, imagining art's autonomy from the market as granting it a privileged political function. The distance between Sartre's position and that of modernist proponents of aesthetic autonomy can be measured, however, through the writer's access to food: while Sartre's writers are not paid, they *are* fed, a distinction that seems to keep them free of the corrupting influence of capitalist exchange, while holding them within and keeping them dependent upon the social body. Sartre's writer *engagé* might retain his autonomy from capitalist modes of exchange, but he is not and cannot be a starving artist.

The rejection of aesthetic autonomy that runs from the CNE through the purge trials to Sartre held a powerful moral and political appeal in a context in which autonomy had been first exposed as impossible and then used as a cover for collaboration. This position, while retaining preeminence throughout the post-war period, was not without its critics. In 1948, in the immediate aftermath of the publication of *What is Literature?*, Jean Paulhan—a wartime member of the CNE and one of the founders of *Les Lettres françaises*—published *De la paille et du grain* (*Of Chaff and Wheat*), a scathing renunciation of the purges. Accusing the advocates of *l'épuration* of hypocrisy for their demand that writers exhibit patriotism, Paulhan's essay attacks the suggestion that writers owe any kind of responsibility to their homeland.[16] His journal, the *Cahiers de la Pléiade*, founded in 1946, sought to put into practice this principle that literature be judged only according to literary standards, publishing work by writers out of favor under the purges alongside those with unblemished records. In an introductory "Note" to the winter 1948 issue, Paulhan

---

[13] Suzanne Guerlac, *Literary Polemics: Bataille, Sartre, Valéry, Breton* (Stanford, CA: Stanford University Press, 1997), 57–94.
[14] Sartre, *What is Literature?*, 81.   [15] Ibid.
[16] Jean Paulhan, *Of Chaff and Wheat: Writers, War, and Treason*, trans. Richard Rand (Urbana, IL: University of Illinois Press, 2004).

affirmed the journal as "a place ... where men and words (and books) can be cleansed of the filth accumulated during the years of war, Occupation, and deliverance."[17] The consecration of an autonomous literary space would, in other words, do the work of national purification that the purges themselves could not.

Paulhan's repudiation of the purges was part of a resurgence of debate over autonomy in the final years of the 1940s. This moment in French intellectual history is captured by the brief post-war run of *Transition*, edited by Beckett's close friend Georges Duthuit and published irregularly from 1948 to 1950, which sought to restage these debates for an anglophone audience. *Transition* placed the debate over literary *engagement* at the center of the field, reprinting extracts from *What is Literature?* in issues 1 and 2, and serializing Duthuit's commentary on the issue, "Sartre's Last Class," across five of its six issues. For Duthuit, however, Sartre's principal antagonist was not Paulhan but André Breton, whom Sartre attacked in the first extract of *What is Literature?* published in *Transition*. In a response, published in the second issue of *Transition*, Breton proclaims that, "ART WILL NEVER TAKE ORDERS."[18] Pitching himself, like Paulhan, against both the rhetoric of treason that surrounded the purge trials and the Sartrean call to commitment that followed, Breton protests that, "No political-military imperative can possibly be accepted or proclaimed in art without treason.... The ignoble word COMMITMENT which caught on after the war, reeks of a servility which both poetry and art can only loathe."[19]

Recalling inter-war surrealism's espousal of the starving artist, Breton's defense of a mode of pure or autonomous art claims that its "categorical rejection of the conditions of life and thought imposed on man in the mid-twentieth century" calls for an "*ascesis*."[20] Other defenders of autonomy likewise countered Sartre's image of a writer "fed, well or badly" by his society with the deployment of hunger and associated tropes of famine and asceticism. In his "Letter—Red," reprinted in the same issue, Henri Pichette claims of the poet that, "If he is genuine, he must and can live on famine."[21] Max-Pol Fouchet, in a reply to Pichette, concurs, linking famine to political refusal. Fouchet praises Pichette for his embrace of rebellion instead of revolution, despite the fact that, "The business of revolution ... is to share out our daily bread, whereas rebellion is

[17] Quoted in Watts, *Allegories of the Purge*, 50.
[18] André Breton, "One Cause, Two-Fold Defense," trans. Francis Scarfe, *Transition Forty-Eight*, no. 2 (1948): 65.
[19] Ibid., 67.   [20] Ibid., 71. Emphasis in original.
[21] Henri Pichette, "Letter—Red," trans. Jack T. Nile and Bernard Frechtmann, *Transition Forty-Eight*, no. 2 (1948): 10.

destructive and brings in no harvests."[22] Whereas Sartre imagines the writer as unprofitable, but fed, Breton, Pichette, and Fouchet, in rejecting the Sartrean call to commitment, return to the modernist trope of the artist as both ascetic in his implicit refusal of food, and unproductive in his inability to generate food or to participate in the kind of political revolution that would distribute it more equitably within society. The modernist starving artist's history as a figure for art's autonomy from the market, in other words, returns in the post-war debates as a refutation of Sartrean commitment and an embrace of the artist's concurrent autonomy from political imperatives.

By the end of the 1940s, autonomy had begun to produce a number of sophisticated defenses, which would pave the way for the emergence of so-called French theory in the 1960s and 1970s. Maurice Blanchot's post-war literary criticism, collected in 1949 as *La Part du feu* (*The Work of Fire*), exemplifies this theoretical repudiation of Sartrean commitment. His influential essay "Literature and the Work of Death" (first published as two essays in 1947 and 1948) sets itself directly against Sartre, opening with a dismissal of the very question— "Why write?"—with which *What is Literature?* begins. Whereas Sartre insists on literature as a form of action, Blanchot claims, to the contrary, "Literature does not act."[23] Instead, literature for Blanchot gives us "a view of the world which realizes itself as unreal using language's peculiar reality."[24] Foregrounding the slippery self-annulment of language, Blanchot suggests that literature can neither refer confidently to the world, nor act successfully upon it—that its ensnarement in language renders it necessarily autonomous. Roland Barthes adopts a similarly anti-Sartrean tone in his 1953 study *Writing Degree Zero*, which draws on essays that date back to 1947, and attacks "intellectual modes of writing" that, being "literary to the extent that they are powerless and . . . political only through their obsession with commitment," "can only give rise to a para-literature."[25] As these names and texts suggest (and as we will see in more detail in Chapter 3), Sartre's call to intellectual commitment cast a long shadow over the history of twentieth-century French thought, prompting a tremendous intellectual outpouring

---

[22] Max-Pol Fouchet, "In Reply to Pichette," trans. J. G. Weightman, *Transition Forty-Eight*, no. 2 (1948): 17.

[23] Sartre, *What is Literature?*, 23; Maurice Blanchot, "Literature and the Right to Death," in *The Work of Fire*, trans. Lydia Davis (Stanford, CA: Stanford University Press, 1995), 340.

[24] Blanchot, "Literature and the Right to Death," 339.

[25] Roland Barthes, *Writing Degree Zero*, trans. Annette Lavers and Colin Smith (Boston: Beacon Press, 1970), 28; see also Sontag's preface, which makes the case for *What is Literature?* as *Writing Degree Zero*'s key antagonist: Susan Sontag, "Preface," in *Writing Degree Zero*, by Roland Barthes (Boston: Beacon Press, 1970), xiv–xv.

in response that laid the early foundations for what would in the 1960s and 1970s become French poststructuralism.

Looking ahead to the rise of French theory two decades later, these debates also looked back to the legacies of modernism. Indeed, the stakes of the struggle over literary *engagement* in post-war France lie in part in their importance for the fate of modernism in the wake of the political compromises, the discrediting of aesthetic autonomy, and the national humiliation of World War II. The centrality of André Breton—an important figure of continuity between the inter-war avant-gardes and the post-war literary field—to this debate, and his own insistence on the continuity between his pre-war and post-war thought, underscores the extent to which debates about the writer's commitment were debates about what was to be done with the modernist heritage. Sartre himself makes this point, positioning Breton and the surrealists as the development of the modernist claim to autonomy, which "radicalizes the old literary claim of gratuity in order to make of it a rejection of action by destroying its categories."[26] Indeed, the identification between aesthetic autonomy and modernist tradition runs through most participants in this debate. Paulhan appeals to Rimbaud and Romain Rolland as his exemplars of literature's inherently traitorous status.[27] Blanchot develops his thought in this period through readings of Kafka and Mallarmé, as well as those, like Lautréaumont, who had been reclaimed for modernism. Barthes's *Writing Degree Zero* works out a literary history that foregrounds writers like Flaubert, Mallarmé, Proust, Céline, and Queneau. For all these writers, the debate between autonomy and political engagement was also a question about whether French literature would continue to be modernist—that is, whether it would retain the assumptions and aesthetic principles that had guided it from the late nineteenth century through to the outbreak of World War II.

For all the urgency of this debate in the late 1940s, the French literary field was surprisingly unified on a key point: from the CNE and Sartre, to Breton, Blanchot, and Barthes, post-war French intellectuals broadly agreed that literature was (or ought to be) oriented towards freedom. In the second installment of "Sartre's Last Class," Georges Duthuit satirizes this surprising convergence between apparent rivals Sartre and Breton: "One frail divinity draws out the full force of love from both men and is defended by both with the same fervor of eloquence from wound and threat: liberty."[28] Duthuit is right. Where Sartre argues that the goal of

---

[26] Sartre, *What is Literature?*, 181–2.
[27] Paulhan, *Of Chaff and Wheat*, 31–4, 52–6.
[28] Georges Duthuit, "Sartre's Last Class (II)," trans. Colin Summerford, *Transition Forty-Eight*, no. 2 (1948): 109–10.

writing is "the reader's freedom," Breton effectively concurs, suggesting that art must espouse "the unconditional defence of a single cause, that of *the liberation of man.*"[29] This conviction that art's principal justification is its capacity to create freedom runs through the entire post-war literary field. On one end of the autonomy/commitment spectrum, the Communists, seeking to use literature as a tool of revolution, imagine it as a path to liberate the workers from their enslavement. On the other, even a writer as committed to autonomous art as Blanchot argues that literature's capacity for negation represents, like the revolutionary Reign of Terror, a desire for "absolute freedom."[30] The understanding of freedom at stake in these positions varies widely, with communist revolution differing markedly from Blanchotian freedom-as-negation and existentialist and surrealist versions of the reader's freedom entailing different versions of the subject and methods for producing liberty. But for all the bitterness of the debates over literature's relationship to politics, the post-war French literary field was united behind its conviction that it provided a route to freedom.

2. THE OBLIGATION TO STARVE: BECKETT'S POST-WAR ART CRITICISM

This fiercely contested literary field forms the backdrop for Beckett's most significant period of literary activity. Between 1945 and 1949 while these debates were raging in Parisian literary journals, Beckett, writing in French for the first time, was undergoing his most prolific and important creative period, during which he wrote three novels (*Molloy*, *Malone Dies*, and *The Unnamable*), two plays (*Waiting for Godot* and the posthumously published *Eleuthéria*), and the *Nouvelles* series of short stories. This outpouring established his reputation as a leading writer in both the French and anglophone literary traditions, and continues to form the basis of his canonicity and critical acclaim. The Beckett of this period is sometimes remembered (particularly in English-language scholarship) as an isolated figure, outliving Joyce and his sphere of influence—so central to Beckett's pre-war writing—without assimilating into an alternate literary scene. This impression has been central to Beckett's reception as a late modernist, which imagines him holding the fort as an increasingly idiosyncratic outpost of modernism into the latter half of the twentieth century.

---

[29] Sartre, *What is Literature?*, 47; Breton, "One Cause, Two-Fold Defense," 65.
[30] Blanchot, "Literature and the Right to Death," 320.

The publication of his collected letters over the last decade, however, has made it increasingly clear that Beckett's turn to French took place against the backdrop of his immersion in the French literary world of the immediate post-war period. During the late 1940s, Beckett's letters show close familiarity with the leading French literary magazines, as well as with the debates outlined in Section 1. Through his friendship with Georges Duthuit, he was closely involved with the production of the post-war run of *Transition*, contributing occasional pieces, performing extensive credited and uncredited translation work, correcting many of the journal's articles, and engaging in an on-going conversation with Duthuit about works published by the journal. Given *Transition*'s investment in restaging the key French literary debates for an international audience, his involvement with this periodical alone would have made Beckett intimately familiar with the intricacies of the post-war disputes over aesthetic autonomy and political commitment. Taken in the larger context of his broader reading in the period, it is clear that, during this crucial period for the development of his aesthetics, Beckett was immersed in the debates and ideas that constituted the post-war French literary field.

Within this field, Beckett's sympathies and commitments lay with those who sought to defend autonomy. Although he had served as an active member of the Resistance during the war, he always remained at a distance from its more literary arm, never becoming involved in the CNE and its organs or with the broader literary Resistance and its clandestine publications. This gave him an ambivalent position in relation to these post-war literary debates. On the one hand, he stood outside the chief engines that sought to insist on the politics of literature in the aftermath of the war. On the other, he had been sufficiently engaged with Resistance activities as to inoculate him against the accusation that his disinterested writing necessarily produced a disengaged politics. Intellectually, he was closest to writers like Blanchot, about whom his partner, Suzanne Dumesnil wrote, in relation to Beckett's nomination for a prize judged by Blanchot: "To have been defended by a man like Blanchot will have been the main thing for Beckett, whatever the outcome."[31] And like Blanchot, Beckett avoided directly engaging the debate over commitment in his published writing, instead mounting a series of implicit defenses of autonomous art through an engagement with modernism.

Beckett's post-war writing about aesthetics primarily takes the form of essays on art, particularly the paintings of his friends Bram and Geer van Velde (his pre-war criticism, in contrast, focuses primarily on literature,

---

[31] Beckett, *Letters*, 2:254.

including substantial critical essays on Proust, Joyce, and Irish poetry). He works out his position in three significant essays, written and published contemporaneously with his period of great literary productivity: "La Peinture des van Velde, ou le monde et le pantalon," published in *Cahiers d'Art* in 1946; "Peintres de l'empêchement," for *Derrière le miroir*, the publication of the Parisian art gallery Galerie Maeght, which appeared in May 1948; and the "Three Dialogues," co-written with Georges Duthuit, which appeared in *Transition* in December 1949. The switch to the visual arts as a medium for thinking through his aesthetics is significant in the light of the contemporaneous French debates over the relationship between art and politics. As Sarah Wilson has observed, "many of the more public battles for Communist ascendency from 1935 to 1954 were waged in paint," making painting an important site for the debate over the relationship between art and politics that raged in France at this time.[32] In the visual arts, as in literature, such debates were shaped around the legacy of modernism. As Kevin Brazil has argued, "This link between realist aesthetics and Communist political humanism permeated the discourse surrounding painting in post-war France."[33] Social realism was by this time the official aesthetic position of the Communist Party, and the "bataille réalisme–abstraction" (the battle between realism and abstraction) was raging—a debate between politically engaged, realist art, on the one hand, and autonomous, abstract art on the other.

Situating Beckett's turn to art criticism within this debate reveals his commitment to both modernism and autonomy. On the one hand, he writes exclusively about abstract painters, whose works lack overt political content and reflect his indifference to the claims of Communist social realism. Bram van Velde's paintings—his favorites in this period—are not only abstract but also eschew the descriptive titles of many of his modernist peers, removing them still further from the threat of political or historical reference. On the other hand, however, Beckett is quite explicit in his letters to Duthuit that his aversion is not just for politically engaged social realist art, but for "the old formalism–realism distinction" as a whole.[34] His embrace of Bram van Velde is premised on the claim that the painter represents "an art of a different order ... from any achieved up to date"—that is, that he represents a definitive break not only from social realism but also, as he argues in the "Three Dialogues," from other

[32] Sarah Wilson, "'La Beauté Révolutionnaire'? Réalisme Socialiste and French Painting 1935–1954," *Oxford Art Journal* 3, no. 2 (1980): 61.

[33] Kevin Brazil, "Beckett, Painting and the Question of 'the Human,'" *Journal of Modern Literature* 36, no. 3 (2013): 88.

[34] Beckett, *Letters*, 2:155.

abstract painters like André Masson and Pierre Tal-Coat.[35] In this, Beckett reprises the modernist language of rupture, locating true artistic novelty not in the high modernist moment of the preceding generation, but in the post-war present. Van Velde's contemporary art represents, Beckett claims, the only truly new art—the only art that fully accomplishes the modernist rupture with the past. At a time when modernism seemed to be on the retreat, Beckett's readings of van Velde insist not only that it is not yet over, but that it is in fact still to be accomplished.

Despite the importance of both literature and the visual arts to debates about aesthetic autonomy and political art, accounts of these two art forms remained surprisingly distinct. Discussions within literature, in particular, often located art outside of the debate about literary commitment. Sartre influentially opens *What is Literature?* by excluding non-literary arts—and ultimately poetry as well—from his call to arms: "No, we do not want to 'engage' painting, sculpture and music 'too', or at least not in the same way."[36] Such a position reflects Sartre's own doubts about the cruder mode of political commitment advocated by Communist social realism. But this segregation in the debates also filters through to the broader literary sphere, where debates over autonomy and politics focus almost exclusively on questions of writing, language, and the proper social role of literature, abandoning the inter-arts emphasis of inter-war modernism. Even *Transition*, despite Duthuit's status as a well-known art critic, keeps these debates surprisingly separate. "Sartre's Last Class," Duthuit's essay about Sartrean commitment, is serialized throughout the magazine's run— failing to appear only in the fifth issue, which is devoted to the visual arts and its intersection with literature, despite the fact that the "Documents" section of this issue is devoted overwhelmingly to precisely the debates about politics and the visual arts outlined earlier in this section.

Beckett, however, not only writes extensively about art in this period, he also does so quite explicitly in order to develop his own positions on *literary* aesthetics. In a letter to Duthuit which contains early versions of the "Three Dialogues," Beckett urges his reader to "bear in mind that I who hardly ever talk about myself talk about little else," underscoring the extent to which his writing on the visual arts functions—as critics have repeatedly assumed—as a testing ground for his own ideas about literature.[37] From his position just beyond the normal remit of literary debates, in a space that has been granted its autonomy in advance, Beckett participates obliquely in these debates, developing a quietly anti-Sartrean

---

[35] Samuel Beckett, *Disjecta: Miscellaneous Writings and a Dramatic Fragment*, ed. Ruby Cohn (New York: Grove Press, 1984), 142.
[36] Sartre, *What is Literature?*, 7.   [37] Beckett, *Letters*, 2:141.

aesthetics. Like Blanchot and Barthes, he signals his distance from Sartre by repudiating the question "What is literature?" itself, which Beckett dismisses in a letter to Duthuit in August 1948 without mentioning Sartre by name.[38] Where Sartre's theory of writing begins with the assumption that "It is we [i.e., humans] who set up a relationship between this tree and that bit of sky" and moves on to locate the impulse to make art in "the need of feeling that we are essential in relationship to the world," Beckett praises van Velde, in direct contrast, for his explicitly non-relational art.[39] As he writes in "La Peinture des van Velde," the year after *What is Literature?* was first serialized, "The history of painting is the history of its relations with its object."[40] Van Velde's innovation, however, is to break decisively with this history, accepting for the first time, as he argues in the "Three Dialogues," "the acute and increasing anxiety of the relation itself."[41] Van Velde's art is, therefore, both radically autonomous and fundamentally anti-Sartrean, founded in a severing of the relation that makes political engagement itself possible.

Nonetheless, if Beckett's decision to write on art partakes of an inter-arts dialogue that seeks to appropriate the autonomy of abstract painting for his own writing and to use art as a testing ground for his non-relational aesthetics, he does so not by claiming an analogy between writing and painting, but rather by underscoring the gap that prevents the two arts from ever truly approaching each other. In his early post-war essays on the van Veldes, Beckett is especially explicit about this, writing that Bram van Velde's paintings "deprive [the spectator], even the quickest to commentary, of the use of speech," and produce "a silence . . . like that which we keep, even as we ask ourselves why, in the presence of a mute."[42] He goes on to suggest that this problem is a product of the exemplary visuality of the painter's work, observing that, "To write purely visual apperception, is to write a sentence stripped of meaning."[43] By placing art beyond the grasp of writing, Beckett makes the inter-arts dialogue a point not of convergence but of disjuncture, and suggests that this disjuncture is precisely the place where these paintings' autonomy lies.

---

[38] "In defining literature, to one's satisfaction, even brief, where is the gain, even brief?": Ibid., 98.

[39] Sartre, *What is Literature?*, 38–9.

[40] "L'histoire de la peinture est l'histoire de ses rapports avec son object": Beckett, *Disjecta*, 135.

[41] Ibid., 145.

[42] "Ils le privent, même le plus prompt au commentaire, de l'usage de la parole . . . C'est un silence . . . comme celui qu'on garde, tout en se demandant pourquoi, devant un muet": Ibid., 125.

[43] "Écrire apperception purement visuelle, c'est écrire une phrase dénuée de sens": Ibid.

In this, Beckett echoes Clement Greenberg, whose influential theory of modernism in art made a small entrée into the Parisian literary sphere around this time in the form of an essay on twentieth-century American art, published in *Les Temps modernes* in 1946. In this essay, Greenberg is scathing about the corrupting influence of "literature" and "literary paraphernalia" on art in the US, echoing arguments that he had earlier developed in his 1940 essay "Towards a Newer Laocoon."[44] In this earlier essay, Greenberg claims that the history of modern art—both the visual arts and other art forms—is that of "a revolt against the dominance of literature, which was subject matter at its most oppressive."[45] The endgame, he suggests, is modernism: that phase of aesthetic development in which, "The arts have been hunted back to their mediums, and there they have been isolated, concentrated and defined."[46] Greenberg's insistence on autonomy as a mode of medium specificity in which literature is excluded from art resonates with Beckett's attempt to imagine the autonomy of the van Veldes' painting through writing's lack of purchase on them. But in writing across the inter-arts line—indeed, in using the difficulty of this line as a site for theorizing autonomy—Beckett moves towards a way of understanding aesthetic autonomy in literature as a kind of failure of literary resources, a mode of inexpressibility that these essays not only espouse but also perform.

This sense of aesthetic autonomy as the inexpressible attains one of its most emblematic forms in the "Three Dialogues," where Beckett famously espouses an aesthetics founded on, "The expression that there is nothing to express, nothing with which to express, nothing from which to express, no power to express, no desire to express, together with the obligation to express."[47] But if this widely quoted formula in some respects typifies the desire for an inexpressible art that runs through the earlier essays, it also introduces an important variation. Both of the earlier French essays on the van Veldes reflect the desire of the French literary field as a whole to find a way to more successfully link art to freedom or liberty. In "La Peinture des van Velde, ou le monde et le pantalon," Beckett suggests that Bram van Velde "blew up" the "impenetrable block" of composition, "in order to liberate from it what he needed."[48] He repeats the emphasis on the van Veldes' attempt to liberate painting in "Peintres de l'empêchement"

---

[44] Clement Greenberg, "L'Art Américain au XXe siècle," trans. Catherine Le Guet, *Les Temps modernes*, no. 2 (1946): 349–50, 352.

[45] Clement Greenberg, "Towards a Newer Laocoon," in *The Collected Essays and Criticism*, ed. John O'Brian (Chicago: University of Chicago Press, 1986), 28.

[46] Ibid., 32.   [47] Beckett, *Disjecta*, 139.

[48] "Confronté par ce bloc impénétrable, A. van Velde l'a fait sauter, pour en libérer ce dont il avait besoin": Ibid., 130.

two years later, suggesting that, in their work, "What painting is liberated from is the illusion that there exists more than one object of representation."[49]

The Beckett of the "Three Dialogues," however, abandons the language of freedom and liberation, writing scathingly of André Masson's "concern with the amenities of ease and freedom," and instead espouses an art driven by obligation and necessity.[50] Reimagining art as a duty—"the obligation to express"—Beckett breaks sharply with the consensus around art's relationship to freedom that runs through the post-war French literary field, from the political writers of the Communist Party, to Sartrean *intellectuels engagés*, to defenders of autonomy like Blanchot and Paulhan. Indeed, Beckett first advocates a position that would "stick close with necessity" in a letter to Duthuit in August 1948, only weeks after another in which he makes a smirking reference to Duthuit's "Sartre–Breton equation"—that is, to the art critic's claim that the two supposed enemies actually approached each other's positions in their shared embrace of liberty.[51] By March 1949, in the letters that form the basis for the "Three Dialogues," Beckett is celebrating Bram van Velde's "fidelity to the prison-house" and his "refusal of any probationary free-dom," in a decisive break with his earlier sense that van Velde's art constituted a final liberation from painting's limitations.[52] Rejecting the terms of the Sartre-Breton debate that structured the literary field, as he will later reject the "formalism–realism distinction" in painting, Beckett's readings of van Velde locate his novelty in his rejection of the consensus around art's relationship to freedom.

It is probable that Beckett's position as a critic of the visual arts helped to motivate this rejection. As Serge Guilbaut has shown, 1948—the year in which Beckett began moving away from a language of freedom—also saw "the first reconciliation of avant-garde ideology with the ideology of postwar liberalism," as American art critics began to describe formal abstraction and aesthetic autonomy in terms of political freedom.[53] Although these claims emerged from American writing and publications, Beckett's friendship with Duthuit, who had an international profile in this period, as well as his affiliation with *Transition*, which was distributed in the US and therefore involved with the Franco-American intellectual conversation, would likely have made him aware of these developments. Indeed, Beckett's refutation of the claim that "the School of Paris

---

[49] "Ce dont la peinture c'est libérée, c'est de l'illusion qu'il existe plus d'un objet de représentation": Ibid., 136.

[50] Ibid., 141.   [51] Beckett, *Letters*, 2:103, 86.   [52] Ibid., 130.

[53] Serge Guilbaut, *How New York Stole the Idea of Modern Art: Abstract Expressionism, Freedom, and the Cold War*, trans. Arthur Goldhammer (Chicago: University of Chicago Press, 1983), 189.

(meaning to be determined) is finished or almost" in "Peintres de l'empêchement" alludes to US attacks on Parisian artistic supremacy, which Guilbaut links to the emergence of the link between liberalism and aesthetic freedom.[54] In this context, Beckett's rejection of the claim that art might constitute a mode of freedom should also be understood as a defense of non-political art against the "apolitical politicism" that turned artistic freedom to political ends.[55]

The theory of art that Beckett develops through his essays on van Velde is therefore best understood as a particularly trenchant form of aesthetic autonomy. His rejection of relation and expression entails an espousal of autonomy, by emphasizing the irreducibility of the aesthetic experience and its radical divorce from both the exterior world in which politics unfolds, and the interior world of authorial expression. Such a non-relational, inexpressive art not only undoes the foundations on which a political art, be it Sartrean engagement or Communist social realism, would be built; it also refuses the conventional link between aesthetic autonomy and freedom, reimagining autonomy not as an expression of the artist's freedom, but as subjugation to the limitations of the aesthetic or artistic condition. For Beckett, as for the writers discussed in Chapter 1, this new art—unfree, inexpressive, non-relational, and autonomous—is best figured as an art of hunger, as he suggests in the line with which I began this chapter: "Between a Gozzoli as such and a Gozzoli from our exploded categories, I would die of starvation."[56]

Hunger figures two interrelated aspects of Beckett's post-war aesthetics. First, it reflects his commitment to an art that would accept the impossibility of relation. As early as "La Peinture des van Velde, ou le monde et le pantalon," Beckett writes of "l'occasion et l'aliment" of painting.[57] He reprises these terms in very literal English translation in the "Three Dialogues," where he conceives of painting, as imagined by the history of Western art, as having two aspects: "the aliment, from fruits on plates to low mathematics and self-commiseration, and its manner of dispatch."[58] But, he goes on, "All that should concern us is the acute and increasing anxiety of the relation itself."[59] Van Velde's art, as "the first to desist from this estheticized automatism," is non-relational in the sense that it is starved, accepting, for the first time in art history, the inability of art to ingest its "aliment."[60] The acceptance of non-relation entails—this is the second use to which Beckett puts hunger—the acceptance of the impossibility of the artist's position. It is an acceptance, in other words, that

[54] "l'École de Paris (sense à déterminer) est finie ou presque": Beckett, *Disjecta*, 134.
[55] Guilbaut, *How New York Stole the Idea of Modern Art*, 2.
[56] Beckett, *Letters*, 2:156.   [57] Beckett, *Disjecta*, 131.   [58] Ibid., 144–5.
[59] Ibid., 145.   [60] Ibid.

"to be an artist is to fail, as no other dare fail, that failure is his world and the shrink from it desertion, art and craft, good housekeeping, living."[61] The art of hunger, as the opposite of "good housekeeping" and even of "living," is the art of this failure, figuring the simultaneous impossibility and necessity of going on after art has been severed from aliment. As the product of the impossible and doomed attempt to create art in the absence of relation, it figures art as a form of unfree autonomy.

Nonetheless, just as he resiles from thinking of art as a route to liberty, in the context of the increasing politicization of artistic freedom, Beckett is careful to ensure that his art of hunger remains a purely philosophical matter, divorced from the political and socioeconomic uses to which such imagery might give rise. This concern is clear from the way he develops the closely related metaphor of an impoverished art, a trope that dominates Beckett's writing on art in 1948 and 1949. In a letter to Duthuit in July 1948, Beckett links the "acceptance of ignorance, of pure weakness" to a tradition of poverty, running from Francis of Assisi to Arthur Rimbaud and Malcolm de Chazal, and in June 1949, he returns again to this configuration, suggesting that what separates his aesthetics from Duthuit's is "the opposition possible–impossible, wealth–poverty, possession–deprivation, etc., etc."[62] Mapping "impossibility" onto "poverty" and "deprivation," Beckett uses poverty and hunger to imagine an art that does without and is not able to.

By the end of 1949, however, when the "Three Dialogues" finally appear, he has revised this claim, rejecting "the pathetic antithesis possession–poverty" on the grounds that, "The realization that art has always been bourgeois, though it may dull our pain before the achievements of the socially progressive, is finally of scant interest."[63] Poverty, in this new account, draws art too firmly into a politicized realm of class struggle and social progress. It suggests, unacceptably from Beckett's perspective, that the intractability of the artist's position might be analogous to the desperation of the poor person's. Instead, Beckett seeks to abandon the preoccupation with art's bourgeois status that, from Greenberg to Sartre to the Communists to Barthes, has given rise to a push towards a new art that would speak to or from the proletariat, or from an avant-garde position exterior to the bourgeoisie. In contrast, Beckett's aesthetics, conceived as a mode of deprivation, poverty, or hunger, does not, he insists, entail a political claim about art's capacity to engage, represent, or overcome these states as actually lived. Instead, Beckett distinguishes between the "ultimate penury" of an art without an object, an art

---

[61] Ibid.   [62] Beckett, *Letters*, 2:84, 165.   [63] Beckett, *Disjecta*, 144.

stripped of relation, and "the mere misery where destitute virtuous mothers may steal stale bread for their starving brats," claiming that, "There is more than a difference of degree between being short, short of the world, short of self, and being without these esteemed commodities. The one is a predicament, the other not."[64] This distinction rejects the analogy between the art of hunger and real starvation on ontological grounds: the "ultimate penury," unlike physical hunger, is not ameliorable. It represents, therefore, a more absolute form of autonomy—one from which there is no escape—and a final, firm rejection of art's political potential.

The aesthetic of "ultimate penury" that Beckett develops represents a turn away from the demands of post-war French aesthetics, towards a radicalization of the thought of one of his favorite philosophers, Arthur Schopenhauer. Schopenhauer's aesthetics turn around his conviction that the world is governed—and made unbearable—by the pervasiveness of unceasing will, and that art is defined by its capacity to temporarily still the will, creating a brief moment of respite. Because appetite is one of the central engines of the will, his aesthetics follow the broader tradition of German Idealist philosophy discussed in the Introduction in pointedly excluding food and other excessively appetite-provoking "aliments" from representation. The "Three Dialogues," however, goes further than Schopenhauer himself, espousing an art that, severed from its "aliment," rejects the relational conditions of desire and will permanently, not just temporarily. The "ultimate penury" instead approaches the culmination of Schopenhauer's ethics, rather than his aesthetics: the state of "voluntary and intentional poverty" that might "serve as a constant mortification of the will, so that satisfaction of desires, the sweets of life, may not again stir the will."[65] Beckett therefore refuses post-war anti-capitalist art in favor of a radicalization of the Schopenhauerian position. He collapses the temporary reprieve from the will granted by art into the permanent reprieve from its demands which, Schopenhauer believes, will end inevitably in an unwilled starvation. He ends, that is, by turning away from political art towards a quasi-metaphysical autonomy, figured as an art of hunger.

Beckett's art of hunger therefore develops through a sustained dialogue with his immediate literary field, but he writes from a position that is discredited in advance, positioned, as D. says of B.'s aesthetics in the "Three Dialogues," as "a violently extreme and personal point of view."[66]

[64] Ibid., 143.

[65] Arthur Schopenhauer, *The World as Will and Representation*, trans. E. F. J. Payne, vol. 1 (New York: Dover Publications, 1969), 381–2.

[66] Beckett, *Disjecta*, 139.

Writing against the overwhelming dominance of Sartrean commitment and other contemporary calls to make art political, he insists on an art that is not only apolitical, but devoid of all relation; not only ineffectual at changing the world, but intrinsically marked by failure on its own terms; not only autonomous, but devoid of any move towards freedom. Situating himself outside both the late 1940s' demand for art to be responsible, and the period's broader consensus on art's liberating potential, Beckett instead reprises the modernist trope of the art of hunger as a figure for the impossibility of his aesthetics, and for his aesthetics of impossibility. Positioning himself in the line of Rimbaud's "self-devouring, ever-reducing thought" and Schopenhauer's starved aesthetics, Beckett's art of hunger allows him, like the writers discussed in Chapter 1, to figure the unviability of his preferred form of autonomy at this moment in history.[67] Assembling a personal canon from figures such as van Velde, Schopenhauer, and Rimbaud, Beckett produces a transhistorical counter-field, one in which his art of hunger finds company in failure.

3. AUTONOMY FROM NATION: HUNGER BEYOND FRANCE AND IRELAND

Beckett's attempt to imagine aesthetic autonomy as unfree represents an attempt to remove art from the grasp of politics. It seeks, as we have seen, to deny both the Cold War-era repurposing of aesthetic autonomy as the literary form of liberalism, and the potential link between his evocation of hunger and Communist or social democratic political advocacy for the poor. Hunger's potential political reach for Beckett, however, emerges not just from its potential to signify socioeconomic inequalities, but also from its intense politicization in both his national contexts. In both France and Ireland at this time, hunger forms part of a narrative of national liberation. It is imagined as a collectivizing experience, whose great suffering will spur the liberation of the oppressed and occupied people: the Irish from English colonization, the French from German occupation. Beckett's art of hunger works assiduously against both these nationalist uses of starvation, capitalizing on his expatriate status to develop a form of what Goldstone calls "autonomy from nation."[68] In the process, he denies hunger's capacity to provide a path to freedom or a communal

---

[67] Beckett, *Letters*, 2:83, 86.
[68] Andrew Goldstone, *Fictions of Autonomy: Modernism from Wilde to de Man* (Oxford: Oxford University Press, 2013), 110–48.

social experience, holding starvation within the ambit of his anti-social and unfree mode of autonomy.

The most immediate context for hunger was the privation of the war years and their immediate aftermath in France. From the early stages of World War II, France suffered serious rationing and food shortages. Ration cards began in 1940 below the recommended daily intake of calories and fell dramatically over the course of the war, while food shortages and poverty meant that people were not always able to access even these meager portions.[69] Even after the war, the combination of high rates of poverty and on-going rationing (which lasted in France until 1949) meant that hunger remained a pressing concern for the rest of the decade. Against this backdrop, hunger became an important way of imagining the shared national experience. Paul Éluard, a member of the Resistance who became one of the leading literary Communists after the war, opens his poem "Courage," published in 1943 in the clandestine Resistance publication *Les Lettres françaises*: "Paris a froid Paris a faim" (Paris is cold Paris is hungry).[70] Hunger here is part of the collectivizing experience that transforms Paris's inhabitants into a mythologized "Paris," figured conventionally through images of feminized suffering, languishing under occupation but poised, the poem assures us, to liberate itself (another of Éluard's poems, entitled "Liberté," was airdropped all over France by the Allies during the war). In a context in which, as Watts observes, "The Resistance writers divided literary history into two groups of writers: patriots and traitors," this tendency to collectivizing liberation was immediately assimilated into a narrative of patriotism and national regeneration.[71]

While Beckett lived through these wartime and post-war privations—James Knowlson reports him suffering through France's rationing and arriving back in Ireland after the war "looking emaciated"—he vehemently denies their accompanying rhetoric of nationalism.[72] His position as an Irishman in France already made this assimilation of collectivity to nation a problematic one, amplified by his pre-existing suspicions about nationalism and collectivism. Thus, while several critics have remarked on

---

[69] When rationing was first introduced in 1940, ration cards for healthy adults not undertaking manual labor allowed 1,800 calories a day, already below the general recommended daily intakes of 2,000 calories for women and 2,500 for men. As the war continued, they quickly fell, and at one point rations were as low as 900 calories per day. See Shannon L. Fogg, *The Politics of Everyday Life in Vichy France: Foreigners, Undesirables, and Strangers* (Cambridge: Cambridge University Press, 2009), 5–6.

[70] Paul Éluard, *Au rendez-vous allemand* (Paris: Les Éditions de Minuit, 2012), 10.

[71] Watts, *Allegories of the Purge*, 34.

[72] James Knowlson, *Damned to Fame: The Life of Samuel Beckett* (New York: Grove Press, 1996), 277–8, 312.

the ways in which the war—especially rationing and food shortages—found their way into Beckett's writing, he nonetheless writes against its contemporary use in post-war France, fracturing the collectivizing, liberating narratives of French hunger.[73] In the French text of *En attendant Godot* (*Waiting for Godot*), Beckett explicitly evokes the time he spent in the south of France, picking grapes for a man named Bonnelly at Roussillon, in the French department of Vaucluse, having fled Paris after his Resistance cell was exposed by the Germans:

> ESTRAGON. Mais non, je n'ai jamais été dans le Vaucluse! J'ai coulé toute ma chaude-pisse d'existence ici, je te dis! Ici! Dans le Merdecluse!
>
> VLADIMIR. Pourtant, nous avons été ensemble dans le Vaucluse, j'en mettrais ma main au feu. Nous avons fait les vendages, tiens, chez un nommé Bonnelly, à Roussillon.
>
> ESTRAGON. (*plus calme*) C'est possible. Je n'ai rien remarqué.[74]
>
> ESTRAGON. No, I was never in the [Vaucluse]! I've puked my puke of a life away here, I tell you! Here! In the [Merdecluse]!
>
> VLADIMIR. But we were there together, I could swear to it! Picking grapes for a man called [Bonnelly], at a place called [Roussillon].
>
> ESTRAGON. (*a little calmer*) It's possible. I didn't notice anything.[75]

This exchange, however, highlights not the collectivizing experience of starvation, but rather the incommensurability of Vladimir and Estragon's experiences, as they argue over memories and histories that don't match up. The failure of cultural memory represented by this exchange is underscored in Beckett's English translation, where the historical echoes are replaced by hesitations and ellipses instead of references to Bonnelly and Roussillon, and where the Vaucluse becomes the Mâcon country, privileging the scatological pun (Cackon) over historical accuracy. Reorienting the play towards an audience lacking the French experience of wartime rationing, Beckett preserves only the decaying, diverging memory that prevents the formation of a triumphant or redemptive communal narrative.

Indeed, although hunger is pervasive among Beckett's characters in his post-war texts, his characters, especially in the novels, mostly starve alone. In *Molloy*, the title character seems to subsist on little whenever he is left to his own devices, while Moran, who begins the novel following Molloy and

---

[73] Ibid., 278; Marjorie Perloff, "'In Love with Hiding': Samuel Beckett's War," *Iowa Review* 35, no. 1 (2005): 76–103; Allison Carruth, "War Rations and the Food Politics of Late Modernism," *Modernism/Modernity* 16, no. 4 (2009): 767–95.

[74] Samuel Beckett, *En attendant Godot* (Paris: Minuit, 1952), 86.

[75] Samuel Beckett, *The Grove Centenary Edition: Volume III, Dramatic Works*, ed. Paul Auster (New York: Grove Press, 2006), 54. Edited to more closely mirror the French.

ends it by resembling him, gradually loses his hearty appetite over the course of the novel, in parallel to his growing separation from family and community. The expiring protagonist of *Malone Dies* survives, alone in a room, on a bowl of soup every two or three days, until even this meager diet disappears towards the end of the novel. These characters, starving alone, experience none of the solidarity or potential for revolutionary sociability with which French writers in this period invested hunger. Even the somewhat more sociable exchanges over turnips and carrots in *Godot*, which Knowlson ties to the post-war French context, reflect a failure to achieve the subsumption of the individual within a larger collective whole. In these passages, Didi and Gogo negotiate and bicker over the distribution of root vegetables, trading them back and forth, putting them into pockets and bringing them out again, rejecting them, eating them, and generally clowning with them. If these exchanges are fundamentally cooperative, sometimes even tender and loving, they nonetheless require, like all clown acts, the point of distinction between Didi and Gogo to sustain the tension and get the laughs. Humorous and repetitive, they lack Éluard's sense that hunger might have a narrative dimension, that it might lead to collective freedom. Like Beckett's aesthetics more generally, they instead imagine a static closed system, in which collective identities cannot form and freedom—or any other form of progress—is unimaginable.

The anti-communal impulse embedded in Beckett's representation of hunger is complicated and amplified by his position between two cultures and two histories of hunger. The French context is countered and at times undermined by Beckett's equally ambivalent, equally anti-nationalist evocation of the long and brutal Irish history with hunger. The contours of this history are well known. Its emblematic moment is the Great Famine of 1845–52, a national catastrophe that "killed at least 1 million people and led more than that number to emigrate," with far-reaching implications for Irish national identity and national self-conception.[76] Within a decade of the famine's end, nationalists had begun to use its memory to attack English colonialism and to mobilize a collective sense of aggrieved Irish nationalism. John Mitchel's 1861 history of the famine, *The Last Conquest of Ireland (Perhaps)*, makes this case eloquently and influentially, arguing that "The Almighty, indeed, sent the potato blight, but the English created the famine."[77] He ends his work on a note of nationalist

---

[76] Timothy W. Guinnane, "The Great Irish Famine and Population: The Long View," *The American Economic Review* 84, no. 2 (1994): 303.

[77] John Mitchel, *The Last Conquest of Ireland (Perhaps)* (Glasgow: R. & T. Washbourne, 1882), 219.

and anti-imperial defiance, producing a vision of national identity out of the recent experience of famine with the promise that "The passionate aspiration for Irish nationhood will outlive the British Empire."[78] The collectivizing power of the famine persisted well into the twentieth century, both in nationalist politics and in oral folklore. When the Irish Folklore Commission decided in 1945 to collect accounts of the famine to mark the centenary of its onset, they found plentiful stories. While these accounts, unlike Mitchel, tend not to blame the British government for the famine, many stories nonetheless attribute the suffering to a form of divine collective punishment, emphasizing the famine's role as a collectivizing experience even where they do not imagine it to be an explicitly political one.[79] Meanwhile, as the republican movement gathered momentum in the twentieth century, the nationalist use of hunger strikes as a weapon against British rule reanimated the political stakes of Ireland's history of privation. Staking a claim to literally embody the suffering of the Irish people, nationalist hunger strikes relied on this collectivist belief, devolving the nation's shared suffering onto the representative body of the exemplary republican. In Ireland as in France, hunger is imagined as a state of suffering so extreme that it both produces Ireland as a nation, and presents the strongest possible moral and political case for its liberation.

Irish modernism of the generations immediately preceding Beckett is steeped in this history of famine and hunger strikes. Several of Yeats's plays seek to elaborate an Irish national mythology through images of hunger and famine, relocated to a medieval Irish past. His first play, *The Countess Cathleen* (1892), is set in the midst of famine and envisages its self-sacrificial protagonist as a heroine attempting to save her people. Lodging famine at the beginning of his attempt to generate a political community through theatre, Yeats imagines hunger as a central fact of Irish national identity. *The King's Threshold* (1904) shifts the focus specifically to the writer, telling of a medieval poet's self-starvation on the king's doorstep in protest at his demotion within the court. While Beckett is on record mocking Yeats's claim that "the 'sense of hardship borne and chosen out of pride'" is "the ultimate theme of the Irish writer," Emilie Morin has shown that the use of scarcity, both formal and thematic, in Yeats's late plays was a significant influence on Beckett's theatre.[80] An even more direct influence, of course, was Joyce who, as Julieann Ulin has shown,

---

[78] Ibid., 220.

[79] Niall Ó Ciosáin, "Famine Memory and the Popular Representation of Scarcity," in *History and Memory in Modern Ireland*, ed. Ian McBride (Cambridge: Cambridge University Press, 2001), 104.

[80] Beckett, *Disjecta*, 72; Emilie Morin, *Samuel Beckett and the Problem of Irishness* (Houndmills: Palgrave Macmillan, 2009), 103.

was himself deeply—if less overtly—immersed in the iconography of the
famine, as derived from nineteenth-century nationalist histories. Joyce's
deployment of this iconography in *Ulysses* explores the community-
forming legacy of famine for the Irish people, even if, as Ulin argues, it
is ultimately Bloom, the Jewish outsider, who is able to move beyond the
paralysis engendered by catastrophe and act pragmatically to foreclose
eviction and hunger in the novel.[81]

From *Godot's navets* to the barren landscapes and begging paupers of
Endgame (1957), Beckett's post-war writing, like that of his chief Irish
interlocutors, returns repeatedly to scenes evocative of the Irish famine.
As with the allusions to World War II, however, these allusions to Irish
cultural memory are degraded to the point that they are no longer
straightforwardly locatable within an Irish context. This effect is apparent
in one of the more explicit references to the Irish history of hunger, one
which focuses not on famine but on hunger striking. Towards the end of
Malone Dies, as Malone wonders about the likelihood of his surviving as
his soup disappears, he evokes the specter of the "Lord Mayor of Cork"
who "lasted for ages."[82] This Lord Mayor of Cork is Terence MacSwiney,
an Irish republican who died in Brixton Prison in 1920 after an internationally publicized seventy-four-day hunger strike. His role in *Malone
Dies* is to exemplify all that Malone is not: the latter lacks the Lord Mayor
of Cork's "political convictions," his "human convictions," and even his
thirst.[83] Without "political convictions" to make his starvation signify,
without "human convictions" to allow him to identify with his "fellow
creatures," and without thirst to offer a minimal connection between self
and world through desire or appetite, Malone is the absolutely anti-social,
non-relational antithesis to MacSwiney. The Irish republican, identified in
this passage only as "the Lord Mayor of Cook," is wholly identified with
the place and the people of Cork, as their chief representative. His
historical function, and his capacity to act as a point of comparison for
Malone, rests on his taking on the burden of history and political community on behalf of his people, and on retaining a connection to a specific
locale. Malone, uncertain as to his location, disinterested in his origins,
and unable to identify with his only visitor, is the antithesis of such a
regional and national representative.

---

[81] Julieann Ulin, "'Famished Ghosts': Famine Memory in James Joyce's *Ulysses*," *James Joyce Annual* (2011): 57–9.

[82] Samuel Beckett, *Trilogy: Molloy, Malone Dies, The Unnamable* (London: Calder, 1959), 275.

[83] Ibid.

MacSwiney, who is reputed to have said, "It is not those who can inflict the most, but those that can suffer the most who will conquer," embodies precisely the Irish republican tendency to turn suffering into triumph and liberation that Beckett despised in Yeats.[84] In this sense, Malone's difference from MacSwiney replicates at the level of national politics the distinction that Beckett draws in his art criticism between the painting of Bram van Velde, devoid of occasion, and that of painters like André Masson, for whom "anything and everything is doomed to become occasion, including... the pursuit of occasion."[85] Like van Velde, Malone refuses the redemptive gesture that would make his hunger into a new occasion, whether for politics or art. Both politically and aesthetically, Beckett's writing insists on preserving hunger as the site of unredeemed failure, failure that cannot lead to either aesthetic or political freedom.

Beckett's hunger therefore writes against both its French and Irish contexts, erasing and negating historical reference, and—through the interference between these two national frames—playing historical contexts off against one another. This contextual negation produces Beckett as an outsider to both Ireland and France, outside of their literary as well as their political traditions and conversations. In this, Beckett continues what Andrew Goldstone identifies as one of the key strands of inter-war modernist autonomy: autonomy as a mode of expatriate "cosmopolitanism... that keeps communal political programs at a distance," and that forces "a choice between a relatively autonomous artistic practice and the solidarity of political community."[86] Like Djuna Barnes and Joyce himself, who Goldstone takes as his examples of this mode of autonomy, Beckett's expatriatism allows him to assert his autonomy as a negation of political community—but one which, in keeping with Beckett's aesthetics of unfreedom, fails to free him from the constant creeping reassertion of both national frames.

Hunger is a particularly important site for this assertion of autonomy, because of its role within a project of political community-formation in both Ireland and post-war France. In denying his and his characters' straightforward insertion into these communities, Beckett also denies hunger's capacity, evident in both France and Ireland, to be transformed into a spur to freedom. Instead, Beckett's characters remain trapped, interminably and often alone, within their starvation, subjugated not to the oppressive machinations of Nazi occupiers or British colonial government,

---

[84] Quoted in Anna Pilz, "Lady Gregory's *The Gaol Gate*, Terence MacSwiney and the Abbey Theatre," *Irish Studies Review* 23, no. 3 (July 3, 2015): 286.
[85] Beckett, *Disjecta*, 144.   [86] Goldstone, *Fictions of Autonomy*, 113, 112.

which might yet be overthrown, but to the hopeless, inexorable conflict between the apparently irremediable scarcity of their world and the physical needs of their bodies. As a result, Beckett's denial of political community throws his characters back into the world of necessity and obligation engendered by his aesthetics of hunger.

4. SUCKING STONES: BODY, FORM, NECESSITY

Instead of understanding hunger as a form of oppression, which would link it to the possibility of freedom and the political uses of art, Beckett imagines it in terms of necessity. His unfree autonomy in fact arises from the intersection of two modes of necessity: bodily necessity, and abstract formal laws, such as those generated by the laws of mathematics or the logic of prescriptive patterns. We have already seen the formal results of this subjugation to necessity in the exchanges between Vladimir and Estragon in *Waiting for Godot* over the distribution of turnips, radishes, and carrots, where the bodily demands of hunger give rise to highly regular, conventionalized verbal and physical exchanges. Similarly, in *Malone Dies*, the protagonist's slow starvation is structured around the two "poles" of "dish and pot, dish and pot," an oscillation that is echoed in the novel's own structural alternation between passages of intense focus on Malone's body and his surrounds, and flights of imaginative fancy.[87] These structures produce textual form as a byproduct of the starving characters' subjugation to abstract laws: to the oscillation of *Malone Dies* and the permutation of root vegetables in *Waiting for Godot*. The product is a kind of formal autonomy, the production of fixed, closed systems that develop through movement within the system around a fixed point. Their refutation of freedom is both thematic—these structures are experienced as unchosen and confining by the characters themselves—and structural, negating the possibility of movement beyond the status quo that would be necessary to produce the prospect of freedom.

Such structures pervade Beckett's writing, constituting one of its most readily identifiable formal characteristics. Their paradigmatic instance is the sucking stones episode in *Molloy*, where the eponymous hero attempts to organize a system for rotating the sixteen stones he has collected to suck on through his four pockets, in such a way that he can be certain to suck every one of the stones in turn. The description of the various systems that

---

[87] Beckett, *Trilogy*, 185.

he devises in his attempt to achieve this takes some six pages in my edition of the novels, a carefully enumerated set of solutions that allows mathematical abstraction to entirely derail plot progression.[88] The conditions for the permutation of the sucking stones lie in Molloy's hunger. As he rhapsodizes early in the novel, "A little pebble in your mouth, round and smooth, appeases, soothes, makes you forget your hunger, forget your thirst."[89] Sucking on stones, for Molloy, is a calmingly sensuous activity, a substitute for food that makes hunger bearable by shifting focus from consumption to bodily sensation. The permutations of sucking stones that so preoccupy him later in the novel prolong his hunger by giving it (mathematical) form.

By conjoining bodily sensation with abstract form, the sucking stones episode—like other hunger-linked permutations in Beckett's writing—recalls Friedrich Schiller's influential definition of the aesthetic. Schiller understood aesthetics to reside in what he calls the "play-drive," that is, "a bond of union between the form-drive and the material drive."[90] This definition of the aesthetic as a mediation between the recalcitrant materiality of our bodies and the abstract laws of logic and morality would seem to find expression in Molloy's sensuous but rigorously logical permutations of sucking stones. Schiller differs sharply from Beckett, however, in finding the aesthetic to be the exemplary site of freedom, because "the opposition of two necessities [the form-drive and the material drive] gives rise to Freedom."[91] For Molloy, in contrast, the multiplication of different modes of necessity produces not freedom but impossibility. Molloy finds himself caught between "two incompatible bodily needs, at loggerheads": on the one hand, the need for "equal distribution" of stones between his pockets, which he describes as both a "principle" and a "bodily need"; and, on the other, the need "to suck the stones in the way I have described, not haphazard, with method."[92] Both of these impulses begin as the demands of the form-drive—the demands of principle and method—before being redescribed as "bodily needs," the demands of the material drive. The move from form to body, however, produces not the "free play" that Schiller finds in the aesthetic, but a greater and more profound sense of necessity—until finally, torn between these two irreconcilable formal–bodily demands, he simply abandons the game entirely, throwing away all the stones but one, "which of course I soon lost, or threw away, or gave away, or swallowed."[93] This passage, in other words, imagines the

---

[88] Ibid., 69–74.   [89] Ibid., 26.

[90] Friedrich Schiller, *On the Aesthetic Education of Man, in a Series of Letters*, ed. and trans. Elizabeth M. Wilkinson and L.A. Willoughby (Oxford: Oxford University Press, 1982), 103.

[91] Ibid., 137.   [92] Beckett, *Trilogy*, 74.   [93] Ibid.

aesthetic—the intersection of body and form—as a site of intersecting and competing modes of necessity, soluble only in the admission of the impossibility of the task at hand. Like the aesthetics B. espouses in the "Three Dialogues," the sucking stones episode uses hunger as the occasion for an aesthetic experience that fails to lead to freedom, collapsing instead under the recognition of its own impossibility.

Beckett's use of permutation to mediate between matter and form, between the body and the laws of logic and number, predates World War II. In the aftermath of war and in the context of the post-war debates over literature and politics, however, these permutations become much more invested in both hunger as the engine of permutation, and the autonomy of the systems that they produce. The shift can be traced through the difference between the sucking stones episode of *Molloy* and the well-known "biscuit scene" in Beckett's major pre-war text, *Murphy* (1938). In the latter scene, the eponymous Murphy, lunching in a park, considers the five biscuits that he habitually eats after lunch: "a Ginger, an Osborne, a Digestive, a Petit Beurre and one anonymous." With a preference for the Ginger and a distaste for the anonymous, he despairs of the "paltry six" permutations available to him with the remaining three biscuits and dreams of conquering his preferences and aversions so as to access the full range of possible combinations, to "partake [of the biscuits] in their fullness."[94] Like the sucking stones scene in *Molloy*, this passage drama-tizes the tension between the exigencies of formal permutation, on the one hand, and of the body, on the other. But while in *Molloy* the demands of the body always resolve into a question of form (and vice versa), Murphy's stubborn tastes represent simply the limits of the permutational system, the spoiler that prevents the full realization of the biscuits' formal poten-tial. For Murphy, unlike Molloy, bodily necessity has no formal potential.

The roots of this difference lie in the old aesthetic question of disinter-estedness. Where Molloy, aided by the fact that all his stones "tasted exactly the same," can approach them with an appropriately disinterested attitude, Murphy's sensuous, material relationship to his biscuits is entirely governed by his deeply interested tastes and preferences.[95] To access the biscuits' full aesthetic potential, to experience the biscuits as simultaneously form and matter, Murphy needs to learn "not to prefer any one to any other."[96] But Murphy is too invested in actually eating the biscuits; he cannot approach them aesthetically. The substitution of permutational eating for permutational hunger in the shift from *Murphy* to *Molloy* moves, in this sense, towards a more aesthetic—because more

---

[94] Samuel Beckett, *Murphy* (Montreuil: Calder, 1938), 57.
[95] Beckett, *Trilogy*, 74.   [96] Beckett, *Murphy*, 57.

indifferent—experience. But Murphy's lingering attachment to interested consumption also allows him to envisage a liberation-to-come, in which his suppression of bodily wants would unlock the full range of formal possibilities. Unlike Molloy, Murphy retains a desire to be freed from his body, an aspiration that is echoed elsewhere in the novel—perhaps most memorably in Murphy's penchant for binding himself to a rocking chair, in order to "appease his body" and thus to "set him free in his mind."[97] Molloy, in contrast, knows that even a state of properly aesthetic disinterest, even a state of contemplation in which the body's whims and preferences are muted, is not a state of freedom. Instead, as his disinterested appreciation of the stones reveals itself to be subject to multiple, mutually exclusive forms of necessity, he foregrounds the unfreedom inscribed in disinterest. Moreover, because for Kant and Schiller disinterest is the foundation of aesthetic autonomy, he similarly suggests that autonomy too is unfree.

The sucking stone episode expands the site of this disinterested autonomy, from the art object's reception (where it is primarily located for Kant and Schiller) to the art object's own internal composition. Disinterested autonomy in Beckett's post-war writing becomes a formal principle, producing texts that function as closed systems and that collapse only under the weight of their own impossibility. While Molloy's abandonment of his sucking stones is the result of his system's internal contradictions, in *Murphy* the dilemma of how to order the eating of the biscuits is only solved through an intrusion from outside the system, in the form of a small dog who eats everything but the Ginger while Murphy is occupied in conversation. *Watt* (1953), which was written during the war, provides an even starker point of contrast to the closed system of the sucking stones. This most permutational and accumulative of Beckett's novels insistently links these modes to eating. From the character of Mary who "ate all day . . . I mean that at no moment during this period was Mary's mouth more than half empty, or if you prefer, less than half full,"[98] to the soup that Watt cooks for his master Mr Knott, "a dish that contained foods of various kinds, such as soup of various kinds, fish, eggs, game, poultry, meat[,] cheese, fruit, all of various kinds, and of course bread and butter, and it contained also . . . " (and so forth in this vein),[99] *Watt*'s engagement with food repeatedly gives on to lengthy lists and systems for consumption. If Murphy dreamed of a release from taste that would allow the full range of permutation to open before him, *Watt* seems to offer just such an escape. These passages present consumption unrestrained by preference or

[97] Ibid., 6.   [98] Samuel Beckett, *Watt* (New York: Grove Press, 1953), 54.
[99] Ibid., 87.

discrimination, to the point that, as in the description of Watt's soup, they are often less permutational than accumulative. Whereas Molloy's sucking stones, in their literal indigestibility, circulate within a closed system to which no new elements are added or subtracted, the food in *Watt* is constantly accumulated and consumed, constantly expanding the bounds of its system. In contrast to both Murphy's biscuits and Watt's foodstuffs, then, Molloy's sucking stones produce a formal image of autonomy, in a system that, governed by indifference, is entirely self-contained, admitting neither ingress nor egress.

In these respects, the sucking stones episode of *Molloy* exemplifies the shift in Beckett's aesthetics in the post-war period towards a new kind of autonomous art, generated out of the application of an attitude of indifference to closed, self-contained systems that inevitably fail, collapsing under the pressure of their own impossibility. In this, the scene begins to produce a literary art that brings together the non-relational, impossible, inevitably failing aesthetics elaborated in his post-war art criticism, with the emphasis on autonomy as unfreedom that runs through his accounts of both hunger and art in the later 1940s. As in the art criticism, hunger is central to this aesthetic stance, because, imagined as isolated and isolating, opposed to political communities of all kinds, it translates the self-containment of the closed system, the indifference of Molloy's lack of appetite or taste, into an embodied experience. Molloy's hunger provides the occasion for permutation and form. In the process, Beckett begins to refigure the "ultimate penury" of the "Three Dialogues" as an experience that takes place at the intersection of formal laws with the body. In doing so, the sucking stones episode recasts the unfreedom of the art of hunger as an experience that is both formal (in the double sense of manifesting at the level of textual form, and obeying the laws of logical, mathematical form) and embodied.

5. STARVING THE TEXT: BODILY RHYTHMS IN THE LATE PROSE

The sucking stones episode translates Beckett's theories of aesthetics—his commitment to a mode of autonomy that is unfree and that takes hunger as its model—into form. In this, it lays the foundations for the late prose, written between the 1960s and the 1980s, which experiments with texts that are formally unfree and produce closed systems. This move aligns with the critical commonplace that Beckett's writing is starved, that it goes hungry. As Terry Eagleton has it, in keeping with a broadly held consensus, Beckett writes "anorexic texts," crafted from "starved words, gaunt bodies and sterile landscapes."[100] The late prose exemplifies this textual emaciation, doing away with character and plot, radically narrowing its vocabulary and simplifying its grammar, and stripping bodies and settings back to their bare, geometric minima. But this starved writing also implements the art of hunger in the narrower and more complex sense of the sucking stones episode, working on this poverty of literary resources to produce a permutative form that reflects the subjugation and manipulation of the body by rigid principles of logic and form. Taking the permutations of sucking stones as its model, the late prose explores what an unfree but autonomous art—an art of hunger—might look and feel like.

The exemplary text of this shift is *How It Is*, published in French as *Comment c'est* in 1961 and then in Beckett's English translation in 1964. Like much of Beckett's writing of the post-war period, *How It Is* depicts a world in which food and appetite vanish in step with one another: a world built around a foundational condition of hunger. It follows an unnamed speaker who crawls through the mud of the text's grim demi-monde, seeking out a companion, Pim, to torture into speech. Like all the inhabitants of the mud, the speaker drags with him a sack containing tins of food and a can-opener, prized possessions that, with no obvious method of restocking, point towards the speaker's eventual starvation. His finite, ever-diminishing food stock, however, does not seem to pose a problem for the speaker, for whom, "my tins all sorts dwindling but not so fast as appetite."[101] In fact, the speaker's lack of appetite is a constant refrain, beginning as early as the second page where the observation "no appetite" is accompanied by the reassuring claim, more explicit in the English, "no need to worry I won't die I'll never die of hunger."[102]

Like Malone and Molloy, the mud-dwellers of *How It Is* tend towards an "ultimate penury" in which starvation is accompanied by indifference, lack of nutrition by a lack of desire. More explicitly than earlier texts, however, *How It Is* imagines this gathering penury as a question for form and language, as much as it is a question for the text's wider relationship to context or politics. Comparing his language (that is, the language of the text), to Pim's, the speaker observes, "I talk like him I do we're talking of me like him little blurts midget grammar."[103] The speaker's

[100] Terry Eagleton, "Edible Ecriture," *Times Higher Education*, 1997, <http://www.timeshighereducation.co.uk/story.asp?storyCode=104281&sectioncode=26>.

[101] Samuel Beckett, *How It Is* (New York: Grove Press, 1964), 17.

[102] Ibid., 8; the French reads "inappétence...allons j'en ai j'en aurai toujours pour un moment"—roughly, "I have I will always have a moment left"—which omits both the direct reference to death and its overt connection to hunger: Samuel Beckett, *Comment c'est* (Paris: Minuit, 1961), 11.

[103] Beckett, *How It Is*, 76.

"midget grammar" redescribes his language through his starving body, which we learn earlier weighs "four stone five stone" and which he imagines shrinking further as he projects himself into an increasingly tin-less—that is to say, increasingly starved—future: "centuries I can see me quite tiny the same as now more or less only tinier quite tiny no more objects no more food and I live the air sustains me the mud I live on."[104] His "midget" stature, in other words, is a function of his starvation, shrinking as his need for food passes. Speaking a "midget grammar," the narrator of *How It Is* translates his shrinking, starving body into language.

The "midget grammar" translates the "grammaire d'oiseau" (bird grammar) of the French, which also contains the implication that the language of the text is a language of hunger. Birds have a strong idiomatic connection to small appetites, both in the English expression "to eat like a bird" and in the French "manger comme un oiseau" or "comme un moineau" (to eat like a bird or like a sparrow) and "avoir l'appétit d'un oiseau" (to have the appetite of a bird). Beckett draws extensively on this trope in the *Trilogy*, where we hear that Molloy "ate like a thrush," that Moran's chickens are refusing to eat, that Malone has "all sorts of birds" at his window which come "asking for food . . . I never give them anything," and that Macmann overhears "the dreadful cries of the gulls that evening assembles, in paroxysms of hunger, round the outflow of the sewers."[105] In this context, the "grammaire d'oiseau" of the French, like the "midget grammar" of the English, imagines the peculiar rhythms of the text to emanate from hunger, from the dwindling of food and the diminishment of appetite.

How It Is's "midget grammar" formalizes the art of hunger as a kind of textual indifference that combines the permutational logic of the sucking stones with the diminution of textual resources of Eagleton's "anorexic texts." Both *How It Is* and *Comment c'est* are entirely unpunctuated, with small phrasal sense units instead organizing meaning. As Leslie Hill observes, these units tend to omit "hierarchical relations between clauses or phrases."[106] The result is a text composed of a highly simplified grammar whose key feature is a relative sameness of individual components, and whose interpretability relies heavily on recapitulation, repetition, and recombination. The grammar of *How It Is* therefore replicates some of the key features of the permutations and combinations that characterize Molloy's sucking stones: the lack of preference, the lack of hierarchy, and the reliance on a repetitive recombination of diminished

---

[104] Ibid., 39, 17.   [105] Beckett, *Trilogy*, 53, 101, 185, 230.
[106] Leslie Hill, *Beckett's Fiction: In Different Words* (Cambridge: Cambridge University Press, 1990), 136.

resources. In *How It Is*, this non-hierarchical, indifferent, repetitive language—this "midget grammar"—becomes the decisive textual feature, inscribing the art of hunger at the level of form.

This textual repetition is amplified by the pervasiveness of permutation to the construction of the world of *How It Is*, and consequently to the structure of the text itself. In part three of the novel, the dyadic act of torture between the speaker and Pim, which is the main content of part two, opens outwards, revealing itself to be one link in a vast chain of torturing couples. Before Pim, the speaker recalls there was Bem: "another part two before part one except that me Pim Bem me Bem left me south I hear it murmur it in the mud."[107] And if there is Bem, then Bem, leaving the speaker, goes onwards to be tortured in turn, so that beyond the individual couples in which the speaker participates there are, he realizes, "millions millions there are millions of us."[108] Much of part three, in fact, is dedicated to parsing the permutations and structures necessary to imagine this vast network of torture, carefully tracing the logical and mathematical strictures to which such a system must be subject. Like the sucking stones, the whole world of *How It Is* unfolds as a vast permutational system, governed by abstract formal laws.

Like Molloy's permutational stones, the mud-dwellers of *How It Is* torture their way through a closed system. Their permutational world ultimately turns back on itself, producing a closed system of torture, "as for example our course a closed curve and let us be numbered 1 to 1000000 then number 1000000 on leaving his tormentor number 999999 instead of launching forth into the wilderness towards an inexistent victim proceeds towards number 1."[109] This self-containment mutates into a form of self-consumption, as the characters drink "this so-called mud" which, it's speculated, might be "nothing more than all our shit."[110] Consuming its own waste, the slowly starving world of the text is imagined as self-consuming—a world that embodies the "ever-reducing, self-devouring thought" that Beckett praised in the 1940s. Textual permutation, therefore, produces the text of *How It Is* as a closed system that eats itself, in an act that Daniela Caselli describes as the "'top to bottom' digestive circularity of the text, in which shit and vomit are food and nourishment."[111] Passing through an emaciated language that Ruby Cohn has described as "peristaltic," the text devours itself,

---

[107] Beckett, *How It Is*, 109.   [108] Ibid., 114.
[109] Ibid., 117.   [110] Ibid., 52.
[111] Daniela Caselli, *Beckett's Dantes: Intertextuality in the Fiction and Criticism* (Manchester: Manchester University Press, 2005), 169.

producing a form of textual autonomy through the self-cancellation of the closed system.[112]

How It Is replicates the unfree autonomy of the sucking stones, with characters subjected to abstract formal laws and confined within a closed system, but it also goes further, imagining the text's unfreedom as a graphic, visceral kind of torture. Part two provides a detailed account of the speaker's violence against Pim, as he hits, beats, and scratches his companion, sticking his can-opener and his nails into various orifices. These scenes of violence are the nodes around which the vast permutational system described in part three is built, literalizing the violence and powerlessness of the more abstract subjugation to formal laws. No character is free from this vicious system, each moving on to helplessly either continue the cycle of violence, or become the tormented in turn, and each perpetuating the cycles of starvation and unfreedom associated with the art of hunger. The process is amplified and underscored by Pim's hunger; as the speaker observes, "Pim has not eaten . . . if he's still nourished it's on mud."[113] In these scenes of torture, Pim (and, in his turn, the speaker himself) becomes an exemplary node in the larger permutational networks, starving but also, by drinking the mud, becoming absorbed into the digestive circularity of the text's closed system.

The torture in these scenes is pedagogical, focused on coercing Pim to speech, as his cries of pain develop slowly into "song," words, and finally narrative. Language and literature in *How It Is* are imagined as the horrifying issue of coercion and violence, an abusive, oppressive form of socialization. The "midget grammar" that both Pim and the narrator speak is reconceived as literally unfree, the direct product of this process of starved torture. In this context, the speaker's repeated insistence that his speech is not his own, but rather a form of quotation—as he says in the opening lines, "how it was I quote before Pim with Pim after Pim how it is three parts I say it as I hear it"—positions the text as a whole as a kind of forced, unfree speech.[114] In this, it continues the trope of language as a kind of force-feeding, something which has been "rammed down my gullet" and which will, inevitably, be regurgitated and vomited back up, a trope that extends back as far as *The Unnamable*.[115] But whereas the attitude of *The Unnamable* is one of disgust and desperation, animated by the frantic impulse to purge oneself of the alien intrusion of language, *How It Is* is indifferent and resigned, reproducing the exemplary attitude of the art of hunger. Unfree and indifferent, *How It Is* speaks the language of the art of hunger.

[112] Ruby Cohn, "Comment c'est: de quoi rire," *The French Review* 35, no. 6 (1962): 564.

[113] Beckett, *How It Is*, 65.   [114] Ibid., 7.   [115] Beckett, *Trilogy*, 300.

While *How It Is* is unusual in both its violence and the explicitness of its connection to hunger, the emaciated syntax, indifferent rhythms, and claustrophobic repetitions of its "midget grammar" are everywhere evident in Beckett's late prose. After *How It Is*, the bodies portrayed in the late works become increasingly devoid of consciousness, ever more subject to the coercive control of the text's internal patterns. In the 1967 text *Ping*, for instance, the "bare white body" at the heart of the text moves only in response to the word "ping," making movement into an effect not of mind or consciousness, but of textual patterns.[116] In *Worstward Ho* (1983), Beckett's last sustained prose work, the text highlights the body's existence as an effect of the text: "First the body. No. First the place. No. First both."[117] As the highly repetitive, highly patterned language of these late texts generates its own formal rules and as the body is increasingly treated as inert material to be worked on, any possibility of agency is increasingly identified with the permutational patterns of the text itself. Extrapolating the sucking stone's sense of the aesthetic as the conjunction of competing necessities of body and form, and *How It Is*'s vision of language as a product of bodily violence, these late texts void their worlds of any possibility of aesthetic or human freedom.

Despite their oddly still, inhuman moods, the late texts are surprisingly affecting—and affective. They seek, as Beckett famously said of his 1972 play *Not I*, "to work on the nerves of the audience, not the intellect."[118] Or as Elisabeth Bregman Segrè says of the experience of reading *Ping*, "On a first reading, one comprehends next to nothing; yet on a first listening (Beckett's texts must primarily be heard), one feels something intensely, something ineffable and far more musical than verbal in quality."[119] As both of these accounts suggest, Beckett's late texts solicit an affective response, distinct from processes of interpretation, which registers first of all as a bodily sensation, an experience that acts "on the nerves." The chief engine of this affect is the language of the late prose, which, with its highly repetitive use of a severely restricted vocabulary and grammar, achieves the quality that Segrè describes as musical, an effect of the principle articulated by the speaker of *How It Is*: "first the sound then the sense."[120]

---

[116] Samuel Beckett, "Ping," in *Samuel Beckett: The Complete Short Prose, 1929–1989*, ed. S. E. Gontarski (New York: Grove Press, 1995), 193–6.

[117] Samuel Beckett, *Nohow On: Company, Ill Seen Ill Said, Worstward Ho* (New York: Grove Press, 1996), 90.

[118] Quoted in Enoch Brater, "The 'I' in Beckett's Not I," *Twentieth Century Literature* 20, no. 3 (1974): 200.

[119] Elisabeth Bregman Segrè, "Style and Structure in Beckett's 'Ping': That Something Itself," *Journal of Modern Literature* 6, no. 1 (1977): 127.

[120] Beckett, *How It Is*, 95.

These texts, privileging language as sound and resonance over its intellectual, hermeneutic, or signifying dimensions, produce what Brian Massumi has called the "autonomy of affect."[121] In Massumi's account, affect describes an autonomous system of intensity, "associated with non-linear processes: resonation and feedback which momentarily suspend the linear progress of the narrative present from past to future" and which register as autonomic bodily responses.[122] Like the "midget grammar" of Beckett's late prose, affect for Massumi emerges independent of and prior to language's capacity to generate meaning and narrative. It therefore constitutes a self-sufficient system, to which emotion—"the sociolinguistic fixing of the quality of an experience which is from that point onward identified as personal"—is opposed.[123] The intensely affective qualities of Beckett's late prose, emerging from systems outside of narrative and explicitly named emotions, therefore restage his commitment to autonomy at the level of linguistic resonance. Autonomy in this account becomes a property of aural language acting on the body, restaging and relocating Beckett's emphasis on a mode of aesthetic autonomy that will act on and through the body by placing bodily needs in tension with—and subject to—the demands of a text, itself bound to the abstract, formal rules of permutation.

These texts rely for their affective qualities on what Enoch Brater has described as the eminently "speakable" quality of Beckett's late prose— that is, the demand for vocalization and performance that they seem to place on the reader by virtue of their highly regular, highly metrical patterning.[124] Indeed, the speakability of the prose from *How It Is* onwards is necessary for producing not just textual affect, but also meaning. The parsing of the texts' semantic units relies on their organization according to verbal rhythms, and as a result, the production of meaning requires the reader to speak the text or imagine it spoken. Given the significance of the motif of citation to *How It Is*'s indifferent narrative voice and its general pervasiveness in the post-*Trilogy* prose, this verbalization implicates the reader from the outset in the proliferation and collapse of narrative and textual voices that mark these texts, as the reader becomes yet another iteration of the voice that "say[s] it as I hear it."[125]

As we have seen, the production of speech in *How It Is* is by no means a free act. Instead, coerced and tortured into language, *How It Is*'s speakers literalize the "obligation to express" that Beckett locates at the heart of

[121] Brian Massumi, *Parables for the Virtual: Movement, Affect, Sensation* (Durham, NC; London: Duke University Press, 2002), 23–45.
[122] Ibid., 26.   [123] Ibid., 27–8.
[124] Enoch Brater, *The Drama in the Text: Beckett's Late Fiction* (New York; Oxford: Oxford University Press, 1994), 4.
[125] Beckett, *How It Is*, 7.

aesthetic production in the "Three Dialogues." The intense speakability of these texts therefore implicates the reader in these chains of coerced speech, making them subject to the requirement to speak, and to the irresistible link between bodily sensation and linguistic production. Even in other late texts where speech is not linked explicitly to violence and torture, Beckett's privileging of "nerves" over "intellect" locates textual effects at the site of autonomous bodily reaction that precedes and escapes the "free" operation of the mind, and that produces language and meaning as an after-effect of sound. Like the starving figures of the art of hunger, therefore, readers of Beckett's late prose experience themselves as subject to the dictates of the body, forced on through the texts by the demands of insistent metrical progression ("On. Say on. Be Said on."), experienced as the compulsion to speak and thus to embody the text. Staging the irresistible compulsion to produce and reproduce language as a kind of "bodily need," these late prose texts make the autonomy of affect into a practice of unfreedom, embedded within the experience of reading.

Beckett's art of hunger therefore stages aesthetic autonomy as the subjugation of both writer and reader to abstract laws of text and form, establishing the autonomy of the text at the expense of the autonomy of the reader. This late prose of obligation and unfreedom is the elaboration of ideas that emerged in Beckett's writing of the 1940s, arising as a reaction against the demand that both art and hunger be made political and made to serve the ultimate end of liberation. Beckett's response is the development of an art whose forms and processes bear witness to art as a site of constraints and limitations, of coercion and embodied necessity. In place of a vision of hunger as a collectivizing experience, preparatory to a great liberation, Beckett reimagines it as producing isolated individuals or viciously antagonistic relationships, which foreground the static, una-meliorable state of an art that is at once autonomous and unfree. The absorption of this aesthetic stance into a set of formal principles is Beckett's peculiar innovation, one which later authors do not follow in precisely the same way. But his development of the art of hunger into a position that allows aesthetic autonomy to outlive its delegitimization sets an important precedent for late twentieth-century writing. Writing out of the aftermath of the 1968 student protests and the late years of apartheid respectively, both Paul Auster and J. M. Coetzee return to the art of hunger to provide a way of imagining art as autonomous from political demands, in social contexts where such positions appeared irresponsible or unreasonable. In these new contexts, the art of hunger leaves open a space for art that persists through its impossibility, by imagining art as a practice of unfreedom.

3

The Starving Artist as Dying Author

Paul Auster and Aesthetic Autonomy after 1968

> Before speech, the hunger of a dissident scribe, attendant eye at banquets, carving his name into the edge of the table: precursor of famine.
>
> To found a self among the morsels, from what is swept away, and leaves the table bare.
>
> Paul Auster, "Stele"[1]

In the second half of 1970 Paul Auster was living in Paris, a young poet who had recently graduated with an MA from Columbia University for a thesis entitled "The Art of Hunger." As he tells it in later memoirs, he was poor and stubborn, caught between an inability to earn a living as a writer and a refusal to supplement his income with more financially sound employment. In this account, the young Auster is an exemplary participant in the art of hunger tradition, an exemplary "starving artist," beating his retreat from the demands of the literary market without a plausible alternative structure to catch his fall. His poems of the period—of which the lines quoted above are an example[2]—replay this reticence on the level of form, troubling modernist claims to impersonality in the echo they establish between poem and poet. They assert their status as literature through their abstraction and heavy symbolism, divorcing themselves from the specifics of their historical moment and the details of material

[1] Paul Auster, "Stele," n.d., 10, Box 67, Folder 1, Paul Auster Archive, 1963–1995 Papers, Berg Collection, New York Public Library.

[2] This extract, from a collection entitled "Stele," is unpublished and probably dates from late 1970. Several of the poems contained in "Stele" are republished as the collection "Spokes," which, in Auster's *Collected Poems*, is dated to 1970. Earlier drafts contained in the same archival folder are written on French-style writing paper, suggesting composition in France. David Lehman, in a poem entitled "Paris, 1971," recalls being given a copy of "Stele" by Auster, which implies that it was written in or before 1971: Paul Auster, *Collected Poems* (London: Faber and Faber, 2004), 19; David Lehman, *New and Selected Poems* (New York: Scribner, 2013), 69.

existence. The hostility of this early poetry to any co-optation by a mass market or broad readership replicates and reinforces the biographical claim to autonomy from the market, and it achieves this by simultaneously claiming its autonomy from both history and politics. Framing his writing as "the hunger of a dissident scribe," Auster positions these overlapping claims to autonomy within the tradition of hunger and asociality that he described in his MA thesis as having Hamsun, Kafka, and Beckett as its central proponents.

This account of Auster as an exemplary starving artist is complicated by his belatedness with respect to the modernist tradition. Auster's claim to write an art of hunger takes place under the shadow of his historical distance from modernism itself, a distance of fifty years, which separates the high point of anglophone modernism in Europe from the beginning of Auster's writing career in the early 1970s. The aspiration in the lines above to "found a self among the morsels, from what is swept away" recalls Nietzsche's excoriation of second-generation Greek tragedians, whom he condemns to "eat your fill on the crumbs of the masters of a previous age."[3] Like these tragedians, Auster, in his attempt to affiliate himself with modernism at the height of the period we subsequently came to call postmodern, is coming too late to the modernist feast. Rejecting the forms in which modernism and aesthetic autonomy had been institution-alized in the mid-century, Auster seeks to retain his affiliation to a previous generation of the literary field at a moment of generational change.

For a brief but defining moment as Auster was coming of age, the situation appeared even more grave: not merely that Auster was taking an unfashionable and outdated position in the literary field, but that the field itself lacked the autonomy on which modernist literature had depended. In the milieu of 1960s student radicalism, aesthetic autonomy was judged to be complicit in the violent status quo that produced the Vietnam War and racial segregation. The student protestors, like the post-war French intellectuals of Chapter 2, developed a theory of art that took politics to be inescapable, and autonomy itself merely a ruse. At the same time, their protests briefly threatened to destroy the structural conditions of the university that permitted the literary and intellectual fields' autonomy in mid-century US. Auster's aesthetics, formed in this moment of historical crisis, sought to de-institutionalize autonomy, investing it instead in the figure of the author, the "dissident scribe" who attempts to "found a self" among the ruins of modernism. Even as the immediate crisis of 1968 passed without destroying the institutions or ideology of aesthetic

[3] Friedrich Nietzsche, *The Birth of Tragedy*, trans. Douglas Smith (Oxford: Oxford University Press, 2000), 62.

autonomy, Auster retained the innovation within the art of hunger that developed in response to this moment: his equation of aesthetic autonomy with the personal autonomy of the artist. As his writing career developed across the 1970s and 1980s, he reimagined the art of hunger of his 1970 Masters thesis as a commitment to the figure of the starving artist—a figure who, as we saw in Chapter 1, represents the domestication of the art of hunger within a literary field.

This chapter focuses on Auster's writing of the 1970s and 1980s, the period during which his interest in both hunger and aesthetic autonomy are at their height. This period covers his entire output of poetry, his most important critical essays, his prose memoir, *The Invention of Solitude* (1982), and his first three novels, *The New York Trilogy* (1985–6), *In the Country of Last Things* (1987), and *Moon Palace* (1989). Despite their relatively late publication dates, these novels share a manuscript genesis that dates to Auster's college years in the late 1960s, when he penned a series of abortive novel drafts that provide many of the characters, situations, and plot points of his early published novels. Given their roots in this earlier historical moment, I read these novels of the 1980s, along with the earlier poetry and non-fiction prose, as engaged in a two-decade-long investigation of the aesthetic consequences of the social and intellectual tumult of the 1960s and 1970s. This investigation develops in the context of lively transnational exchange between French and US intellectual cultures, with thought on both sides of the Atlantic seeking new ways of understanding art's relation to society and literature's relation to non-literary language. In this context, Auster uses the art of hunger to stake out a position that defends aesthetic autonomy by investing it in the figure of a dying, but not yet dead, author.

1. AESTHETIC AUTONOMY IN THE UNIVERSITY

By the 1960s, a version of aesthetic autonomy, commonly attributed to modernism, had become firmly institutionalized within the American university. The key agent of its institutionalization was the New Criticism, whose methodological emphasis on "the text itself" and on what Douglas Bush critically described as its tendency "to analyze the work *in vacuo* as a timeless autonomous entity," translated modernism's perceived promotion of aesthetic autonomy into a critical principle.[4] Indeed, the New Criticism

---

[4] Gerald Graff, *Professing Literature: An Institutional History* (Chicago: University of Chicago Press, 2007), 173; Douglas Bush, "The New Criticism: Some Old-Fashioned Queries," *PMLA* 64, no. 1, Part 2, Supplement (1949): 14.

itself helped to construct this perception of modernism's autonomy, by taking modern literature, especially modern poetry, as its favored object of study and by setting out to defend contemporary writing against the indifference or hostility of the historicist "scholars" to whom the New Critics opposed themselves.[5] But if its roots were initially in modernism, by the 1940s this method had expanded to colonize literary studies more broadly, reading "earlier literature in the light of a modernist poetics that said poetry is neither rhetorical persuasion nor self-expression but an autonomous discourse that cannot be reduced to its constituent concepts or emotions."[6]

From the beginning, this New Critical investment in literary autonomy was as much an institutional as a critical stance. John Crowe Ransom's influential article "Criticism, Inc.," for instance, laid the groundwork for the New Criticism in its linkage of "the autonomy of the work itself as existing for its own sake" to the autonomy of the English department (especially its autonomy from the claims of historicism) and of scholarly inquiry generally.[7] In this period of academic professionalization, literary studies departments established themselves in opposition to departments of history, sociology, philosophy, and related disciplines, entrenching the aesthetic claim to autonomy as a brute fact of the institutional landscape. Meanwhile, over the same period, the university as an institution was asserting its own claims to autonomy from society, with the bedding down of the concept of academic freedom and its eventual acceptance as a bedrock of the post-war university. As the New Criticism went from "rags to riches to routine" over the course of the post-war period, this increasingly dominant methodological approach combined with the disciplinary and institutional autonomy of the English department within the university and the university within the society, to wrap university-level literary studies in several layers of autonomy. In the process, aesthetic autonomy became an increasingly institutional and institutionalized affair.[8]

The lingering effects of this link between institutional and aesthetic autonomy were felt most forcefully in the field of undergraduate education. At Columbia, where Auster was an undergraduate from 1965 to 1969 and a Masters student in 1969–70, this institutionalized autonomy achieved perhaps its most paradigmatic form in the division between the two compulsory Core (general education) courses, Contemporary Civilization (CC)

---

[5] See, for example, René Wellek and Austin Warren, *Theory of Literature* (New York: Harcourt, Bryce and Company, 1942), 36.

[6] Graff, *Professing Literature*, 198; the most influential example of this expansive gesture is probably Cleanth Brooks, *The Well-Wrought Urn* (London: Denis Dobson, 1947).

[7] John Crowe Ransom, "Criticism, Inc.," *Virginia Quarterly Review* 13, no. 4 (1937): 598.

[8] Graff, *Professing Literature*, 226.

and Literature Humanities (Lit Hum). The English faculty at Columbia represented a range of methodological stances, including some, like Lionel Trilling's liberal humanism, that do not fit comfortably within the broad-brush debates between "critics" and "scholars" of the era. But despite this faculty-level diversity, the compulsory Literature Humanities sequence, like many general education and introductory English courses in the period, cleaved closely to the New Critics' preferred method of decontextualized close reading. In this, as Daniel Bell argued in a 1966 review of Columbia's Core sequence, Lit Hum failed in its original intention "to parallel the Contemporary Civilization course: to provide in the realm of ideas and imagination a concurrent sense of the movement of thought with events."[9] Instead, he worried, "The temptation of this approach is that it leads to an extreme 'New Criticism,' of reading the work *in se*, without reference to any external context."[10]

Auster's relationship to the critical and institutional consensus around aesthetic autonomy was somewhat ambivalent. Despite Bell's concerns, Auster was an extremely enthusiastic student of Literature Humanities, which he has described in a recent memoir (written in the second person) as "without question the most invigorating intellectual challenge of your life so far."[11] Indeed, from *Paradise Lost*, which appears in his MA thesis as a touchstone for his theory of language, to *Don Quixote*, which is the subject of an extensive meditation in *City of Glass*, to Dostoevsky's *Notes from Underground*, whose spirit and attitude pervade Auster's early writing, the set texts of Lit Hum have proven formative for Auster's writing and thought.[12] It would not be an exaggeration to say that Auster's early writing is in part the history of his creative and intellectual engagement with the readings of this course, an engagement that was in turn shaped by the treatment of these texts as decontextualized aesthetic objects.[13]

[9] Daniel Bell, *The Reforming of General Education: The Columbia Experience in its National Setting* (New Brunswick, NJ: Transaction Publishers, 2011), 212.

[10] Ibid., 213.

[11] Paul Auster, *Report from the Interior* (London: Faber and Faber, 2013), 184.

[12] For a complete list of Literature Humanities set texts, see Columbia College, "Literature Humanities: Texts 1937–2013," Columbia College: The Core Curriculum, accessed August 31, 2014, <http://www.college.columbia.edu/core/1937.php>.

[13] Auster's teacher for Lit Hum and for at least one other early undergraduate course was Angus Fletcher, a disciple of Northrop Frye, who may have brought a more archetypal angle to this course. Nonetheless, Frye followed the New Critics in their commitment to the "intentional fallacy," and, as one review of Fletcher's 1964 book on allegory noted, his approach shared with the more New Critical approach to Lit Hum an "essentially non-historical" orientation: Northrop Frye, *Anatomy of Criticism: Four Essays* (Princeton: Princeton University Press, 1957), 86; Russell Fraser, "Review of *Allegory: The Theory of a Symbolic Mode* by Angus Fletcher," *Modern Language Review* 62, no. 2 (1967): 298; for Auster's discussion of Fletcher, see Auster, *Report*, 184.

The environment in which Auster studied in the late 1960s was already marked by the generational decline of the New Criticism, in anticipation of the discipline's slow shift towards the "French theory" that would transform literary studies in the 1970s and 1980s.[14] Despite his enthusiasm for Lit Hum, Auster's early essays suggest incipient reservations about the New Critical methods he was encouraged to follow. He opens an undergraduate essay on one of Beckett's French poems, for instance, by ironically declaring his intention to "hack it to pieces, in the best tradition of the academy"—a disparaging allusion to New Critical close reading—while retaining a New Critical conviction that the work's internal integrity will render it "capable of bearing the blows of the butcher's cleaver."[15] Similarly, while in the paper itself he has "confined myself as rigorously as possible to the text," the paper's extensive notes, which he commends as "no doubt more interesting and readable than what precedes them," contextualize the poem in relation to Beckett's other writing and the sources and intertexts of his work, combining New Critical approaches with an author-centric historicism. Auster's very early solution to the critical vacuum created by the decline of the New Criticism supplements attention to the text as an autonomous object with attention to the author. It prefigures Auster's characteristic defense of aesthetic autonomy, which breaks with the New Criticism in its identification between the formal autonomy of the work and the personal autonomy of the author.

2. ART AND POLITICS IN 1968: THE AUTONOMOUS UNIVERSITY IN CRISIS

The shift from New Criticism to French theory represents a generational changing of the guard, a jostling for positions within a Bourdieusian literary field. The unrest that swept university campuses in the late 1960s, however, mounted a more serious challenge to the concept of

---

[14] I call this movement French theory, following François Cusset, in order to foreground its reception in the US as a peculiarly French way of thought. This does not, of course, fully reflect the nationality or origins of many of its key thinkers, from Kristeva to de Man: François Cusset, *French Theory: How Foucault, Deleuze, Derrida & Co. Transformed the Intellectual Life of the United States*, trans. Jeff Fort (Minneapolis: University of Minnesota Press, 2008).

[15] Paul Auster, "College Essays: Explications: The Third Poem of *Quatre Poèmes*," TS, 1966–7, Box 79, Folder 2, Paul Auster Archive, 1963–1995 Papers, Berg Collection, New York Public Library.

autonomous art, casting doubt not just on the old positions but on the structural autonomy of the field as a whole. In the spring of 1968, Auster's junior year of college, Columbia erupted in protest, making headlines nationally and internationally and becoming synonymous with college unrest across the US (the slogan "One, two, many Columbias," adapted from Che Guevera's "one, two, many Vietnams," emphasized the university's germinal role in nationwide student protest). Between 23 and 30 April, students occupied five buildings on the central university campus, forcing the suspension of classes and other university business. After the university sent the police to violently break up the occupation, university closures and a student strike persisted through the first weeks of May.

The protests were driven by the students' realization of the university's complicity in the major political struggles of their day. They were reacting against, on the one hand, Columbia's plans to construct a new university gym in a local park, which was seen as extending the largely white university's colonization of the poor black Harlem neighborhoods that surrounded it, and, on the other, the administration's involvement in government and military research, which was seen as providing covert support for the Vietnam War. These events suggested that the university's role as a guarantor of both intellectual and aesthetic autonomy was a fraud—that it was instead deeply invested in and complicit with the politics of segregation and militarism. In this context, autonomy itself seemed, from the students' perspective, to lose both its institutional grounds and its intellectual legitimacy.

As a junior at Columbia in the spring of 1968, Auster participated in the occupation as an occupant of the Mathematics Building, one of the more radical, primarily undergraduate buildings.[16] After the university called police to end the occupation, sporadic protests and campaigns continued throughout the remaining years of the decade and into the early 1970s, shaping the academic environment of the second half of Auster's college life. Auster himself was fully immersed in this environment. His 1997 memoir *Hand to Mouth* recounts his friendship with several leading activists, including Mark Rudd, the leader of the student protests, whom Auster describes as "a childhood friend and Columbia dorm neighbor."[17] As the leaders of the protests radicalized and went underground, he recalls standing in a post office, studying "the posters of the

---

[16] "Math Commune," n.d., Box 11, Folder 21, Occupiers of Buildings, Student Statements and Correspondence, Group Positions, Protest and Activism Collection, 1958–99, Columbia University Archives.

[17] Paul Auster, *Hand to Mouth: A Chronicle of Early Failure* (London: Faber and Faber, 1997), 34.

FBI's ten most wanted men pinned to the wall. It turned out that I knew seven of them."[18]

Coming of age in this radicalized environment, Auster's understanding of autonomy—personal, aesthetic, and institutional—was shaped by the assumptions of the student protests. Critics of the protests, especially among faculty, saw them as direct attacks on the autonomy of the university. Lionel Trilling, a professor of English at Columbia, found the students to be "wrong in dealing with the university as if it were perfectly continuous with the society," worrying that under such circumstances, "the academic life will soon be made impossible."[19] Sidney Hook, a philosophy professor, concurred: "If the university is conceived of as an agency of action to transform society in behalf of a cause, no matter how exalted, it loses its relative autonomy, imperils both its independence and objectivity, and subjects itself to retaliatory curbs and controls on the part of society on whose support and largesse it ultimately depends."[20] For these faculty members, the student protests threatened to undermine and undo the structural autonomy that the university was afforded.

These writers are correct in their sense that the autonomy of the university was a central preoccupation for student protestors, but their analysis does not capture the depth of the activists' concerns. Where Trilling and Hook saw student protestors as attacking university autonomy, the student protestors instead believed that there was nothing to attack: that the university had always been complicit in systems of US inequality and militarism. By highlighting the ways in which the university's professed autonomy masked its actual complicity in the defense of a violent status quo, student protestors sought to show that neither the administration nor the research of universities was in fact autonomous, and that claims to autonomy functioned merely as a smokescreen for the university's political activities. At the same time, they reinterpreted these professions of autonomy as themselves political gestures. When the 1966 French Situationist pamphlet "On the Poverty of Student Life"—which was influential in both the US and France—attacked the university as "totally cut off from historical reality, both of the individual and of society," the implicit accusation was that to profess to stand apart from "historical reality" during what both French and American students took to be a period of profound crisis was to adopt a political stance that

---

[18] Ibid., 34–5.

[19] Stephen Donadio, "Columbia: Seven Interviews," *Partisan Review* 35, no. 3 (1968): 392.

[20] Sidney Hook, "Is Fanaticism in the Saddle?," *Columbia College Today* 15, no. 3 (1968): 90.

defended the status quo.[21] What the students propose here is not merely a new position of autonomy that will supersede that of the previous generation, but rather a new conviction that autonomy itself is structurally impossible under current circumstances. They maintain that in the 1960s US, as in France under German occupation, there is no position from which autonomy can be practiced, no position free from the contamination of the field's over-politicization. The students made this analogy to the hyper-politicized social context of World War II explicit, warning each other against being a "good German," one of "the great mass of Germans who, in their ignorance, in their denial, and especially in their silence, allowed the Nazis to do their work."[22] While such an analogy may seem somewhat overblown from a contemporary vantage point, its considerable influence persuaded student protestors that their intellectual field, like that of wartime and post-war France, was experiencing an acute crisis in its structural autonomy.

In place of the complicity that student protestors found in the university's commitment to autonomy, their own "liberation classes"—held by students and sympathetic faculty during the May strike—envisioned an open, democratic university, an educational institution devoid of the traditional university's structural or conceptual commitment to autonomy. Crucial to this vision was an emphasis on the "relevance" of education to the world beyond academia. One document outlining the rationale for these classes argues that, "In order to be responsive to the interests of its real constituency—students, faculty, employees, and community—the university has to be a critical, participatory institution which prepares people to control their own lives and change society."[23] Another affirms that, "In all cases, the relevance of the topics to the participants' lives will be constantly examined and emphasized."[24] These classes, in other words, sought to provide an alternative to what they saw as the discredited, impossible fiction of the autonomous university, advancing a new model of education in which specialist knowledge was to be alive

[21] Members of the Situationist International and Some Students at the University of Strasbourg, *On the Poverty of Student Life, Considered in its Economic, Political, Psychological, Sexual, and Particularly Intellectual Aspects, With a Modest Proposal for Its Remedy* (Detroit: Black and Red, 2000), 4.

[22] Mark Rudd, *Underground: My Life with SDS and the Weathermen* (New York: Harper Collins, 2009), 11.

[23] Strike Education Committee and Liberation School, "Why Have Liberation Classes?" May 7, 1968, Box 12, Folder 12, Strike Education Committee and Liberation School, Protest and Activism Collection, 1958–99, Columbia University Archives.

[24] Strike Education Committee and Liberation School, "For Immediate Release," May 5, 1968, Box 12, Folder 12, Strike Education Committee and Liberation School, Protest and Activism Collection, 1958–99, Columbia University Archives.

to students' experiences and active in producing social change, and in which the heteronomy of the university would be harnessed to foment political change.

If the activists' critique of the autonomy of the university was grounded in an analogy between the contemporary US and World War II-era Europe, its solution had a similar provenance, in the students' rediscovery of the French existentialists' post-war concept of authenticity. In their goal of overthrowing the "authoritarian structures" of the university in order to allow students to "take control of their own lives," the organizers of the liberation classes foresaw a new form of education that would allow students to nurture their authentic selves. This educational philosophy supported the broader orientation of the New Left towards the "search for authenticity," which Doug Rossinow has argued "lay at the heart" of 1960s radicalism.[25] As the Port Huron Statement—the 1962 manifesto of the Students for a Democratic Society—proclaimed, the organization advocated for "finding a meaning in life that is personally authentic."[26] The liberation classes, by reorienting education towards the goal of self-determination and relevance, opposed the autonomous university in crisis with a new model of authentic education, and of education for authenticity.

Given the institutionalization of aesthetic autonomy in this period, this challenge to the autonomy of the university also threatened the structural basis for the autonomy of art. And as the autonomy of the literary field—to the extent that it was institutionalized in the university—was called into question, so too was the philosophical concept of aesthetic autonomy. Quentin Anderson, a Columbia English professor who chaired its Joint Committee of Disciplinary Affairs in the aftermath of the unrest, makes the link between the decline of aesthetic and university autonomy explicit in the preface to his 1971 study of nineteenth-century American literature, *The Imperial Self*: "In our very different period—post-modernist, post-new-critical—there are no hedges about the sacred realm of art. Like the formerly sacrosanct plot of green on the university campus, it is now crisscrossed by the paths made by those who are rather frantically seeking to define their humanity, and in the process find art rather more a means than a refuge."[27] Similarly, when Mark Rudd, leader of the Columbia Chapter of activist organization Students for a Democratic Society, traces

---

[25] Doug Rossinow, *The Politics of Authenticty: Liberalism, Christianity, and the New Left in America* (New York: Columbia University Press, 1998), 4.

[26] Richard Flacks and Nelson Lichtenstein, eds., "The Port Huron Statement," in *The Port Huron Statement: Sources and Legacies of the New Left's Founding Document* (Philadelphia: University of Pennslyvania Press, 2015), 242.

[27] Quentin Anderson, *The Imperial Self: An Essay in American Literary and Cultural History* (New York: Knopf, 1971), xii.

his frustration with Columbia's mode of education to a poetry class where he recalls being "overcome by a wave of despair," he makes the teaching of literature into the paradigmatic site of the university's problematic autonomy.[28] Despite their very different politics, Rudd and Anderson agree that the attack on the autonomy of the university necessarily entails an attack on the aesthetic autonomy that has been identified with it in this period. In this new environment, "The 'New Criticism' will not be tolerated," as one liberation class proudly advertised.[29] Both the institutional structure of the autonomous university and the philosophical and critical commitment to aesthetic autonomy that this structure housed were placed in question by the student protestors' claims.

Art did remain an important feature of the student protests, but it was a form of art that explicitly sought to undo both the institutional and the philosophical supports on which aesthetic autonomy rested. The organizers of the liberation classes were careful to emphasize that their vision of a relevant education included cultural and aesthetic subjects and not merely practical, applied, or scientific ones. As one of their pamphlets insisted, "Balkan Dancing is just as relevant as chemical engineering"—and indeed, Balkan Dancing was a charmingly persistent presence on liberation class schedules.[30] In their aesthetic and cultural education, they attempted to bring literature into contact with their world and concerns. Literary offerings featured strongly on the programme, including classes on modern poetry from Kenneth Koch, on Victorian and avant-garde literature by Kate Millett, and several classes led by Paul Zweig, then a junior faculty member in the English and Comparative Literature department. Many of these classes, in keeping with the strike committee's goals of providing a "relevant" education, sought to tie their literary subjects to politics and revolution. Students were offered classes on "Literature and Revolution," "Thoreau on the Duty of Civil Disobedience," "The Methodology of Marxist Literary Criticism," and "Wm. Blake: A Radical Discussion of the Songs of Early Prophetic Books." Another, entitled "Our Own Poems," promised to discuss poetry "in ways that relate directly to our own lives and thoughts and the events around us."[31]

[28] Rudd, *Underground*, 4.
[29] Strike Education Committee and Liberation School, "Four New Courses of Special Interest," May 1968, Box 12, Folder 13, Strike Education Committee and Liberation School, Protest and Activism Collection, 1958–99, Columbia University Archives.
[30] Strike Education Committee and Liberation School, "The Future of Education," 1968, Box 12, Folder 12, Strike Education Committee and Liberation School, Protest and Activism Collection, 1958–99, Columbia University Archives.
[31] Strike Education Committee and Liberation School, "Liberation Classes," May 1968, Box 12, Folder 13, Strike Education Committee and Liberation School, Protest and Activism Collection, 1958–99, Columbia University Archives; Strike Education Committee and Liberation School, "Four New Courses of Special Interest."

Through poetry readings and theatre, literature also became an important feature of the protests and associated fundraising activities at Columbia. The activists' literary preferences inclined strongly towards engaged and performative modes. "Guerilla theatre" was popular, as were readings by poets like Allen Ginsberg, Kenneth Koch, David Shapiro, and Ron Padgett, suggesting a preference for literary forms that privileged the poet's voice and the physical presence of actors or writers. This preference is in line with what Mark McGurl has called the "*phonocentric* literary historical moment*" of the 1960s, with its emphasis on "a textual performance of vocal authenticity."[32] In this, the Columbia student movement inclined towards what Marjorie Perloff has called "the dominant poetic of the sixties, a poetic...of strenuous authenticity, the desire to present a self as natural, as organic, and as unmediated as possible."[33] As Kenneth Koch, a poet and teacher at Columbia who emerged as one of the dominant literary voices in the Columbia student protests, writes in his 1975 verse manifesto "The Art of Poetry," poetry aspires towards "the perfection of an original style which is yours alone" and whose quality is measured by the extent to which it is "in my own voice."[34] The students' belief that they were living through the de-institutionalization of literature, and the consequent loss of the structural conditions on which literary autonomy was based, thus engendered a shift in the conceptual frameworks to which literature was subjected. As the quest for an authentic poetics of voice came to replace the New Critical admiration for impersonal, textual poetry, authenticity replaced autonomy as the chief value by which literary prestige and success were measured.

In France—where Auster lived from 1970 to 1974, in the wake of the May '68 student protests—the literary field also saw the decline of aesthetic autonomy, in favor of a more relevant, revolutionary art. The events of May 1968 have frequently been understood as primarily aesthetic or linguistic. Both Roland Barthes and Michel de Certeau have called the protests a "prise de parole," a taking or seizing of speech, on analogy to the "prise de Bastille" of an earlier French revolution.[35] As Barthes argued: "Not only did the crisis have its language, the crisis was language."[36] This "verbal revolution" was

---

[32] Mark McGurl, *The Program Era: Postwar Fiction and the Rise of Creative Writing* (Cambridge, MA: Harvard University Press, 2009), 230.
[33] Marjorie Perloff, *Radical Artifice: Writing Poetry in the Age of Media* (Chicago: University of Chicago Press, 1991), 20.
[34] Kenneth Koch, "The Art of Poetry," *Poetry* 125, no. 4 (1975): 189, 192.
[35] Roland Barthes, "L'Écriture de l'événement," *Communications* 12 (1968): 109; Michel de Certeau, *La Prise de parole et autres écrits politiques* (Paris: Seuil, 1994).
[36] "Non seulement la crise a eu son langage, mais encore la crise a été langage": Barthes, "L'Écriture de l'événement," 109.

allegedly shaped—and has certainly been remembered—as taking place in and through the creative use and appropriation of language, of "words on tracts, on posters, on walls, on banners, on placards, words of protests, of speeches, spoken and stuck to the wall, hurled, transcribed in the heat of the moment."[37] In its creativity, its spontaneity, its imaginativeness, and its formal inventiveness, this revolutionary language is frequently understood as a kind of avant-garde poetry: as one of the iconic pieces of graffiti from this period proclaimed, in the revolution, "poetry is in the streets."[38] Like the Columbia protests, May '68 in France insisted that poetry was not autonomous but revolutionary.

As at Columbia, the French retreat from the philosophical commitment to aesthetic autonomy was intimately related to the student protestors' attack on university autonomy. Gérard Fromanger, a member of the Atelier Populaire des Beaux-Arts, the group of artists responsible for the iconic posters of May '68, describes the protests as a crumbling of aesthetic autonomy, recalling that, "'68 comes to prove that we [artists] must necessarily have a relation to the real and no longer only to the imaginary of the museum, the imaginary of painting, solitude, the indeterminate universe of shapes, absolute theorisation, the coldness of the minimal... We are finally necessary."[39] The Atelier Populaire linked this collapse of aesthetic autonomy to a collapse in the autonomy of the university. In a manifesto from July 1968, they profess their aim of "better connect[ing] artists] to all other categories of worker," a goal which forces them outside the university, for "No professor can help us to better attend to [mieux fréquenter] this reality."[40] Kristin Ross has argued that the collapse of aesthetic autonomy in France in 1968 was part of a larger revolt against the compartmentalization of society into discrete "sociological categories," a social division of labor that permits both aesthetic and university autonomy. As a result, she sees May '68 as a period in which "politics was exerting a magnetic pull on culture, yanking it out of its specific and

---

[37] Maurice Tournier, *Les Mots de mai 68* (Toulouse: Presses Universitaires de Mirail, 2007), 4.

[38] Andrew Feenberg and Jim Freedman, *When Poetry Ruled the Streets: The French May Events of 1968* (Albany, NY: State University of New York Press, 2001), iv.

[39] "'68 arrive pour faire la preuve que nous devons obligatoirement avoir un rapport au réel et non plus seulement à l'imaginaire du musée, l'imaginaire de la peinture, la solitude, l'univers indéterminé des formes, la théorisation absolue, la froideur du minimal... On est finalement nécessaire": Gérard Fromanger, "L'art, c'est ce qui rend la vie plus intéressante que l'art," *Libération*, May 14, 1998, <http://www.liberation.fr/cahier-special/1998/05/14/special-mai-68-gerard-fromanger-28-ans-peintre-militant-actif-de-l-atelier-populaire-des-beaux-arts-_235995>.

[40] "...les reliera mieux à toutes les autres catégories de travailleurs...Aucun professeur ne peut nous aider à mieux fréquenter cette réalité": "Document: L'Atelier Populaire," *Cahiers de mai*, 2 (July 1, 1968): 16.

specialized realm."[41] For Ross, in other words, the Atelier Populaire's repudiation of the twinned realms of aesthetic and university autonomy was not merely a position in a literary field, but part of the field's new precariousness *as* a field—that is, as a sociological category or a world apart. In France, as in the US, then, the upheaval of the late 1960s imagined a new, more relevant art, born of the demise of aesthetic and university autonomy not only as ideas, but also as structural positions. The post-war consensus around the overlapping categories of aesthetic and academic autonomy, epitomized in the US by the hegemony of the New Criticism and the modernist literary canon that it promoted, was temporarily replaced by an avant-gardist commitment to literature's acting in and on the world.

Auster's 1997 memoir, *Hand to Mouth*, revisits these early years of his writing career, retrospectively constructing his youthful self along the model of the starving artist. While he was personally and politically sympathetic to the student activists, in *Hand to Mouth* he constructs an image of himself as a young man "temperamentally unfit for group activities," endowed with "loner instincts," who, throughout the campus unrest, "went on paddling my little canoe—a bit more desperately, perhaps, a bit less sure of where I was going now, but much too stubborn to get out."[42] Investing his fledgling writing career in the trope of a beleaguered craft paddling against the stream, Auster's memoir persistently identifies writing with brooding isolation. He recalls of his final years at Columbia that, "In spite of the distractions and constant turmoil, I managed to do a fair amount of writing," a claim whose "In spite of" jars sharply against activist hopes for the integration of protest and art.[43] While the leaders of the Columbia strikes sought ways of understanding literature as continuous with the "distractions and constant turmoil" of social activism, Auster imagines writing as intrinsically opposed to, even imperilled by, such activity.

In rejecting the activists' socially engaged theory of art, Auster insists on the writer's autonomy from political and social demands, as well as from community itself. In fact, *Hand to Mouth* folds together several different modes of autonomy. Not only does Auster maintain his autonomy in political and social terms by resisting the student activists' incorporation of art into social activism or politics, he also refuses the New Critical position that preserves aesthetic autonomy by linking it to institutional autonomy, arguing that "on principle, it felt wrong to me for a writer to hide out in a university." At the same time, *Hand to Mouth* as a whole is a classic story

---

[41] Kristin Ross, *May '68 and its Afterlives* (Chicago: University of Chicago Press, 2002), 15.
[42] Auster, *Hand to Mouth*, 34.   [43] Ibid., 35.

of "the life of a starving poet," defined by a persistent refusal of work and the market and a consequent "constant, grinding, almost suffocating lack of money."[44] Auster, in other words, imagines himself to be simultaneously autonomous from the market, from politics, from social contexts, and from the institution of the university. His claim to this multiply inflected personal autonomy functions as a simultaneous assertion of the autonomy of his writing, while suggesting, in line with the student protestors' conviction that autonomy is undergoing a structural crisis, that there are no more institutions and no more social contexts within which this autonomous writing might take place.

By translating his claims for the autonomy of art into the realm of the personal, Auster's autonomy becomes bound up with an appeal to authenticity. His suggestion that any affiliation with an institution or group represents a necessary compromise of autonomy is born, as we have seen, of the student activists' conviction that structural autonomy was never actually autonomous, that it was always a mask for complicity and suspect politics. But this rejection of autonomy as a structural force also allows him to reimagine autonomy as a form of authentic selfhood, in the mode of the post-war culture of authenticity that, according to Abigail Cheever, "separates the individual from the social world" and embraces "that which might be uniquely one's own rather than a product of social influence."[45] By conceiving of his autonomy as a mode of authenticity, Auster both justifies his rejection of the politicized aesthetics of the student movement on its own terms, and reconfigures aesthetic autonomy in the terms of one of the decade's most influential ideas. In the process, he forges a new line of continuity between the modernist concept of aesthetic autonomy and the sixties' embrace of authenticity.

In fact, Marshall Berman suggested in the preface to his 1970 book *The Politics of Authenticity* that a concern with "the political consequences of the search for personal authenticity" provided a rare point of intergenerational continuity between student radicals (among whom he counted himself) and the professors who had taught him at Columbia College a decade earlier.[46] Two years after Berman's book was released, Lionel Trilling confirmed Berman's evaluation of the Columbia faculty with the release of *Sincerity and Authenticity*, still a landmark study of authenticity in literature. In this book, Trilling traces the emergence of

[44] Ibid., 23, 3.

[45] Abigail Cheever, *Real Phonies: Cultures of Authenticity in Post-World War II America* (Athens, GA: University of Georgia Press, 2010), 3.

[46] Marshall Berman, *The Politics of Authenticity: Radical Individualism and the Emergence of Modern Society* (New York: Atheneum, 1970), xii.

authenticity as a literary value to eighteenth-century aestheticians' disdain for art's capacity to please and, with it, their disdain for the audience of the artwork.[47] Like Auster, Trilling imagines authenticity to be intimately bound up with aesthetic autonomy and sees this union as inhering in the person of the artist, whose "reference is to himself only" and who "regards his audience with indifference, or with hostility and contempt."[48] Equating the oppositional authenticity of student activism with the autonomous authenticity described by his professors, Auster's portrait of the young artist imagines a writer whose "imaginative desocialization" (as Quentin Anderson described the attitude of the student activists and their nineteenth-century American precursors) allows him to carve out an authentically autonomous art that crosses the generational gulf of the 1960s.[49] In doing so, Auster reimagines the relation between personal autonomy and authenticity to include *aesthetic* autonomy. In contrast to student protestors for whom authenticity was opposed to aesthetic autonomy, Auster offers a Trilling-esque model of authenticity in art as the conjunction of personal and aesthetic autonomy.

Auster, however, breaks with both his professors and his peers on the point of authenticity's relationship to freedom. Both Trilling and the student movement take it for granted that the quest for authenticity is a quest for freedom. This is what Berman means by evoking the "political consequences of the search for personal authenticity." It lies behind Trilling's extensive engagement with Hegel, whose conception of positive freedom approaches the notion of authenticity, as well as the Port Huron Statement's claim that "The goal of man and society should be human independence," which the authors define as "finding a meaning in life that is personally authentic."[50] But Auster, in the tradition of earlier writers of the art of hunger, describes authenticity in the language of necessity, not freedom, appealing to his "need to affirm myself as an outsider," and wrestling with the problem of "how to reconcile the needs of the body with the needs of the soul."[51] This account of autonomous authenticity as a form of necessity, not of freedom—and as one that might have a plausible claim to compete with such basic necessities as the need to eat— explains the narrative trajectory of *Hand to Mouth*, which moves unstoppably towards not liberation, but suffering and catastrophe. As the first page of the memoir announces, this book describes a period in which the

---

[47] Lionel Trilling, *Sincerity and Authenticity* (Cambridge, MA: Harvard University Press, 1972), 92–105.

[48] Ibid., 97, 98.   [49] Anderson, *The Imperial Self*, 4.

[50] Trilling, *Sincerity and Authenticity*, 26–52; "The Port Huron Statement," 242.

[51] Auster, *Hand to Mouth*, 46, 106.

"constant, grinding, almost suffocating lack of money... poisoned my soul and kept me in a state of never-ending panic."[52] Conceding that "There was no one to blame but myself" but suggesting, through the language of necessity, that he could nonetheless not do otherwise, Auster's problems arise not from any external oppression, but from his incapacity to experience an authentic life as a free life. *Hand to Mouth*, in other words, describes the impossibility of imagining an authentic autonomy, an autonomy that is conceptual but not structural, as a path to freedom.

The starving artist, which dramatizes Auster's dual commitment to autonomy and authenticity, is both a legacy of modernism and a mark of Auster's negotiation with his immediate context, where hunger played a small but persistent role in the student protests. The Columbia SDS used fasts as a tool of protest, a way of "draw[ing] people's attention to the immorality of the Vietnam War," and at least one liberation class promised to discuss "Vegetarianism and Fasting."[53] At the same time, hunger sometimes featured as a metonym for poverty in SDS propaganda material, as in one flyer that railed against "Humans starving in Mississippi, animals gorging in Scarsdale."[54] The Port Huron Statement similarly declares that "The United States' principal goal should be creating a world where hunger, poverty, disease, ignorance, violence, and exploitation are replaced as central features by abundance, reason, love, and international cooperation."[55] For these students, hunger is a dramatization of shared oppression. Its use in activist literature and protest was intended to demonstrate solidarity with, and to recognize the shared humanity of, those suffering this most basic of catastrophes.

In this collectivizing model of hunger, some of the students—who, as Mark Rudd has observed, were disproportionately Jewish—were drawing on a much longer religious and ethnic tradition.[56] Both Josh Cohen and Derek Rubin have argued that Auster's sense of hunger as that which "must be preserved at all costs" reflects a Jewish experience of endlessly deferred longing, derived from the long experience of exile.[57] Moreover,

---

[52] Ibid., 3.

[53] Rudd, *Underground*, 24; Strike Education Committee and Liberation School, "Liberation Classes."

[54] Students for a Democratic Society, "Dare We Be Heroes?" n.d., Box 13, Folder 8: Students for a Democratic Society, Protest and Activism Collection, 1958–99, Columbia University Archives.

[55] "The Port Huron Statement," 268.

[56] Mark Rudd, "Why Were There So Many Jews in the SDS? (Or, the Ordeal of Civility)," markrudd.com, November 2005, <http://www.markrudd.com/?about-mark-rudd/why-were-there-so-many-jews-in-sds-or-the-ordeal-of-civility.html>.

[57] Josh Cohen, "Desertions: Paul Auster, Edmond Jabès and the Writing of Auschwitz," *The Journal of the Midwest Modern Languages Association* 33, no. 3 (2001 2000): 94–107;

for Jewish-Americans born around the end of World War II and entering university in the late 1960s, images of the emaciated Jews of the Holocaust were haunting symbols of an atrocity that was evolving in this period, as Herbert Gans has argued, into "a new symbol for the threat of group destruction."[58] As a marker of both shared humanity and a specific ethnic identity—and as a symbol for the threat of the annihilation of both— hunger recurs throughout Auster's various social contexts as a powerful symbol of oppression. Auster's portrayal of his younger self as a starving artist activates this association between hunger and the loss of freedom, but it does so by removing the connotations of collectivity that attach to both hunger's activist and Jewish lineages.[59]

The role of Auster's Jewish identity in informing his use of hunger gestures towards the changing meaning of authenticity in the late 1960s. Cheever describes authenticity as shifting in this period "from an existential emphasis on self-constitution to a more postmodern view of the self as an embodiment of culture."[60] As Auster began his literary career, individualist notions of authenticity were losing ground to the argument that authenticity inhered in group or ethnic identifications. Hunger, with its group associations, locates Auster on the cusp of this movement, showing where he could tip forward into a mode of authenticity defined by cultural identifications. His insistence on autonomy as the vehicle of authenticity, however, keeps him wedded to the individualist, existentialist version of the idea. Holding aesthetic autonomy, personal autonomy, and authenticity together in a single gesture, Auster's early work tells the story of modernism made new through its commitment to 1960s' modes of authentic individuality.

3. THE DYING AUTHOR: "FRENCH THEORY" AND THE AUTONOMY OF THE ARTIST

Unlike either post-Vichy France or late-apartheid South Africa, the shock that the literary field experienced in the aftermath of 1968 was short-lived

---

Derek Rubin, "'The Hunger Must Be Preserved at All Costs': A Reading of *The Invention of Solitude*," in *Beyond the Red Notebook: Essays on Paul Auster*, ed. Dennis Barone (Philadelphia: University of Pennsylvania Press, 1995), 60–70.

[58] Herbert J. Gans, "Symbolic Ethnicity: The Future of Ethnic Groups and Cultures in America," *Ethnic and Racial Studies* 2, no. 1 (1979): 11.

[59] I deal with Auster's complicated relationship to his Jewish heritage in more detail elsewhere. See Alys Moody, "Eden of Exiles: The Ethnicities of Paul Auster's Aesthetics," *American Literary History* 28, no. 1 (2016): 69–93.

[60] Cheever, *Real Phonies*, 3.

and localized. While in both the US and France 1968 is often taken to have marked a major turning point in political and social life, it did not necessarily have an equally profound impact on the structure of the literary field. To the contrary, the sense of crisis that shaped the student activists' attitudes to university and aesthetic autonomy did not endure substantially beyond this period, nor did it spread much beyond the university milieu in which it originated. Nonetheless, within this milieu, the crisis was serious and profound. The intense and rapid radicalization of the Columbia activists—Mark Rudd and others in his circle progressed from student protests to domestic terrorism in less than eighteen months— reflected the gravity of Auster's peers' belief that supposedly autonomous institutions were in fact complicit in the violence of the state. This crisis, then, is best understood as simultaneously real and formative from the perspective of Auster and his peers, and ephemeral and minor from the perspective of the US literary field as a whole. This double perspective clarifies the historical provenance of Auster's aesthetics, which were formed in the crisis years around 1968, but subsequently imported into a literary field in which autonomy was being readily recuperated as both a concept and an institutional position. The starving artist, as we saw in Chapter 1, embodies this domestication of the art of hunger within a fully constituted literary field; its return in Auster's mid-career work, such as the 1994 memoir *Hand to Mouth*, is a product of his attempt to bring a theory of autonomy developed in the period of its crisis into a field whose autonomy had been reconstituted.

As we saw in Section 2, the theory of autonomy that Auster develops during and in the aftermath of the 1968 crisis invests aesthetic autonomy in the personal authenticity of the author. Despite the claims of modernist impersonality, this personalization of aesthetic autonomy is a characteristically modernist move. Andrew Goldstone's *Fictions of Autonomy* suggests that modernist aesthetic autonomy is as often imagined to inhere in the life of the author as in the status of the text, and we have already seen how this impulse creates the iconic figure of the starving artist in inter-war modernism. By the time Auster took up this theme in the late 1960s and 1970s, however, the intellectual climate had shifted. The New Criticism influentially reimagined aesthetic autonomy as a purely textual affair, contingent on the excision of the author from the poem. Wimsatt and Beardsley's influential "intentional fallacy" epitomizes this shift, elevating evidence "internal" to the poem over the "private or idiosyncratic" evidence of authorial intention or biography.[61] In a context where the New

---

[61] W. K. Wimsatt and M. C. Beardsley, "The Intentional Fallacy," *The Sewanee Review* 54, no. 3 (1946): 477.

Criticism was understood as part of the university's complicit autonomy, and where students were rejecting institutions in favor of a claim to personal authenticity, Auster's return to a modernist vision of personalized aesthetic autonomy offered an intellectually respectable way of keeping the position alive.

While the twinned autonomies of art and the university managed to outlive the shock of 1968, the new critical approaches that sprung up in its wake did little to rehabilitate the personal vision of aesthetic autonomy. As the student protests raged, the academy was undergoing a generational change in the forms of aesthetic autonomy it enshrined, as the New Criticism was slowly supplanted by the first stirrings of what would come to be known as "French theory." François Cusset traces the latter's arrival in the US—and the invention of poststructuralism itself—to The Languages of Criticism and the Sciences of Man conference at Johns Hopkins in October 1966 (coinciding with the beginning of Auster's sophomore year of college).[62] Although it would not be fully absorbed into the US academy until well after 1968, Auster, as a French-speaker and student of French literature, was better positioned than most to feel its first reverberations in the US. Indeed, his Masters thesis, submitted in May 1970, supervised by Edward Said, and drawing heavily on Roland Barthes, reveals his early engagement with then-recent French thought.

As a young poet in Paris between 1970 and 1974, contemporary French thought was central to his professional and social life. Working as a translator during the 1970s, he translated works by Bataille and Blanchot; a book-length study by Pierre Clastres, one of Lévi-Strauss's disciples; a collection of essays and interviews from the 1970s by Sartre; and what he describes as "op-ed pieces" by Foucault and Sartre.[63] Lydia Davis, his girlfriend and then wife until their divorce in 1979, who frequently collaborated with him on translations (including several of those listed above), has gone on to become one of Blanchot's major translators. His social circles in Paris reinforced this professional familiarity with current French thought. Although not highly theoretical, the French poets of his acquaintance were woven into—if, like Auster, generally intent on holding themselves apart from—the milieu out of which theory sprang. Edmond Jabès, whom Auster admired, befriended, and

---

[62] Cusset, *French Theory*, 28–32.

[63] Maurice Blanchot, *Vicious Circles: Two Fictions and After the Fact*, trans. Paul Auster (Barrytown, NY: Station Hill Press, 1989); Pierre Clastres, *Chronicle of the Guayaki Indians*, trans. Paul Auster (New York: Zone Books, 2000); Jean-Paul Sartre, *Life/Situations: Essays Written and Spoken*, trans. Paul Auster and Lydia Davis (New York: Pantheon Books, 1977); Auster, *Hand to Mouth*, 69.

interviewed, is the subject of one of the essays in Derrida's *Writing and Difference* (1967). André Du Bouchet and Jacques Dupin, friends whose aid Auster has described as "essential" to his survival in Paris, edited the journal *L'Ephémère* (1967–72), which regularly published essays by Bataille and Blanchot.[64] Working closely as a translator with the work of such a wide range of leading writers of this period, and active in social and literary worlds that intersected theirs, Auster was immersed in the major debates and themes of French thought of the 1970s.

France offered Auster the promise of expatriation as a form of autonomy, allowing him—like Andrew Goldstone's modernists and like Beckett himself—to reject the "solidarity of political community" that, in the US context, denied art's autonomy, in favor of "a relatively autonomous artistic practice."[65] Auster reinforced this effect by assembling around himself a notably autonomous version of the French literary field. His MA thesis relies heavily on the Barthes of *Writing Degree Zero* and his translation work privileged writers like Blanchot. He thus built a para-literary career around writers who, as we saw in Chapter 2, were and remained the chief theorists of aesthetic autonomy in the post-war period. At the same time, the circle of poets around *L'Ephémère* represented one of the more autonomous poles of the French literary field among the younger generation. A 1976 study of the journal in the inaugural issue of *French Forum* described the review as standing for "the case of *Littérature*," a position that was emphasized by both Du Bouchet's and Dupin's relative silence on the events of May '68 and, in the aftermath of these events, the question of politics itself. As Dupin explained in an interview in the 1990s, espousing a position whose roots critics have traced to the 1960s, "I do not believe for all that that the writer must sign up for a party, for a group, and sign indiscriminately all the circulating letters of protest, manifestos and petitions."[66]

But if France offered Auster a literary field whose distance from his own US context relegitimized aesthetic autonomy for him, it offered little support for the personal autonomy with which he continued to identify it. One of the great themes—by some accounts, *the* great theme—of French thought in the aftermath of 1968 was the intertwined deaths of the subject and the author. As Luc Ferry and Alain Renault argue, the thread that holds together what they call the philosophy of '68 is the belief

---

[64] Auster, *Hand to Mouth*, 69.

[65] Andrew Goldstone, *Fictions of Autonomy: Modernism from Wilde to de Man* (Oxford: Oxford University Press, 2013), 112.

[66] "je ne crois pas pour autant qu'il faille que l'écrivain s'enrôle dans un parti, dans un groupe, et signe à la volée toutes les protestations qui circulent, manifestes, et pétitions"; quoted in Maryann De Julio, *Jacques Dupin* (Amsterdam: Rodopi, 2005), 30.

that "the autonomy of the subject is an illusion."[67] While the central claim of Ferry and Renault's study—that there is a direct line between the philosophy of '68, especially the death of the subject, and 1980s individualism—is hotly contested, their basic characterization of its dominant philosophical thrust is much more widely accepted. Julia Kristeva remembers *Tel quel*, the journal around which so much of this thought gravitated in the 1970s, as "the privileged link where the structuralist advance turned into an analysis of subjectivity," and for many, this analysis of subjectivity necessarily entailed the death of the subject.[68] In the closing pages of *The Order of Things*, Foucault famously proclaims "the death of man," by which he means the death of the autonomous subject, "the subject as foundation of Knowledge, of Freedom, of Language, of History."[69]

The death of the subject naturally casts the author—the autonomous subject conceived as foundation and origin of a text—into doubt. Barthes's famous proclamation of the "death of the author" and Foucault's of the "author function" therefore arise as the literary correlates of French theory's broader critique of the subject.[70] Where the New Critical intentional fallacy amplified the autonomy of the text, the poststructuralist death of the author has more ambiguous consequences for aesthetic autonomy. Barthes opens his essay by attributing the death of the author and the beginning of *écriture* to a version of aesthetic autonomy in which writing exists "no longer with a view to acting on reality but intransitively, that is to say, outside of any function."[71] This link between the death of the author and literary autonomy is quickly eroded, however, and within a few pages we find Barthes "[l]eaving aside literature itself (such distinctions becoming invalid)" to argue that it is not literature but language which "knows a 'subject,' not a 'person,'" and which makes this subject "empty outside of the very enunciation which defines it."[72] Although the death of the author begins as a specifically literary affair, a way of distinguishing literary from other uses of language, it ultimately entails the end of literature

[67] Luc Ferry and Alain Renaut, *French Philosophy of the Sixties: An Essay on Antihumanism*, trans. Mary H. S. Cattani (Amherst, MA: University of Massachusetts Press, 1990), xxiii.

[68] Julia Kristeva, "My Memory's Hyperbole," in *The Portable Kristeva*, ed. Kelly Oliver (New York: Columbia University Press, 1997), 10.

[69] Michel Foucault, *The Order of Things: An Archaeology of the Human Sciences* (London: Routledge, 2002), 373; Michel Foucault, "The Birth of a World," in *Foucault Live: Interviews 1961–84*, ed. Sylvère Lotringer, trans. John Johnston (New York: Semiotext(e), 1989), 67.

[70] Roland Barthes, *Image, Music, Text*, trans. Stephen Heath (London: Fontana, 1977), 142–8; Michel Foucault, "What Is an Author?," in *Aesthetics, Method, and Epistemology*, ed. James D. Faubion, trans. Josué V. Harari (New York: New Press, 1998), 205–22.

[71] Barthes, *Image, Music, Text*, 142.   [72] Ibid., 144–5.

as a specialized mode of language. Without the capacity to separate literary uses of language from language in general, aesthetic autonomy becomes unthinkable in the domain of literature. At the same time, Barthes erodes the New Critical defense of textual autonomy, imagining the text as dissolving into a "tissue of quotations drawn from the innumerable centres of culture."[73] Thus while poststructuralism, and Barthes himself, retain an ambivalent attachment to aesthetic autonomy, the logic of the death of the author tends to erase the autonomy of art in general and any given literary text in particular, by removing the borders of both.[74]

In this context, Auster's early theory of aesthetics identifies the structural crisis in aesthetic autonomy precipitated by the 1968 protests with the poststructuralist and New Critical critique of authorial autonomy, which posed an intellectual, but not a structural, challenge to his thought. Like other writers in this book, Auster records what he takes to be autonomy's crisis in the figure of hunger. The besieged aesthetic that he develops out of this trope has its fullest theoretical elaboration in his 1970 Masters thesis, "The Art of Hunger," on Hamsun, Kafka, Céline, and Beckett, and in a 1970 essay of the same title, which adapts the material on Hamsun. *The Art of Hunger* subsequently becomes the title of his collected essays, in which he works through the key aesthetic problems of his early writing career, pointing to the centrality of hunger, especially his theoretical elaboration of the art of hunger, to his early writing.

For Auster, hunger allows the prolongation of the author's survival in the face of the twin threats of the New Criticism and the emergent poststructuralism. Where Barthes had declared the death of the author in 1967, Auster in 1970 emphasizes that "hunger presupposes dying, but not death."[75] His art of hunger develops in the space where the author's death is imminent but deferred, the autonomous subject on the point of collapse but, in the defiant final words of his thesis, "Not Dead Yet."[76] The dying author foregrounds the writer as the site of aesthetic autonomy's crisis and of Auster's resistance to this crisis. It offers a prehistory for *Hand to Mouth*'s equation of aesthetic autonomy with the personal autonomy of the author, which, in its emphasis on authorial will and intention, departs from earlier writers in the art of hunger tradition. Where Beckett's B. sees van Velde as "the first to admit that to be an artist is to fail," a formulation that implies that failure is inherent in the

[73] Ibid., 146.

[74] For an account of theory's relationship to autonomy, see Suzanne Guerlac, *Literary Polemics: Bataille, Sartre, Valéry, Breton* (Stanford, CA: Stanford University Press, 1997), 2.

[75] Paul Auster, "The Art of Hunger" (Columbia University, May 1970), 6, Box 10, Folder 1, Paul Auster Archive, 1963–1995 Papers, Berg Collection, New York Public Library.

[76] Ibid., 48.

nature of art itself, Auster proposes instead that Hamsun "does not want to succeed. He wants to fail," recasting authorial failure as a willed, personal choice.[77] Auster's account of Hamsun's novel, in particular, repeatedly highlights the protagonist's active choice to starve: he is "wag-[ing] a hunger strike against himself" and "refusing to live the life he has been given."[78] The result for Auster is "an art that is indistinguishable from the life of the artist who makes it," in which "the radical subjectivity of the narrator effectively eliminates the basic concerns of the traditional novel."[79] Positing the author's "radical subjectivity" as the loci of the art of hunger, Auster suggests that, even in the shadow of the death of the author, aesthetic autonomy presupposes authorial autonomy.

Auster's starving author keeps alive the intricacy and depth of the author's interiority, making the introverted exploration of self into the site of aesthetic autonomy. Replacing "historical time" with "inner dur-ation," he presents hunger as precipitating an inward turn that makes the text coextensive with the author's interiority.[80] In this sense, Auster can be read as using hunger to negotiate between different commonplaces of modernism's reception, rejecting the New Critical touchstone of imper-sonality in favor of the novelistic exploration of inner subjectivity and consciousness. For Auster, however, this turn reflects not an interest in psychology or subjectivity per se, but, more specifically, a fascination with the author's interiority as the site and source of art. In this, Auster finds a way of reading modernism against both the New Critics, for whom the author was beside the point, and the poststructuralists, whose theories of the "scriptor" and the "author function" reject authorial interiority in favor of an understanding of the author as an effect of discourse or the depthless point at which discourses intersect.

The interiorized author produced by the experience of starvation is, in Auster's reading, at once autonomous and authentic. His "radical subject-ivity" echoes the "radical individualism" that Marshall Berman sees as the source of authenticity, and, like Lionel Tilling's artist, he "seeks his personal authenticity in his entire autonomousness."[81] Like these contem-poraries, Auster imagines the author's authenticity as residing in his capacity to hold himself apart from society—as Trilling writes, "what destroys our authenticity is society."[82] The risk of this position is that,

---

[77] Samuel Beckett, *Disjecta: Miscellaneous Writings and a Dramatic Fragment*, ed. Ruby Cohn (New York: Grove Press, 1984), 145; Paul Auster, *The Art of Hunger: Essay, Prefaces, Interviews and The Red Notebook, Expanded Edition* (New York: Penguin, 1997), 18.

[78] Auster, *Art of Hunger*, 12, 13.   [79] Ibid., 18, 10.

[80] Auster, "Art of Hunger [1970]," 19.

[81] Trilling, *Sincerity and Authenticity*, 99–100.

[82] Berman, *The Politics of Authenticity*; Trilling, *Sincerity and Authenticity*, 93.

in their refusal of the social, these artists might come to embody not authenticity but, instead, its opposite: alienation.[83] For a theorist like Berman, the "radical individualism" of authenticity is distinguished from alienation by its promise of "a dream of an ideal community in which individuality will not be subsumed and sacrificed, but fully developed and expressed."[84] Auster's "radical subjectivity," in contrast, relies for its autonomy on the fact that it is staunchly anti-communal and anti-communitarian—even anti-social. As he argues of Hamsun's narrator, the dying author becomes "introverted to a degree that precludes the possibility of human contact."[85] The hunger of the dying author therefore preserves the writer's interiorized subjectivity at the center of the creative act, but in the process it turns this gesture of authenticity into alienation: "the suicide that is the search for the Self."[86]

The question of alienation's relationship to authenticity is what, for Auster, distinguishes hunger from nausea—those two great metaphors of non-consumption and social isolation. Throughout his thesis, he develops this theme through a sustained comparison between Hamsun's narrator and Roquentin, the protagonist of Sartre's *Nausea*. The disanalogy is sufficiently belabored that one reader of his thesis, presumably his thesis adviser Edward Said, wonders with some exasperation in the margins, "Why do you always refer to Roquentin?"[87] But Roquentin—the hero of existentialist alienation and its overcoming in the discovery of personal authenticity—is an important counterpoint to Auster's reading of Hamsun's narrator. As Auster argues, "Whereas Roquentin wants nothing more than to be cured of his nausea, to escape from the ambiguities that fetter him, Hamsun's hero embraces his own confusion and systematizes it to a degree that almost transforms it into an art."[88] Sartre—like the student activists described by Rossinow—imagines alienation and authenticity to exist in an essentially narrative relation, where alienation, becoming intolerable, prompts the subject to search for and eventually attain authenticity. But, Auster suggests, Hamsun and his fellow hunger artists accomplish quite a different feat, turning inward to find authenticity within their alienation, in a move that, he implies, can be productive of art itself.

As Auster's reference to Roquentin's fetters implies, the equation of authenticity with alienation forecloses on the possibility of freedom. For both the existentialists and the 1960s student radicals, the narrative movement from alienation to authenticity is the process by which the freedom of authenticity emerges from the unfreedom of alienation. By

[83] Rossinow, *The Politics of Authenticity*, 4.
[84] Berman, *The Politics of Authenticity*, ix.   [85] Auster, "Art of Hunger [1970]," 2.
[86] Ibid., 40.   [87] Ibid., 11.   [88] Ibid., 8.

equating these states, Auster closes off the path by which freedom might be realized. Instead, his reading of the art of hunger tradition dispenses with the "assumption that art is an essentially free enterprise" in favor of an art—the art of hunger—that "emerges from the viscera as a necessary act."[89] The hunger artist's autonomy, in Auster's reading, keeps him imprisoned within his own interiority, subject to a visceral necessity and an "inner compulsion."[90] If this sense of necessity remains "a matter of choice" for Auster's hunger artists, it does so in order to dramatize the impossibility of their situation, caught between a commitment to autonomous subjectivity and the extinction of that position.[91] Auster's paradoxically chosen necessity, his willed unfreedom, reflects his theory of art's impossible attempt to unite opposites, producing an art that is simultaneously alienated and authentic, embracing the personal autonomy of the author in the moment of his death and the aesthetic autonomy of the work in an era of relevant art. Auster's theory of the starving author as a *dying* author is his solution to this impossibility: a theory of art that imagines aesthetic autonomy as the author's imprisonment within his own interiority, figured through an account of hunger that sees it as radically isolating and interiorizing.

4. POETRY AND UTOPIA

"The Art of Hunger" is unusual among Auster's essays from this period in its focus on fiction rather than poetry. Nonetheless, to the extent that it describes what Barthes, in *Writing Degree Zero*, calls "the inhuman experience of the poet, who accepts the most momentous of all breaks, that from the language of society," Auster's thesis might be understood as laying out an essentially poetic theory of literature.[92] Where for Beckett the art of hunger approached painting, for Auster it finds its home in poetry. His decade-long body of poetic work—which spans the 1970s but remains relatively neglected by critics—stands at the center of his attempt to develop an art of hunger, reflecting poetry's importance for debates about aesthetic autonomy at this time. While for both Barthes and the New Critics, modernist poetry was the privileged site of aesthetic autonomy, for the student radicals, poetry was in the streets, the genre reimagined as the site of socially relevant, engaged art. Poetry therefore became the primary site of the scuffle over the viability of aesthetic autonomy

---

[89] Ibid., 12–13.   [90] Ibid., 2.   [91] Ibid., 3.

[92] Roland Barthes, *Writing Degree Zero*, trans. Annette Lavers and Colin Smith (Boston: Beacon Press, 1970), 40.

during Auster's formative years; in the late 1960s, settling the question of poetry's autonomy meant settling the question of literary autonomy per se.

Auster's own poetry—tight, spare, and abstract, in the cast of the American Objectivists and the French school of André Du Bouchet and Jacques Dupin—stakes its position with those for whom poetry epitomizes an autonomous and asocial literature. It carries forward the doubling of personal and aesthetic autonomy in a body of writing that is rife with images of hunger and its cognates. Auster's use of hunger in the poetry follows the logic of the starving artist that he develops in his thesis, imagining the poet or the speaker to be caught in the suspended state of a dying that defers death. In the poetry, however, this role for hunger is bound up with a theory of language's fallen state. In "Notes from a Composition Book," written in 1967 and collected with his poetry, he describes the "fall of man" as "a question of language conquering experience: the fall of the world into the word, experience descending from the eye to the mouth."[93] The mouth's dual function as the site of speaking and of eating structures Auster's argument. The descent from eye to mouth is a way of describing an alienated language, one that no longer perfectly expresses the world it seeks to describe, but it also ties this fallenness to the act of eating, alluding to the Biblical story that locates the Fall in Eve's eating of the fruit. The art of hunger, then, becomes an art that takes place in the hiatus before the fruit is eaten, in the suspended state in which eating is deferred and language remains temporarily and impossibly whole.

This understanding of the art of hunger as an imperfect attempt to preserve or re-create a perfect language runs throughout Auster's poetry. In an untitled poem from the 1970–2 collection *Unearth*, for instance, Auster writes:

> Night, as though tasted
> within. And of us, each lie
> the tongue would know
> when it draws back and sinks
> into its poison.
> We would sleep, side by side
> with such hunger, and from the fruit
> we war with, become the name
> of what we name.[94]

These lines work through the different faces of a fallen language: from night, the time of unseeing, in which the prospect of speaking a perfect language that comes "from the eye" is foreclosed; to the lie, which "The

---

[93] Auster, *Poems*, 204.   [94] Ibid., 41.

Art of Hunger" reads as the final, wilful rupture of word and world, in which language's imperfection is harnessed in a violent repudiation of society and ethics; to the fruit, symbol and source of the biblical Fall and thus, in Auster's mythology, the origin of language's imperfection. Each phase of this fallen language is linked to eating—to taste, to the tongue, and finally to the implied consumption of "the fruit | we war with"—but the moment of eating is always held in suspense, deferred to the ambivalence of the simile ("as though") and the conditional tense. By suspending eating, Auster prolongs the moment of hunger, allowing it to emerge as an almost physical presence, that which we sleep "side by side | with." But the deferral of eating also collapses the distinction between eating and speaking, so that taste becomes metaphor, and the tongue, in a gentle pun on *sapere*, the Latin for both knowing and tasting, "knows" the lie—that is, "knows" language. Hunger becomes the prolonged moment, then, before the Fall of the authentic language of the prelapsarian world into the inauthenticity of a world where everything is named falsely. By suspending the act of eating, this poem seeks to hold off the moment of the Fall, holding the poem in the moment of hunger, when word and thing are still coextensive. Its suspension of eating is reimagined as the dream of holding open a precarious moment of full linguistic autonomy, in which the utopia of language might emerge.

As the plural first person of this poem suggests, the uni-vocality of the Adamic poet holds the germ of a new sociality. Whereas both *Hand to Mouth* and "The Art of Hunger" are militant in imagining the author as a singular, isolated figure, Auster's early poetry makes frequent use of the collective voice and the intimacy of the second person, both of which imply forms of relation that are largely absent from his other theorizations of the art of hunger. On the one hand, this "we" is a mark of the utopian orientation of the poetic work, signaling the poet's desire to speak on behalf of many. In this sense, it returns the art of hunger to the orbit of student activism, with its hopes for a transformative poetics and its imagination of hunger as a symbol of solidarity. It connects with other early works that imagine Auster's poetry as participating in a poetic uprising, such as the first poem of *Unearth*:

> Your ink has learned
>   the violence of the wall. Banished,
> but always to the heart
> of brothering quiet . . .
>   . . . Each syllable
> is the work of sabotage.[95]

[95] Ibid., 37.

Here, the banishment of exile is imagined as maintaining a kind of solidarity, a "brothering quiet," and the act of writing is described in the language of subversive violence. In this context, the "violence of the wall" evokes the graffiti—poetry on the walls—of the May '68 Paris uprisings. It implies that "wall writing," the title of one of Auster's collections, might be read as suggesting its affiliation to this tradition of activist literature.

But the plural first person (as well as the second person that also runs through this poetry) also suggests a pluralization of the self that marks the perpetual frustration of the poet's desire for "uni-vocal expression." Instead, the poet experiences the traumatic process of writing described by Maurice Blanchot in *The Space of Literature*, in which the writer "does not discover the admirable language which speaks honorably for all. What speaks in him is the fact that, in one way or another, he is no longer himself; he isn't anyone any more."[96] This sense that writing, far from attaining the universal, instead represents a crisis for the self, a form of self-alienation that entails the collapse of the unitary subject, is widespread in the poetry. In "Scribe," "he talked himself | into another body." "Viaticum" speaks of "your voice, | your other voice," and poem 13 of *Unearth* of the "Other of I."[97] The "we" in this context—as well as the "you" that often seems addressed back to the poet or speaker himself—represents a desperate attempt to hold the multiplying subject together, a plural Adam that approaches not the voice of the people but instead the dying (but not yet dead) author, fracturing on his way out. As Blanchot goes on to argue, "he who sings must jeopardize himself entirely and, in the end, perish, for he speaks only when the anticipated approach toward death, the premature separation, the adieu given in advance obliterate in him the false certitude of being."[98] Ultimately, the utopian voice that would make Auster's poetry a truly new language, one that could provide the foundation for a new collectivity, is indistinguishable from the fracturing first person that cannot even speak on his own behalf. The promise of an authentic language that would unify word and world is attainable only through the collapse of the author into a state of permanent self-alienation. The slipperiness of the voice in these poems gestures towards the self-annulling paradoxes inherent in Auster's formulation of the art of hunger—the need to create an asocial language so as to open the way for a new sociality; the attempt to harness alienation towards the end of authenticity—paradoxes that reflect Auster's attempt

---

[96] Maurice Blanchot, *The Space of Literature*, trans. Ann Smock (Lincoln, NE: University of Nebraska Press, 1982), 28.

[97] Auster, *Poems*, 69, 76, 49.   [98] Blanchot, *The Space of Literature*, 156.

to create an autonomous language and an autonomous subject in an intellectual environment that disavows both.

This complex, multiple interiority is an art of hunger in the sense that it is an art of the dying author. It achieves its completion and its annulment in the figure of the stone, one of the central images of Auster's poetry and a metaphor for both death and the absoluteness of the Edenic language. In the art of hunger tradition, the eating of stones has a long history as a kind of anti-eating that keeps hunger alive, as in Rimbaud's declaration that "If I have any *taste*, it is for hardly | Anything but earth and stones" ("Si j'ai du *goût*, ce n'est guères | que pour la terre et les pierres") or the sucking stones in Beckett's *Molloy*. In Auster, however, the stone is a figure not for the prolongation of hunger but for its annulment. The stone is what does not consume and what cannot experience hunger. Whereas Auster's starving writers are always in the deferred process of dying, his stones are metaphors for death, for the end of the multiplying and collapsing interiority of hunger. This is why Auster's critics have tended to gloss the stone in terms that evoke the self-reflexive opacity of his art of hunger, describing it as "the irreducible element which refers to nothing but itself" and a trope that "stand[s] variously for material fragments, the impermeability of language and resistance to interpretation."[99]

Like the art of hunger, Auster's stones are identified with the possibility of an Edenic language in which words and things conform fully to one another. As he writes in an early poem, the poetry seeks to make the transition from "one stone touched | to the next stone | named," performing the Adamic leap by which word and thing are brought together, which is also the leap by which the poem assumes the stone's perfected autonomy.[100] But whereas the art of hunger's attempt to undo the Fall of language is provisional, temporary, and imperfect, the stone's materiality represents a state of perfected, absolute meaning. In this, Auster's use of the trope differs from the more common late twentieth-century figure of what Walter Benn Michaels calls the "meaningless stone," where the stone becomes a figure for the text's polysemy, its endless availability for interpretation.[101] While Michaels and Auster both probe the implications of imagining a text as a stone, and a stone as a text, the significance of this material language ends in quite different formulations: for Michaels, the stone represents materiality without meaning; for Auster, it represents the

---

[99] Änne Troester, "'Beyond This Point, Everything Turns to Prose': Paul Auster's Writing between Poetry and Prose," *Amerikastudien/American Studies* 47, no. 4 (2002): 529; James Peacock, "Unearthing Paul Auster's Poetry," *Orbis Litterarum* 64, no. 5 (2009): 416.

[100] Auster, *Poems*, 40.

[101] Walter Benn Michaels, *The Shape of the Signifier: 1967 to the End of History* (Princeton: Princeton University Press, 2004), 110.

infusion of materiality with absolute meaning. When he imagines that "our voice | is in league | with the stones of the field," Auster imagines a state in which the poet's voice acquires the materiality of the stone, but also a state in which the stone acquires the meaningfulness of language.[102] The autonomy, in other words, that Auster imagines in the stone is not one that destroys language or leaves it open to endless interpretation, but one that sees language perfected, meaning fixed in the perfect identity between word and thing.

For both Auster and Michaels, what is ultimately at stake in the figure of the stone is an anxiety about the speaker's relationship to the text—a concern, ultimately, about intentionality. Michaels borrows the image of the stone from Paul de Man, who distinguishes between "intentional objects," exemplified by the chair, which are organized around the use for which they are intended (for chairs: to be sat on), and "natural objects," exemplified by the stone, whose "'meaning' . . . could only refer to a totality of sensory appearances."[103] The stone, in this account, is the paradigmatically intention-less object. Its meaningless materiality and its openness to interpretation are both functions of the fact that it is an object without an author, one whose meaning is not determined at the point of production, but rather at the point of reception. Auster's stone, as we have seen, offers a third model of interpretation, locating the stone's meaning within the stone itself. On the one hand, this departs from the reading of both Michaels and de Man in that, insofar as the stone is a figure for perfect and immanent meaning, it is not open to endless interpretation and the reader, therefore, has no more purchase on the stone than on the intentional object. But Auster also agrees with Michaels and de Man that the stone is a figure for the author-less text. Because the stone, in Auster's ideal language, contains its own perfectly self-sufficient meaning, it has no need of an author. In this Edenic "language of stones" there is only one conceivable word for each thing and therefore no choice to be made, no space for the governing consciousness of the speaker or writer.[104]

In this sense, the language of stones is the endpoint for poetry and for the art of hunger, insofar as Auster imagines both as vehicles of autonomous subjectivity. It is the point at which Auster's poetry perfects itself out of existence: the death of the author. If the dream of a prelapsarian language implies a poet-Adam who alone can speak it, the image of the stone suggests that the realization of this perfect language requires that the

[102] Auster, *Poems*, 40.

[103] Paul de Man, *Blindness and Insight: Essays in the Rhetoric of Contemporary Criticism*, 2nd edn (New York: Oxford University Press, 1971), 23–4.

[104] Auster, *Poems*, 107.

speaker be already dead—beyond the prolongation of the dying author's hunger. In "Viaticum," for instance, he describes:

> the second
> and brighter terror
> of living in your death, and speaking
> the stone
> you will become.[105]

In a poem whose title evokes eating preparatory to death—a viaticum is the Roman Catholic term for the administration of the Eucharist as part of last rites—the stone is a placeholder for the still impenetrability of impending mortality, as it moves within the liminal time of "living in your death," the time of the art of hunger, in which the author is not dead yet. The act of "speaking | the stone | you will become"—both speaking death, and speaking the Edenic language that entails the author's death—suggests that the approach to this perfect materiality of language is simultaneously an approach towards death. Neither speech nor the speaker can survive the achievement of this literary goal, the perfection of the language of the stone. Poetry itself, therefore, exists in the attempt to manifest the stone at a remove, in the approach towards but not the achievement of the Edenic language, and in the suspended time of the art of hunger. Poetry, like the art of hunger, is the not-quite of the author's death and the not-quite of the text's self-cancelling autonomy. Auster's stone, in this sense, is simultaneously a figure for a perfectly inhuman—unconsuming and unconsumable—language, devoid of author or reader, as well as an image for an absolutely authentic language, perfectly true to the nature of the thing being expressed. It is the end point of the art of hunger, replacing the prolongation of dying with the finality of death and the intricate interiority of hunger with the blank impenetrability of stone.

5. A GENEALOGY OF SOLIPSISTS: INHERITING MODERNISM IN THE NOVELS

Auster's Eden is a utopian project, one that looks back to a lost paradise in order to orient itself towards an unachievable language-to-come. In this, it distinguishes itself both from more purely nostalgic Edens, shaped out of the lament for a lost Golden Age, as well as those more optimistic, typically American versions, for which the trope implies a

---

[105] Ibid., 76.

realizable—perhaps already realized—paradise.[106] In fact, this recursive temporality, the hope for novelty through recuperation, structures Auster's early writing. It underpins, in particular, his relationship to literary history, with his implicit claim for a modernist lineage in "The Art of Hunger" and other early essays, and the subsequent attempt, through tropes such as the stone and Eden, to reanimate this modernist tradition and work through its implications and legacies in the poetry.[107]

This recuperative relationship to modernism appears in Auster's early writing as a problem of filiation. In an unpublished interview with James Knowlson, Beckett's biographer, Auster evokes Harold Bloom's "anxiety of influence" to explain his relationship with Beckett, writing that "in a way you have to kill off your father in order to do your own work."[108] Auster's representations of fathers and fatherhood, however, suggest that questions of inheritance and descent are complicated matters in his work. In a late poem, written on the occasion of his own father's death, Auster describes his father as "Stone wall. Stone heart," implying a continuity between paternity and the stone of the poetry.[109] But the stone, as a figure for that which is self-contained and devoid of a reader, is an intrinsically anti-social and therefore anti-genealogical figure. As Auster writes of his father in his memoir *The Invention of Solitude*, he was, "A man without appetites. You felt that nothing could ever intrude on him, that he had no need of anything the world had to offer."[110] His father's self-sufficiency is related to the solipsism of the modernist writers in Auster's Masters thesis as the stone is related to the art of hunger: the former standing as the perfection and the end of the latter's impossible quest for autonomy. As the memoir makes clear, however, the autonomous father is a bad father, a figure whose opacity and self-containment risks making filiation and inheritance impossible. Against this backdrop, the Bloomian anxiety of influence morphs into a new form of anxiety specific to the modernist inheritance. If the art of hunger is solipsistic and solitary, if autonomy is

---

[106] Compare Auster's utopian Eden with Stevenson's account of the nostalgic Edens of British modernism: Randall Stevenson, "Not What It Used to Be: Nostalgia and the Legacies of Modernism," in *The Legacies of Modernism: Historicising Postwar and Contemporary Fiction*, ed. David James (Cambridge: Cambridge University Press, 2012), 23–39; for an account of the American uses of Eden, see J. Lee Greene, *Blacks in Eden: The African-American Novel's First Century* (Charlottesville, VA: University of Virginia Press, 1996).

[107] On modernism's Edenic preoccupations, see, in addition to Stevenson, Sean Pryor, *W. B. Yeats, Ezra Pound and the Poetry of Paradise* (Farnham: Ashgate, 2011).

[108] Paul Auster, "Extract of Interview, Enclosed with Letter from James Knowlson to Paul Auster," September 1, 2004, Box 88, Folder 2, Paul Auster Archive, 1999–2005 Papers, Berg Collection, New York Public Library.

[109] Auster, *Poems*, 102.

[110] Paul Auster, *The Invention of Solitude* (London: Faber and Faber, 1982), 17.

conceived as intrinsically anti-social, then Auster's attempt to position himself as the son to modernism's father engenders not just the anxiety that Auster might end up too close to these literary patriarchs, but also the fear that by organizing them into a genealogy he will undo the tortured isolation that he seeks to replicate. This is a variant of the familiar problem of modernist inheritance, the fact that, as Derek Attridge puts it, "nothing could be less modernist than a repetition of previous modes."[111] But for Auster, the problem is not so much that modernist novelty, once repeated, is no longer new, but instead that his formulation of modernist autonomy brooks no society, while literary genealogy is by definition a way of conceptualizing relation.

This problem of establishing a literary genealogy pervades Auster's early oeuvre. We find traces of it in "The Art of Hunger," where Auster links the modernist hunger artists according to a logic of analogy and resemblance, producing a configuration that evades issues of genealogy and influence in favor of something more like Deleuze's "community of celibates."[112] It is also present in the suspended Eden of the poetry, which avows the impossibility of inheriting the lost, dreamed-of paradise. But Auster's early novels, where an explicit concern with failed paternity intersects with a sustained interrogation of Auster's modernist forebears, show the most sustained and complex theorization of the difficulties of positioning oneself as heir to the art of hunger. Reflecting back on the theories of literature developed through his early essays and poetry, novels such as *The New York Trilogy* (especially *City of Glass*, the first novel of the trilogy) and *Moon Palace* inscribe the equation of failing literary autonomy and failing authorial autonomy, which I traced in Sections 2–4, onto this problem of modernist inheritance.

Studded with failed fathers and interrupted genealogies, these novels are centrally concerned with the problem of paternity. *City of Glass* features a reclusive protagonist, Quinn, who "had once been a father," until the death of his wife and son. Quinn finds himself caught up in the disastrous father–son relationship of two men, both named Peter Stillman, the elder of whom is recently released from prison, where he had been held for keeping his young son in complete isolation in a bid to discover "God's language."[113] Quinn's task—to protect the younger Stillman from his

---

[111] Derek Attridge, *J. M. Coetzee and the Ethics of Reading: Literature in the Event* (Chicago: University of Chicago Press, 2004), 5.

[112] Gilles Deleuze, *Essays Critical and Clinical*, trans. Daniel W. Smith and Michael A. Greco (London: Verso, 1998), 84.

[113] Paul Auster, *The New York Trilogy* (London: Faber and Faber, 1987), 1, 20.

father—speaks to the complete breakdown of this abusive father–son relationship. *Moon Palace* features a different kind of genealogical anxiety, with a melodramatic story of an apparent orphan, Marco Stanley Fogg, who through a series of coincidences comes to find both his father, who had been unaware of Marco's existence, and his grandfather, who had abandoned his own son at a young age. Similarly, in *The Locked Room*, the last book of the *Trilogy*, the narrator acts as an adoptive father to the protagonist, Fanshawe's, abandoned son, while Fanshawe himself has a father who is described as a "cipher" and who dies when his son is in his late teens.[114] These narratives collectively imagine paternity as unstable and impermanent, presenting filiation and fatherhood not as givens but as tasks to be achieved and endlessly renewed.

Once uncoupled from these father–son relationships, however, Auster's abandoned sons and bereaved fathers become taciturn, solipsistic recluses. In the aftermath of his family's death, Quinn retreats from social interaction, embarking on what he describes as a "posthumous life."[115] Fanshawe, concluding that "I wasn't meant to live like other people," abandons his family and dies a recluse in Boston, where "no one knows who I am. I never go out."[116] Marco in *Moon Palace*, after the death of his uncle, enters a downward spiral marked by "a militant refusal to take any action at all" until he can see his life becoming "a gathering zero."[117] Each of these retreats resembles the isolation that Auster has long associated with writers in general, and the art of hunger in particular, but—as Quinn's "posthumous life" suggests—each goes beyond it, entering the perfected state of the stone or the death of the author. In this state, Quinn, formerly a poet, becomes a pseudonymous detective writer, who "did not consider himself to be the author of what he wrote," while Fanshawe disavows his large body of writing.[118] Marco, never a writer, instead marks his downward spiral by divesting himself of the books he inherited from his uncle. At the extremity of family breakdown, where genealogy disappears or is renounced entirely, Auster's protagonists become so isolated that they stage a different kind of authorial death, a social death. Just as the perfected Edenic language ends in the author's obsolescence, the severing of all genealogical ties entails such a renunciation of society that authorship is no longer possible. The end of genealogy, in other words, repeats on the plane of authorial biography the same dilemma that the stone represents in the domain of poetic language, recasting the author's isolation,

---

114 Ibid., 218.   115 Ibid., 5.   116 Ibid., 312, 310.
117 Paul Auster, *Moon Palace* (London: Faber and Faber, 1989), 20, 24.
118 Auster, *Trilogy*, 4.

like the poet's language, as fundamentally unperfectable and therefore in some sense unachievable.

The anxiety about genealogy has a specific valence for a writer who came of age in the late 1960s. Kristin Ross has written that the "official story" of the 1960s and their mass revolts "is one of family or generational drama," an interpretation that she rejects but that has nonetheless been tremendously influential in shaping contemporary and later understandings of the period.[119] Herbert Marcuse, one of the defining thinkers of the 1960s student revolts in both France and the US, hailed the prospect of breaking "the chain which linked the fathers and the sons from generation to generation."[120] Quentin Anderson, one of Columbia's senior professors during the protests, agrees with Marcuse's evaluation, despite their vastly different politics, observing among both his students and American writers of the nineteenth century "an alternate mode of self-validation that openly proclaims its independence of the fostering and authenticating offices of the family and society."[121] Indeed, one way of understanding the contested fate of modernism and modernist autonomy in this period is as a generational conflict: modernism, particularly in its institutionalized form, has become the literature of the fathers, both literally in that modernists belong to these students' fathers' or grandfathers' generation, and symbolically, in that its writing and its reading practices are now being taught by the institutions, acting *in loco parentis*, against which the students are rebelling. In this context, Auster's early interest in modernists who sit on the margins of modernism's genealogical narratives can be understood as an attempt to establish a genealogy of the anti-genealogical, mimicking Anderson's project in *The Imperial Self* (1971).

In the novels, where Auster frames these questions in more explicitly familial terms, modernist intertexts make their appearances precisely where genealogy is collapsing but not eclipsed. Most prominent here is Marco's early flirtation with solipsism in *Moon Palace*, a project that he describes as "nihilism raised to the level of an aesthetic proposition," echoing the claims in "The Art of Hunger" that see Hamsun's protagonist as "the living embodiment of nihilism itself" and Céline as "the first novelist to fully accept nihilism as the inheritance of the twentieth century."[122] Indeed, several critics have pointed out that the plot and intensely focalized characterization of the opening section of *Moon Palace*

[119] Ross, *May '68 and its Afterlives*, 5.
[120] Herbert Marcuse, *An Essay on Liberation* (Boston: Beacon Press, 1969), 24–5.
[121] Anderson, *The Imperial Self*, vii–viii.
[122] Auster, *Moon Palace*, 20; Auster, "Art of Hunger [1970]," 19, 21.

echo the catastrophic starvation of Hamsun's *Hunger*.[123] While the immediate context here is the severing of familial ties, however, the broader narrative focuses on recuperating the Hamsunian Marco into an intergenerational saga. It therefore emphasizes the long, if sometimes hidden, roots of modernist solipsism, even as, in resocializing Marco, it irrevocably removes him from the Hamsunian narrative. This novel, the last of Auster's career to engage substantially with the thematics of hunger, is in some ways his farewell to the towering role the art of hunger played in his earliest writing, but it bids this adieu, not by repudiating the logic of modernist autonomy but simply by pulling back to recontextualize it within a larger genealogical arc.

Where *Moon Palace* rewrites Hamsun as the prelude to a family reunion, *City of Glass* inscribes modernist texts within a genealogical project in order to produce a surprisingly coherent literary history. At the head of this lineage stands Peter Stillman the father, who, before his incarceration, presents as an American Milton: his thesis develops an absolutist version of the Edenic language theory, through a fabricated historical figure, Henry Dark, a supposed disciple of Milton who emigrated to the New World. Stillman's fire-and-brimstone religiosity, which fuels his quest for a perfect language and his delusional faith that it is within reach, has its roots in Auster's own thesis, where Milton functions as Auster's embodiment of the belief, impossible for modern writers, that "with the Second Coming...language will be restored to its prelapsarian unity."[124] Stillman never loses his faith in this ideal language, but on his release from prison he abandons the providential faith in the son who will be born speaking a new language, preferring instead "to confine myself to physical things, to the immediate and the tangible."[125] Setting himself the task of creating a new language through a careful process of observation, Stillman comes to identify with the more limited, secular aspirations of poetry after the loss of religion—the aspirations, in short, of modernist and, for Auster, specifically Objectivist poetry, as worked out in his essays on Reznikoff, George Oppen, and Carl Rakosi. In fact, the late Stillman strongly resembles a Christianized Reznikoff, with both sharing a penchant for meandering walks through New York City as the foundation of their linguistic and literary activity.[126] Stillman the father, in other words, embodies a literary historical transition from early modern to modernist

---

[123] Christopher Donovan, *Postmodern Counternarratives: Irony and Audience in the Novels of Paul Auster, Don DeLillo, Charles Johnson, and Tim O'Brien* (New York: Routledge, 2005), 74; Ilana Shiloh, *Paul Auster and the Postmodern Quest: On the Road to Nowhere* (New York: Peter Lang, 2002), 97.

[124] Auster, "Art of Hunger [1970]," 33.   [125] Auster, *Trilogy*, 76.

[126] Auster, *Art of Hunger*, 40.

poetry, all the time working towards the impossible task of realizing a perfect language. He stages Auster's theory of poetry as a utopian gesture, and suggests that the Objectivist strand of modernism is a secularization of a tradition of religious poetry with roots in Milton.

The younger Stillman, as both the elder's son and the product of his single-minded quest for God's language, tests the genealogical implications of this poetic tradition. The results are disturbing, suggesting that the quest for the Edenic language issues in both great damage to the subject and the end of genealogy itself (the young Stillman declares himself "the last of the Stillmans . . . the end of everyone, the last man").[127] The son, therefore, is a living critique of the disastrous side effects of poetry's totalizing aspirations, in a text that marks Auster's final and definitive turn to novels and away from poetry. But he also embodies a development internal to poetry itself—he describes himself as "mostly now a poet"—that issues in something disturbingly like the modernism of the art of hunger.[128] Like the writers of the art of hunger who have obliterated "historical time . . . in favor of inner duration," the younger Stillman "know[s] nothing of time. I am new every day."[129] And like Hamsun's narrator, whose invention of new words such as "Kuboaa" Auster discusses at length in "The Art of Hunger," the young Stillman writes poems in which "I make up all the words myself . . . I am the only one who knows what the words mean."[130] More generally, the young Stillman's halting speech, which revels in the sound of words, in their materiality ("Peter could not think. Did he blink? Did he drink? Did he stink? Ha ha ha"), and which delights in formal inventiveness, suggests a rather juvenile parody of the self-corrective, aggressively formal language of modernist experimentation, particularly late Beckett. *City of Glass*, therefore, traces the issue of the poetic quest for a utopian language to two related strands of modernism: the Objectivists, who secularize this tradition but retain its utopian orientation; and the art of hunger, which lives in the shadow of this utopianism's failure. It presents both as not just literary, but also ethical dead ends, flawed in both their comical unreadability, and their broken and disturbing renunciation of society in all its forms—flawed, in other words, in the way they insist on the autonomous writer as the vehicle for an ideal language.

The closest *City of Glass* comes to depicting a path out of the modernist impasse lies with Quinn, who is hired, in effect, to run interference between the Reznikoffian father and the Beckettian son. With a background as

---

[127] Auster, *Trilogy*, 19.   [128] Ibid., 19.
[129] Auster, "Art of Hunger [1970]," 19; Auster, *Trilogy*, 18.
[130] Auster, *Trilogy*, 19.

both a poet and a pseudonymous detective writer, Quinn's mixed literary heritage lacks the purity of the Stillmans', a position that grants him a liberating distance from their destructive literary and linguistic ideals. Indeed, the writing that Quinn produces which features most centrally in *City of Glass* is neither a literary text nor an attempt at a new language, but simply his notebook, a record of his involvement with the case, which the narrator uses as the basis for reconstructing the narrative. This document, which has parallels in Blue's reports in *Ghosts* (the second novel of *The New York Trilogy*) and the narrator's biography of Fanshawe in *The Locked Room*, signals a shift to new, more observational, more quotidian—one might even say more prosaic—modes of writing.

But while this new mode represents a shift away from the poetry and its quest for a perfect language, it does not imply a wholesale rejection of modernism. Instead, Quinn might better be understood as a figure who brings together the Objectivists' observational aesthetics with the art of hunger. On the one hand, Quinn, like the older Peter Stillman, closely resembles Auster's portrayals of Reznikoff. Like both the Jewish poet and the deluded villain, Quinn loves long walks in New York for their capacity to make him "feel that he was nowhere"—an echo of Auster's claim that Reznikoff's identity as a Jewish-American grants him "the condition of being nowhere."[131] On the other hand, however, the intense, anti-social isolation with which Quinn opens the novel recalls not Reznikoff and the Objectivists—who always have ethnic and national affiliations to ground them, in Auster's reading—but the solipsists of the art of hunger. These two strands come together most clearly in the novel's climax, in which Quinn embarks on an obsessive stake-out of the older Peter Stillman, disintegrating physically and mentally in the process. Like the modernists of "The Art of Hunger," Quinn's stake-out moves him asymptotically towards complete starvation, always deferring its fatal end but keeping "the total fast in his mind as an ideal, a state of perfection he could aspire to but never achieve."[132] Quinn's art of hunger, however, only serves to bring him more firmly into the orbit of Auster's Objectivists, combining the art of hunger's experience of "the true nature of solitude" with such intense and devoted observation that "It was as though he had melted into the walls of the city," following what Auster elsewhere describes as "[t]he Reznikoff equation, which weds seeing to invisibility."[133] This combination of solitude, observation, and invisibility similarly characterizes Blue and *The Locked Room*'s narrator in the subsequent two books of *The New*

---

[131] Ibid., 4; Auster, *Art of Hunger*, 44.   [132] Auster, *Trilogy*, 114.
[133] Ibid., 117, 116; Auster, *Art of Hunger*, 38.

York Trilogy, placing this quasi-modernist hybrid at the center of Auster's shift to the novel.

What becomes of autonomy in this transition to the novel? The image of the author as an almost tragically autonomous subject, fracturing under the weight of his alienation from society, persists throughout these texts and, in fact, beyond: we see traces of it in later novels, from *Leviathan* (1992) to *Travels in the Scriptorium* (2007) and *The Book of Illusions* (2002). But as Quinn's equation of solitude with observation suggests, the point of this authorial autonomy is increasingly to afford a new vantage point on the world. The fully self-referential, self-contained text that represented the stone-like ideal is increasingly not a goal but a dead end or a false start. Each of the volumes of *The New York Trilogy* turns around a central text that is said to explain everything: Quinn's notebook in *City of Glass*; the manuscript that Blue has watched Black writing in *Ghosts*; and Fanshawe's red notebook in *The Locked Room*, which he leaves for the narrator. Each of these texts, however, remains out of sight of the reader, read only by a single character who, in each case, is himself a loner who has shadowed the text's author through the novel and who ultimately expresses his bafflement before this supposedly explanatory text. As *The Locked Room*'s narrator writes of Fanshawe's red notebook, "Each sentence erased the sentence before it, each paragraph made the next paragraph impossible."[134] These absent centers of the three novels are fundamentally unreadable as texts, standing as late examples of Auster's readerless aesthetics of autonomy. But if the poetry aspired to this condition, to a perfect but unreadable, self-cancelling language, the novels that compose *The New York Trilogy* are neither identical with these texts nor aspire to replicate them. Aesthetic autonomy, at least as Auster had once imagined it, persists into the novels not as the goal or endpoint of literature but as a textual black hole, a series of unreadable texts written in unspeakable, self-consuming languages.

Both the literary history of modernism and the dead-end of aesthetic autonomy appear in these novels not simply as a reflection on philosophical and literary questions, but as a self-reflexive history of Auster's own development as a writer. This is already clear from the above account, where we repeatedly find Auster alluding to, not Reznikoff himself, but his own early essays on Reznikoff; not Hamsun, but his Masters thesis and 1970 essay on Hamsun. In fact, the novels from *The New York Trilogy* to *Moon Palace* (and, to a lesser extent, beyond) draw extensively on Auster's own archive as one of their key intertexts. All three of Auster's

---

[134] Auster, *Trilogy*, 314.

first novels—*The New York Trilogy, In the Country of Last Things,* and *Moon Palace*—spring from a series of abortive early manuscripts that date from Auster's college days in the late 1960s. In revisiting this archive, however, Auster also builds in his own auto-critique of his earlier aesthetic positions. This shift is clearest in the treatment of the ideal of an Edenic language, which passes from a source of earnest fascination in the early drafts to a subject of scathing critique in the published texts, in line with Auster's shifting relationship to the aspirations of the poetry. This self-critique persists down to a very granular level. The young Stillman's halting speech, for instance, with its distant echoes of Beckett, enters more firmly into a Beckettian lineage when we understand this influence as passing through one of Auster's own untitled early typescripts, which experiments with the kind of broken, rhythmical prose that characterizes Beckett's late works: "My mouth is dormant," the young Auster writes. "There is no intake, to eat, and no output, to speak. My hunger is in the words I write, each one, as if the last, dragging my dwindling body to the edge, where there is, no more" (that final Beckettian comma!).[135] From here, the stylistic progression to Stillman the son's speech—"This is what is called speaking. I believe that is the term. When words come out, fly into the air, live for a moment, and die"—is clear, clearer in fact than its echo of Beckett himself.[136] Given this intermediate manuscript, then, Stillman's language emerges less as a direct parody of modernism or Beckett, and more as a parody of Auster's own juvenilia, of his youthful debt to modernism.

Moon Palace stages this self-critique in a more biographical mode, transplanting the plot of Hamsun's *Hunger* to the scene of Auster's own university days. Marco, like Auster, begins at Columbia in the fall of 1965. He reaches his solipsistic breakdown against the backdrop of the "tumult of politics and crowds, of outrage, bullhorns, and violence" that characterized the late 1960s, culminating in a final breakdown in the summer of 1969.[137] On the one hand, Marco replicates Auster's later self-portrait of the author as loner, held apart from the sociality of the student protests, which would emerge in *Hand to Mouth*. On the other, however, he lives out the plot of *Hunger*, the novel that, in the 1969–70 academic year, would serve as the key text of Auster's thesis. This doubling of biographical and literary allusion (and of literary allusion *as* biographical allusion) reimagines modernist aesthetics as a phase of Auster's own life, a point not just in the larger sweep of literary history, but also in the more intimate unfolding of literary biography. The result is something like the process

[135] Paul Auster, "TS 47 pp. Unidentified Prose," n.d., 37, Box 22, Folder 3, Paul Auster Archive, 1963–1995 Papers, Berg Collection, New York Public Library.
[136] Auster, *Trilogy*, 16.   [137] Auster, *Moon Palace*, 24.

that Quentin Anderson finds in nineteenth-century American writers, whom he takes as the precursors to the student protestors of the 1960s and who, in a process that he calls "secular incarnation," perform "the act not of identifying oneself with the fathers, but of catching all their powers up into the self, asserting that there need be no more generations, no more history, but simply the swelling diaspason of the swelling self."[138] If Auster's art of hunger begins by identifying aesthetic autonomy with the autonomy of the author, it ends by suggesting that modernism and its quest for autonomy constitute just a phase in that author's life.

It is not easy in this context to hold firmly to the (ordinarily very useful) distinction that Seshagiri and James make between postmodernism's parodic relationship to modernism, and metamodernism's more earnest, historicist rediscovery of periodization.[139] If we understand what initially seemed to be Auster's parodic relationship to modernist style not as a parody of modernism itself, but as a self-parody of his youthful commitment to modernism, we lose the straightforwardness of postmodernism's supposedly unserious engagement with modernism. Instead, we are redirected towards the young Auster's startlingly earnest attempts to write a late late modernism (or early metamodernism), both in his unpublished early prose and in his published poetry, and towards an engagement with modernism that, in his critical works, is vested in a clear sense of modernism's location as an early twentieth-century phenomenon, with respect to which he is irrevocably belated. Indeed, the preoccupation with genealogy, including genealogies of modernism, testifies to the ongoing role of literary history for Auster. In other words, what a study of the long history of Auster's engagement with the art of hunger finally suggests is that Auster's much-discussed postmodernism is also both a kind of metamodernism, an earnest engagement with the history and the styles of modernism as a lost past, and an "intramodernism," an engagement with his *own* modernist past. In this sense, both the "mischievous self-dissection" of modernism and the "reassertion of integrity" that James identifies with the modernist turn in contemporary fiction are at play in Auster, for whom integrity and self-dissection are merely different facets of the same exploration of self and subjectivity that underpins his writing as a whole.[140]

---

[138] Anderson, *The Imperial Self*, 58.

[139] David James and Urmila Seshagiri, "Metamodernism: Narratives of Continuity and Revolution," *PMLA* 129, no. 1 (2014): 94.

[140] David James, "Integrity after Metafiction," *Twentieth-Century Literature* 57, no. 3–4 (2011): 497.

Reading Auster's early novels as hesitating between postmodernism and metamodernism illuminates the ambivalence of these texts' relationship to autonomy. Most accounts of postmodernism treat it as the final eclipse of modernist autonomy, from Fredric Jameson's sense that postmodernism represents the end of art's capacity for any external critique of society, to Andreas Huyssen's claim that postmodernism is the end of the high/low divide that characterizes his account of modernist autonomy.[141] Auster's turn to the postmodern novel affirms this claim insofar as it provides a way of critiquing and moving beyond the stiflingly extreme modes of autonomy that he develops in the poetry. But modernist autonomy nonetheless remains an object of fascination for Auster in the novels. The unreadable texts that represent the impossibility of absolute aesthetic autonomy may no longer offer a plausible model of writing, but they remain the empty centers around which the novels are organized.

The real problem of aesthetic autonomy in Auster's novels, however, persists as a dilemma not about an autonomous Edenic language, but about the autonomous writer, a figure who is part mythical Adam, part social recluse. As *Hand to Mouth*—which post-dates the novels and represents Auster's last sustained foray into the art of hunger—suggests, the starving artist remains central to his writing long after other modes of autonomy have been relegated to his poetic past. Auster's post-modernist art of hunger, making the author the last bastion of autonomy in the shifting literary landscape of the 1960s and 1970s, therefore affirms an individualist, anti-institutional autonomy. It imagines autonomy as rebellion, as a kind of youthful dissidence, so that the work of his less autonomous novels becomes to integrate the hunger artists of his youth into a social and genealogical framework. In this sense, Auster's novels constitute a kind of reparative project, an attempt to work through the social fractures of the 1960s without losing the era's utopianism and to hold together the subject in the face of the poststructuralist critique. Aesthetic autonomy in Auster's 1980s becomes both that which needs to be cherished and nurtured, kept alive as a last spark of dissidence, but also that which needs to be socialized, woven into communities and genealogies. The art of hunger as a project of authorial autonomy, even of radical individualism, is ultimately set aside in Auster's writing precisely because it resists this socialization, even as the figure of the isolated, ideally autonomous author persists throughout his writing, achieving late-career

---

[141] Fredric Jameson, "Postmodernism, or The Cultural Logic of Late Capitalism," *New Left Review* 146 (August 1984): 53–92; Andreas Huyssen, *After the Great Divide: Modernism, Mass Culture, Postmodernism* (Bloomington, IN; Indianapolis: Indiana University Press, 1986).

manifestations in texts like *Travels in the Scriptorium* (2007) and *Man in the Dark* (2008).

The redefintion of aesthetic autonomy as authorial autonomy that Auster uses the art of hunger to articulate becomes increasingly important in late twentieth-century literature. Authors from Philip Roth and J. M. Coetzee (in his later work) to Ben Lerner and Jonathan Safran Foer insist on their own status as taciturn, reclusive authors, in order to guarantee the literariness of their texts and to invest the texts they write with the aura of the autonomous author-figure lurking behind. As Benjamin Widiss argues, in a study that traces "the persistence of the author" in the face of modernism's and then poststructuralism's attacks, "the hermeneutic strategies we have been taught by modernism, and taught as well that they serve to elucidate texts that at the very least strive to be hermetically sealed, instead derive essential energy from the spectre of the author standing behind and beyond."[142] Auster's writing suggests that the "hermetically sealed" text, in the tradition of modernism, might be not undermined but underwritten by an autonomous "author standing behind and beyond." His reactivation of the art of hunger tradition, therefore, points towards an alternate mode of aesthetic autonomy, one vested not in New Critical form but in the author himself. With its central figure of the dying author who is not beyond the text but *in* it, he reimagines aesthetic autonomy as a form of unfree authorial introversion.

---

[142] Benjamin Widiss, *Obscure Invitations: The Persistence of the Author in Twentieth-Century American Literature* (Stanford, CA: Stanford University Press, 2011), 4.

4

Starving Across the Color Line

J. M. Coetzee in Apartheid South Africa

On December 3, 1971, J. M. Coetzee was newly returned to South Africa from the US, where he had taught at SUNY Buffalo and completed a Ph.D. at the University of Texas at Austin. Seeking a publisher for "The Narrative of Jacobus Coetzee," a novella that would later be published as part of his first novel *Dusklands*, the young Coetzee made his first approaches to the British publisher Calder and Boyars, and to seven American literary agents. Conceding that his novella "is of no historical value, in the narrower sense," he argues that it nonetheless "does trace a line between so-called autonomous fictions and the psychology of the conquistador."[1] The letters go on to underscore this line, comparing his work favorably to "Calley's recent work on My Lai"—a dark joke about the conflicting stories told at trial by a US officer who had been convicted over the My Lai massacres in Vietnam earlier that year—before conceding, in the letters to agents (but not to Calder and Boyars), the likelihood that "it will never win a massive readership."[2] While the absence of a projected readership shows Coetzee aligning himself with a model of aesthetic autonomy that refuses the demands of the market as part of the paradox-ical attempt to sell his work, the analogy between his writing and Calley's fabrications suggests that this autonomy carries potentially significant political import.

Nonetheless, the politics that emerges from Coetzee's "autonomous fictions" is, in its link to the "psychology of the conquistador," not necessarily the politics that many of his readers, past and present, have wished. South African literary culture in the 1970s and 1980s increasingly understood literature's role as part of a larger project of anti-apartheid liberation and, with striking consensus, rejected aesthetic autonomy for its

---

[1] J. M. Coetzee, "Letters to Calder & Boyars; Bach Jr. Literary Agent; McIntosh, McKee & Dodds," December 3, 1971, Container 69, Folder 1: Business Correspondence, 1969–March 1976, J. M. Coetzee Papers, Harry Ransom Center, University of Texas at Austin.

[2] Ibid.

failure to contribute to this project. While many proponents of aesthetic autonomy have, as we have seen, sought to defend it by claiming that it too is a practice of freedom, Coetzee's letters also reject this position, linking aesthetic autonomy to structures of oppression and the worldview of those who uphold such structures. His writing, that is, carries forward the art of hunger's understanding of aesthetic autonomy as fundamentally unfree. Reprising this conviction in the highly politicized literary field of late apartheid South Africa and in a context where hunger itself is a political instrument, he reimagines the unfreedom of this tradition in explicitly political terms. In this sense, Coetzee's art of hunger is a specifically South African one, linking its claim that autonomy is unfree with the anti-apartheid attack on aesthetic autonomy as the tool of a colonial elite.

This chapter assumes that, as Jarad Zimbler has argued, to understand Coetzee's early fiction requires us to read it within the literary field of apartheid South Africa, whose debates and anxieties shape it.[3] In this context, as the 1970s turned into the 1980s, the intense politicization of South Africa's post-Soweto literary field came to echo the dilemma of post-Vichy France, producing a field whose politicization was so thoroughgoing that to declare one's art autonomous was to be taken to occupy a political position. For a white South African with an Afrikaner surname like Coetzee, to insist on the autonomy of art was to risk complicity with the status quo—to risk assent to the apartheid regime. Coetzee's writing in the 1980s therefore develops out of a complex maneuver that seeks to defend an autonomous position, while refusing the co-optation of this autonomy to a conservative politics. This is the context in which Coetzee delivered his widely quoted 1987 address "The Novel Today" as part of the Weekly Mail Book Week. Reprising the commitment to "autonomous fiction" first signaled in the 1971 letters, in the 1987 lecture he mounts a defense of the "novel that operates in terms of its own procedures and issues in its own conclusions . . . a novel that evolves its own paradigms and myths, in the process . . . perhaps going so far as to show up the mythic status of the paradigms of history."[4] Arguing for the specificity of literature as "another, an other mode of thinking," he maintains that such a mode is valuable—and politically powerful—precisely because of its capacity to usurp history's discursive position.[5] The autonomy of literature, in this account, allows literature to reflect upon the discourse of history and, he

[3] Jarad Zimbler, *J. M. Coetzee and the Politics of Style* (New York: Cambridge University Press, 2014).

[4] J. M. Coetzee, "The Novel Today" (TS, 1987), 2, Container 64, Folder 7: Early Works, 1987, J. M. Coetzee Papers, Harry Ransom Center, University of Texas at Austin.

[5] Ibid., 3.

implies, to engage more broadly with contemporary political and cultural concerns from this putatively autonomous position. Autonomy is defensible because it is, after all, political.

"The Novel Today," with its beleaguered tone, testifies to the closing of the structural and intellectual space for literature outside politics in the final years of apartheid. While this lecture attempts to solve the dilemma by politicizing autonomy, however, this chapter focuses on the text and archive of Coetzee's fourth novel, *Life & Times of Michael K* (1983), which, I argue, suggests that literary autonomy, in order to remain autonomous, must embrace a form of anti-politics. The drafts of *Michael K* play out the tension between aesthetic autonomy and political engagement in the evolution of their narrative and intertexts, culminating in a text that, with its starving protagonist in the lineage of Bartleby, Kafka's hunger artist, and Hamsun's *Hunger* narrator, takes up a position within the art of hunger tradition. Like earlier texts of the art of hunger, *Michael K* offers a response to the twinned contemporary crises of aesthetic autonomy and modernism, by way of the figure of starvation. In a political context in which hunger itself carries a powerful political charge, however, Coetzee's manifestation of the art of hunger explores the divergence of aesthetic from political autonomy, reanimating the art of hunger's unfree aesthetic autonomy in a context where such a disavowal of literature's political potency was anathema. By taking the art of hunger as the site for testing the intersection of aesthetic and political autonomy, *Life & Times of Michael K* imports the art of hunger's claims about autonomy into the political sphere. It takes on the schism that the art of hunger establishes between autonomy and freedom, as Michael K, the last of the hunger artists, transforms the aesthetics of the art of hunger into an anti-politics.

Michael K reveals Coetzee triangulating his defense of aesthetic autonomy against two other, less immediate, literary contexts. As I have been suggesting throughout this book, the story of the art of hunger is a story of the collapse and delegitimization of social contexts for aesthetic autonomy. In this context, the modernist legacy of the art of hunger provides an imagined counter-field, an alternate context, in which the notion of aesthetic autonomy can be sustained and extended. At the same time, this constructed modernist canon is embedded within a more concrete and contemporary literary field in Coetzee's address to a transnational literary and academic elite for whom modernism remained an important touchstone. Addressing himself as a provincial writer to the metropolitan centers of power, as he does in the 1971 letters, he seeks to locate himself within literary systems of value that speak above all to the value of autonomy, and to find a global audience that prizes this concept where his local peers do not. For Coetzee, this global audience was to a significant extent an academic one. As a result, his defense of aesthetic autonomy develops by reading South African critiques of the idea through theoretical debates about the relationship between literature, politics, and autonomy that emanated from the US academy during the 1970s and 1980s. These debates taught Coetzee a pessimism about the terms in which political freedom was imagined in South Africa. In doing so, they provided an alternate literary field into which Coetzee could insert his writing, in which both modernism and aesthetic autonomy retained their credibility.

1. MODERNIST AUTONOMY UNDER APARTHEID

The debates over aesthetic autonomy that ran throughout twentieth-century literary culture were perhaps nowhere more vehement than in South African writing during the dying days of apartheid. Against the backdrop of mounting international criticism and growing internal resistance that seemed, to people at all points on the political spectrum, to augur the regime's imminent collapse, politics seeped into all aspects of life. In this context, writers—both black and white—increasingly felt themselves bound by what Afrikaner writer André Brink called "that responsibility one owes to one's society and one's time"—a responsibility almost always conceived in immediately political terms, as the responsibility to describe and critique the injustices of apartheid.[6] Reading South African literary discourse of the 1980s, what is immediately striking is the almost unanimous consensus that political engagement must be the primary locus of literary activity, a consensus that echoes and amplifies the sentiments of the French literary field of the 1940s. Louise Bethlehem remarks on the "rhetoric of urgency" and the "commitment to literary truth-telling" that pervades (and, she believes, constrains) literary discourse of this era.[7] In such a context, claims for autonomous art appear not so much irrelevant as downright irresponsible, a refusal of one's immediate political duties that could only lend succor to the racist status quo. As Nadine Gordimer argued, "In South Africa the ivory tower is bulldozed anew with every black man's home destroyed to make way for a white man's."[8]

---

[6] André Brink, *Mapmakers: Writing in a State of Siege* (London: Faber and Faber, 1983), 204.

[7] Louise Bethlehem, "'A Primary Need as Strong as Hunger': The Rhetoric of Urgency in South African Literary Culture after Apartheid," *Poetics Today* 22, no. 2 (2001): 368, 366.

[8] Nadine Gordimer, *The Essential Gesture: Writing, Politics and Places*, ed. Stephen Clingman (London: Jonathan Cape, 1988), 295.

The consensus over the necessity of literary commitment grew throughout the 1970s, until by the early 1980s aesthetic autonomy had been widely discredited. The emergence of this consensus can be traced in the gradual fall from grace of the Sestigers, a group of experimental young Afrikaner writers, active in the 1960s and influenced by the literary innovations of post-war European writing. The Sestigers were perhaps the most prominent apartheid-era writers to embrace what Jarad Zimbler and André Brink variously call "art for the sake of art" or "l'art pur."[9] By the end of the 1960s, however, their preference for literary experiment over political engagement had led to a split within the group, with Brink, Breyten Breytenbach, and Jan Rabie arguing for "the need for literature to take arms within and against the socio-political realities of South Africa."[10] By 1983, Brink was able to argue that "most of the key figures among the Sestigers, including those who had initially argued very strongly against commitment, have in the course of the 1970s broadened the scope of their writing to include the contemporary South African scene."[11] If the opposition between aesthetic autonomy and political engagement constituted a real debate at the beginning of the 1970s, when Coetzee first described his writing as autonomous, by the early 1980s, when he began writing *Michael K*, autonomy no longer seemed a viable position, even for its formerly most devout adherents. By the final years of the 1980s, the collapsing status of aesthetic autonomy had seriously tarnished the Sestigers' reputation, leading to a growing critical consensus that they represented an unfortunate and embarrassing aberration in South African literature, irretrievably compromised by what Martin Trump calls their "enormous political naivety" and what Neil Lazarus, slightly more generously, suggests was their "failure ... to resist appropriation by a neutralizing tradition."[12]

One of the pressures that paralleled and contributed to this growing politicization of literary discourse was the growth of the state's censorship apparatus over the course of the 1960s, which intensified during the 1970s. As censorship became increasingly draconian, authors not only became politicized in defense of their right to say what they would, but also, as Zimbler argues, came to see "bannings ... as signs of election, as evidence that the publication or person in question had been deemed

[9] Jarad Zimbler, "For Neither Love Nor Money: The Place of Political Art in Pierre Bourdieu's Literary Field," *Textual Practice* 23, no. 4 (2009): 603; Brink, *Mapmakers*, 27.
[10] Brink, *Mapmakers*, 27.   [11] Ibid.
[12] Martin Trump, "Afrikaner Literature and the South African Liberation Struggle," *Journal of Commonwealth Literature* 25, no. 1 (1990): 47; Neil Lazarus, "Modernism and Modernity: T. W. Adorno and White South African Literature," *Cultural Critique* 5 (1986–7): 135.

sufficiently political by the state."[13] In this context, censorship paradoxically increased the importance of political engagement to South African literature. The relationship between censorship and the claim to aesthetic autonomy is a complex one in the South African context. On the one hand, the censor is a figure of the state's denial of literature's privileged social position and its exertion of its power over the literary, and in this sense censorship denies that literature may have any sovereignty or autonomy in its own right. This is Coetzee's position, and he goes so far as to argue that "the censor forces him [the writer] to internalize a contaminating reading," suggesting that censorship compromises literary autonomy not just after the fact, but in the very moment of composition.[14] On the other hand, as Peter D. McDonald has shown in his study of censorship under apartheid, censors saw themselves as "officially certified guardians of the literary" and, in keeping with this position, frequently—if somewhat sporadically and capriciously—passed works that they believed held sufficient literary merit.[15] In this, they espoused a position of qualified support for literature's autonomy, a belief not only that a work's "literariness" merits special consideration, but that it necessarily limits its political power, along with its intended audience. As Zimbler suggests, this situation "inevitably contributed to the general opinion that avant-garde literature was complicit or, at best, politically irrelevant."[16] It had a similar effect on the position of aesthetic autonomy itself, amplifying the politicization of literary discourse by increasing the sense that the recourse to pure art was itself an act of complicity with the apartheid regime.

For all Coetzee's antagonism towards censorship's attack on literary autonomy, he was one of the beneficiaries of the exemption on grounds of literary merit. None of his three novels vetted by the censorship authorities—*In the Heart of the Country*, *Waiting for the Barbarians*, and *Life & Times of Michael K*—was ultimately banned. While in each case the censor flagged potentially problematic elements, each was passed because of their lack of popular appeal, their literary experimentation, and their lack of geographic and historical specificity—all elements of a classic humanist definition of aesthetic autonomy.[17] The censor's report on *Waiting for the Barbarians*, in fact, is striking in its echo of Coetzee's

---

[13] Zimbler, "For Neither Love Nor Money," 609.

[14] J. M. Coetzee, *Giving Offense: Essays on Censorship* (Chicago: University of Chicago, n.d.), 36.

[15] Peter D. McDonald, *Literature Police: Apartheid Censorship and its Cultural Consequences* (Oxford: Oxford University Press, 2009), 11.

[16] Zimbler, "For Neither Love Nor Money," 612.

[17] Peter D. McDonald, "The Writer, the Critic, and the Censor: J. M. Coetzee and the Question of Censorship," *Book History* 7 (2004): 291–2.

own sense of his works' autonomy, pointing out the "Kafkaesque" qualities of the narrative and arguing against banning it in part because, "Though the book has considerable literary merit, it quite lacks popular appeal."[18] The proximity between Coetzee's and the censors' defenses of autonomous literary value was clearly uncomfortable, and it underscored the suspicion, prevalent in South African literary culture of the time, that the appeal to autonomy was not a neutral position but one which, intentionally or otherwise, provided tacit support for the unacceptable status quo.

Nonetheless, Coetzee's discomfort with the tension between autonomy and responsibility was not entirely unique. Despite the vehemence of the disavowal of aesthetic autonomy, statements about literature by white South African writers in this period suggest a contentious, unsettled relationship between the demand for political engagement and the pull towards aesthetic autonomy. In her influential 1982 essay "Living in the Interregnum," Nadine Gordimer finds herself trapped between "two absolutes": "One is that racism is evil... The other is that a writer is a being in whose sensibility is fused what Lukács calls 'the duality of inwardness and outside world,' and he must never be asked to sunder this union."[19] Gordimer's second certainty is not precisely a claim for the autonomy of literature in any absolute sense, but it does maintain that art has its own internal logic whose preservation—even in the face of external demands—is central to its status as literature. Going on to argue that, at least in the contemporary South African context, "the coexistence of these absolutes often seems irreconcilable within one life," Gordimer points up not only the difficulty of carving out a space in which art can operate under its own internal laws, but also the continuing impulse to do so.[20]

This vestigial desire to maintain the autonomy of the aesthetic realm makes sense in light of the literary canon that late apartheid white South Africans constructed for themselves. This canon centers around European modernism, reaching back to its nineteenth-century precursors and forward to its post-World War II heirs, but always gravitating inexorably around writing from Europe, across a range of European languages, from the early twentieth century. In their essays, writers like Brink and Gordimer develop their theories of literature by constant and explicit reference to modernist writers, from Joyce and Eliot to Céline and Kafka. The interweaving of quotations from these Europeans with their own thoughts speaks to the extent to which this tradition has been assimilated into their own thinking about literature. References to South African literature, in

---

[18] Quoted ibid., 290.   [19] Gordimer, *Essential Gesture*, 277.   [20] Ibid.

contrast, are widespread, but tend to be engaged more as an object of analysis than as fully assimilated cultural touchstones.

Given the centrality of European modernism to South African literary culture, it is perhaps unsurprising that later critics should have sought to read South African letters through the lens of theorists whose ideas have developed out of precisely this modernist tradition. But in this electric political environment, the importance of aesthetic autonomy to such theories has posed a particular challenge for critics seeking to bring European modernist thinkers and European thinkers of modernism to bear on apartheid South Africa. Neil Lazarus, for example, has argued that an Adorno-influenced reading of South African modernism requires that "Adorno's preference for 'autonomous' over 'committed' art is seen to be contingently rather than abstractly and aesthetically motivated"—an extraordinary claim, given the centrality of aesthetic autonomy to Adorno's theory of art.[21] More recently, Jarad Zimbler has offered a Bourdieusian account of the apartheid-era South African literary field, which similarly requires a redefinition of aesthetic autonomy so that it describes, not autonomy as a denial of social, commercial, or political claims upon the artist, but rather "a particular state of the literary field, one in which the relevant mode or modes of evaluation are chosen by the artists themselves."[22] By redefining autonomy in this way, Zimbler ensures that it need not entail a retreat from social or political commitment, allowing him to suggest that South Africa's political literature is not the opposite of autonomy, but rather an expression of it. For both critics, the centrality of political art—a category that neither Adorno nor Bourdieu are able to find a place for—to the South African literary environment necessitates a whole-scale reinvention of aesthetic theories with which they engage.

Zimbler and Lazarus both have recourse to theories of literature that have been developed out of an analysis of modernism—out of Beckett and Kafka, in the case of Adorno; and out of the aestheticism of late nineteenth-century France, in the case of Bourdieu—and that, as a consequence, place aesthetic autonomy at their center. The South African critics, however, subvert this equation from within, maintaining the modernist theoretical frameworks while denying the demands of autonomy. In this sense, both Lazarus and Zimbler show how apartheid-era South African literary culture presents a serious challenge to theories of literature that derive from modernism, within which the significance of some model of aesthetic autonomy can seem like a given. Their theoretical revisions reflect autonomy's tortured, delegitimized place in South African

---

[21] Lazarus, "Modernism and Modernity," 143.
[22] Zimbler, "For Neither Love Nor Money," 615.

letters, even as it echoes the extent to which South African literary culture of this period remains deeply and self-consciously indebted to European modernism. The intense ambivalence that aesthetic autonomy generates in these critics is a feature not only of the critics themselves, but also of the white apartheid-era South African literary establishment that they are describing, torn as it is between a political investment in engaged art and an aesthetic commitment to the literary tradition most closely associated with aesthetic autonomy.

The tension between aesthetic autonomy and "responsibility" comes clearly into focus where "engaged" South African writers seek to enter into dialogue with "autonomous" European authors. Here Beckett offers a particularly instructive example, given that he functions as an important figure in both apartheid-era South African literary discourse and the post-war reconfiguration of aesthetic autonomy that I discuss in Chapter 2. Both Brink and Gordimer have recourse to Beckett at moments where they find themselves seeking to work through the relationship between autonomy and engagement. For Brink, Beckett—writing *Watt* while in hiding in Roussillon during World War II—becomes an example of what it is to "*écrire dangereusement*," equating Beckett's political and aesthetic activities in such a way as to efface his impulse towards autonomy.[23] Similarly, in "The Essential Gesture," Gordimer seeks to redefine what I describe in Chapter 2 as Beckett's grappling with autonomy, making it instead into an abstract mode of responsibility. For Gordimer, "Through a transformation by style—depersonalized laconicism of the word almost to the Word—Samuel Beckett takes on as his essential gesture a responsibility direct to human destiny, and not to any local cell of humanity," a position made possible because, Gordimer argues, "His place—not Warsaw, San Salvador, Soweto—had nothing specific to ask of him."[24]

Running through both Gordimer's and Brink's readings of Beckett is the impulse to save him from the unspoken charge of "art for art's sake," or what Martin Trump, writing critically of the European allegiances of the Sestigers, dismisses as "the historically truncated works of Beckett, Artaud, Sartre and Ionesco."[25] Both Brink and Gordimer, in contrast, seek a hidden mode of responsibility in Beckett's writing. Both these readings, however, produce uncharacteristic blind spots: Gordimer's necessitates the effacement of the serious demands placed on writers in France during and immediately after World War II, a situation that her frequent recourse to Camus shows her to be intimately aware of, while Brink's ignores the significant gap between the text of *Watt* and its context of

---

[23] Brink, *Mapmakers*, 183.   [24] Gordimer, *Essential Gesture*, 297.
[25] Trump, "Afrikaner Literature," 49.

production. Such blind spots are symptomatic of the tense attempt to reconcile European modernism with the call to responsibility that characterizes white South African literature's uncomfortable relationship to modernist autonomy.

Coetzee's more ambivalent sense of the author's political responsibility is reflected in his rather different engagement with Beckett's work. Where Brink and Gordimer seek to articulate Beckett's responsibility as a writer, Coetzee's most prolonged engagement with the Irishman's writing is his 1969 doctoral dissertation on Beckett's English fiction, and a series of articles based on this and similar research during the 1970s. All of these articles apply computational stylistics in his quest for "the ideal of mathematical formalization"—a reading of Beckett that maximizes and exaggerates his texts' formalism, reading them as a series of permutations on sets of words.[26] At the same time, Beckett also marks, for Coetzee, the limit case for his espousal of aesthetic autonomy. Since at least the early 1970s, Coetzee has been vicious in his attacks on Beckett's late prose, which he described in a 1973 essay on *Lessness* as "a formalization or stylization of autodestruction" that is also a form of "automatism," and, in the 1992 *Doubling the Point* interviews, as "disembodied" and "posthumous."[27] This repudiation of Beckett's late writing suggests that for Coetzee the living body represents the limit of aesthetic autonomy. Elsewhere in *Doubling the Point*, Coetzee affirms that his own fiction erects "a simple (simple-minded?) standard" in the body, and links this to the South African context, claiming that, "in South Africa it is not possible to deny the authority of suffering and therefore of the body."[28] In dispensing with the body, Beckett becomes, for Coetzee, not a covert practitioner of political commitment, but a cautionary tale of aesthetic autonomy taken too far. More broadly, Beckett's reading of Coetzee shows him participating in his broader literary culture's tendency to form their aesthetic principles by testing European modernism against the political exigencies of contemporary South Africa.

While claims for the "modernism" of South African writing are common, however—Lazarus argues as much as far back as 1989—the importation of the term to Africa, particularly via studies of influence, has been deeply controversial. In an influential 1976 essay on Charles Larson's *The Emergence of African Literature*, Ayi Kwei Armah disputes Larson's claim

---

[26] J. M. Coetzee, *Doubling the Point: Essays and Interviews*, ed. David Atwell (Cambridge, MA: Harvard University Press, 1992), 22; J. M. Coetzee, "The English Fiction of Samuel Beckett: An Essay in Stylistic Analysis" (Ph.D. dissertation, University of Texas at Austin, 1969).

[27] Coetzee, *Doubling the Point*, 45, 23.   [28] Ibid., 248.

that he was influenced by James Joyce, attributing "this language of indebtedness and borrowing and influence" to "a none too subtle way Western commentators have of saying Africa lacks original creativity."[29] Nicholas Brown, more recently, has followed Armah, opening his study of African literature and European modernism by reminding us that, "In the context of African literature and modernism, we have been permanently warned away from influence study by Ayi Kwei Armah's funny but devastating response to Charles Larson's *The Emergence of African Fiction*."[30]

Nonetheless, the stakes and significance of modernism in Africa are quite different when we turn our attention from the black anti-colonial literature that is Brown's primary focus, towards the white South African writing that is mine. While black African literature has often understood the European intellectual tradition, including European modernism, as an extension of colonial hegemony, white South African writing, especially of the apartheid era, is uncomfortably aware that its status as a settler literature leaves it suspended between European and African frames of reference. Coetzee uses the term "white writing" to describe this literature written by "a people no longer European, not yet African."[31] As he acknowledges in a 2003 interview, in response to a question about his relationship to South Africa, he himself is "a late representative of the vast movement of European expansionism," and his "intellectual allegiances are clearly European, not African."[32] The hint of the derivative and the taint of colonialism that make modernism such an uncomfortable frame of analysis for black African literature are, in contrast, constitutive features of white South African writing. White South Africa's fraught relationship to European modernism thus underscores the "provincial" status that Coetzee attributes to South Africa during this period.[33] These white South African writers sit uncomfortably between the poles Tim Woods identifies of "European artists [who] looked to Africa for borrowings to revitalize what was perceived to be a flagging and insipid *aesthetics*," and "African writers [who] borrowed from European modernism for the

[29] Ayi Kwai Armah, "Larsony, or Fiction as Criticism of Fiction," *Asemka* 4 (1976): 6.

[30] Nicholas Brown, *Utopian Generations: The Political Horizon of Twentieth-Century Literature* (Princeton: Princeton University Press, 2005), 2.

[31] J. M. Coetzee, *White Writing: On the Culture of Letters in South Africa* (New Haven: Yale University Press, 1988), 11.

[32] J. M. Coetzee, "An Exclusive Interview with J. M. Coetzee," *DN.se Kultur*, December 8, 2003, n.p., <http://www.dn.se/kultur-noje/an-exclusive-interview-with-j-m-coetzee>.

[33] See, for example, J. M. Coetzee, "Address to UCT Fellows" 1985, Container 64, Folder 3, J. M. Coetzee Papers, Harry Ransom Center, University of Texas at Austin.

purposes of promoting a radical *politics* of counter-colonialism."³⁴ For white South Africans, modernism dramatized not the turn to counter-colonial politics, but the uncomfortable awareness of the colonial frame of their aesthetic preferences and positions.

The claim of a genealogy with European literature thus serves, particularly for Coetzee, as a way of acknowledging the political reality that binds white South Africans to colonization, and therefore a way of gesturing towards the foundational illegitimacy, the original sin, of white settler culture. In this context, the autonomy that these writers acknowledge as the historically specific by-product of a certain moment of European culture is already political in a very specific way, because it enters the South African scene as part of the legacy of colonialism. It is significant, therefore, that the anxieties about aesthetic autonomy belong more or less exclusively to white South African writing. While black South African literature of this period certainly has its debates and controversies, they turn not on the question of whether art should be autonomous, but on how best to engage with the political reality in which they find themselves. Thus, Njabulo S. Ndebele's influential essay "The Rediscovery of the Ordinary," sometimes linked to debates within white South African letters about the status of the aesthetic, is clear that what is at stake for him is not a debate between political and autonomous art, but rather a debate between different modes of political art, a claim not that art shouldn't have political change as its central goal, but rather that "the means of combating the situation have become too narrow and constricting."³⁵ For white South Africans like Gordimer and Brink, in contrast, the assumption that writers have a responsibility to their society, while never disputed, is also made to answer to a separate set of concerns about the value and possibilities of an autonomous aesthetic sphere—and does so as part of the continuing links that bind white South Africa to Europe and white South African writing to European modernism.

2. HUNGER IN SOUTH AFRICA

In Chapters 1–3 I argued that the art of hunger becomes compelling for writers at historical moments when the status of aesthetic autonomy enters a state of crisis. But while modernist autonomy enters what may be one of

³⁴ Tim Woods, "A Complex Legacy: Modernity's Uneasy Discourse of Ethics and Responsibility," in *The Legacies of Modernism: Historicising Postwar and Contemporary Fiction*, ed. David James (Cambridge: Cambridge University Press, 2012), 159.
³⁵ Njabulo S. Ndebele, *South African Literature and Culture: The Rediscovery of the Ordinary* (Manchester: Manchester University Press, 1994), 57.

its most serious crises in the context of apartheid South Africa, hunger is far from a neutral site for exploring this particular crisis. For many South African writers, hunger offers not a metaphor for aesthetic autonomy, but its most troubling indictment. Pondering the line between internally generated and externally imposed modes of responsibility, for example, Nadine Gordimer wonders:

> If the writer accepts the social realist demand, from without, will he be distorting, paradoxically, the very ability he has to offer the creation of a new society? If he accepts the other, self-imposed responsibility, how far into the immediate needs of his society will he reach? Will hungry people find revelation in the ideas his work contains "without his knowledge"?[36]

For Gordimer, "hungry people" emerge as a final arbiter of this debate, implying that the writer's responsibility is, in the final account, always directed towards the hungry and measured against the writer's capacity to reach them. The "impossibility" that Coetzee acknowledges of denying the authority of suffering and the body in the South African context therefore becomes for Gordimer both the limit and antithesis of aesthetic autonomy, the final demand to which the writer must bow. For Sarah Christie, Geoffrey Hutchings, and Don Maclennan, hunger constitutes the paradox that risks destabilizing even the most realist and engaged writing, "for [realist writers] know that if people are hungry or suffering from persecution you feed them and free them from persecution. You do not first write novels about them."[37] Hunger in this reading could not be further from the figure for aesthetic autonomy that it becomes in modernist writing. It is not a trope for literature's distance from the world but the very thing that most forcefully condemns such distance.

Conversely, South African writers also use hunger metaphorically, to make the case for literature as a necessity of human life. In an essay from 1969, André Brink argues that art "satisfies a need in man as vital as hunger . . . Like hunger, it is a personal need."[38] This analogy echoes Antonin Artaud's claim in the 1939 preface to *The Theater and its Double* that "What is important, it seem to me, is not so much to defend a culture whose existence has never kept a man from going hungry, as to extract, from what is called culture, ideas whose compelling force is identical with that of hunger."[39] Brink's version, however, introduces a more humanist note, using the analogy with hunger to

---

[36] Gordimer, *Essential Gesture*, 295.
[37] Sarah Christie, Geoffrey Hutchings, and Don Maclennan, *Perspectives on South African Fiction* (Johannesburg: A. D. Donker, 1980), 100.
[38] Brink, *Mapmakers*, 46.
[39] Antonin Artaud, *The Theater and its Double*, trans. Mary Caroline Richard (New York: Grove Press, 1958), 7.

suggest the possibility of a synchronicity between the artist's personal impulses and his or her universal responsibilities, a synchronicity that ultimately makes the writer into "a conscience in the world."[40] Meanwhile, by 1989, when Leon de Kock reprised this figure, hunger was no longer a metaphor for Artaud's dream of a compelling culture, nor for Brink's sense of a universal human desire for expression, but instead a figure for the realist obligation to testify and document: "There was a desire to tell, from the individual's point of view, to reveal the lie behind the moral sanctimony of separate development. This was an immediate, primary need as strong as hunger."[41] Taken together, these references reveal that hunger was already— quite independently of the art of hunger tradition—an important figure in late apartheid South African literary discourse, where it functioned to generate what Louise Bethlehem has called a "rhetoric of urgency."[42] Linked to the realist, politically engaged impulses that dominate late apartheid writing, hunger in South Africa is repeatedly cast not as a figure for, but as the opposite of aesthetic autonomy.

Hunger's importance to South African literary discourse reflects its centrality to South African political discourse in the final years of apartheid. Among black and Coloured people, poverty and the associated food privation was one of the more common forms of devastation wrought by apartheid. The authors of *Uprooting Poverty*, a landmark 1989 study of poverty in South Africa, estimated that one-third of all non-white children suffered from malnutrition and that in 1975 between 15,000 and 27,000 children had died from starvation.[43] As the authors note, this is particularly striking in a country that habitually exported food, and was a direct consequence of the highly racialized economic inequality that was a feature of apartheid society.[44] In this context, hunger came to be firmly identified with non-white racial groups, especially black and Coloured people. As Coetzee recalls of a rare encounter with a young Coloured boy in his fictionalized memoir *Boyhood*, the boy "is also Coloured, which means that he has no money, lives in an obscure hovel, goes hungry."[45] The bareness of the equation of this racial category with poverty

[40] Brink, *Mapmakers*, 46.

[41] Leon de Kock, "A Prison-House of Mirrors?," *Journal of Literary Studies = Tydskrif Vir Literatuurwetenskap* 5, no. 2 (1989): 230.

[42] Bethlehem, "Rhetoric of Urgency."

[43] Francis Wilson and Mamphela Ramphele, *Uprooting Poverty: The South African Challenge: Report for the Second Carnegie Inquiry into Poverty and Development in Southern Africa* (New York: W. W. Norton & Co., 1989), 101.

[44] Ibid., 100, 17.

[45] J. M. Coetzee, *Boyhood: Scenes from Provincial Life* (London: Vintage, 1998), 61.

and hunger speaks to the racialization of deprivation that underwrote apartheid society.

In this context, hunger played an important role in shaping how South Africans thought about and discussed racial inequality. As Diana Wylie has argued, debates over "whether the first cause of African hunger lay in ignorance or poverty" shaped much twentieth-century discourse about hunger in South Africa.[46] Until the 1960s, the former theory—that Africans lacked the knowledge to feed themselves adequately—held sway, as "Cultural racism succeeded in making modern black poverty appear to be a cultural trait rather than the result of political and economic policies."[47] In the final two decades of apartheid, however, this consensus began to shift. Research increasingly linked hunger to poverty, and this linkage ultimately became central to anti-apartheid campaigns both within South Africa and internationally. Grace Davie has shown that, from the early 1970s, the poverty line became a central tool in black trade union campaigns, while her interviews with participants in the 1973 Durban Strike show them pointing to their "empty stomachs" and the simple fact that "we were hungry" as the root causes of their activism.[48] This interaction between social scientific measurements of poverty and its lived experience—understood and remembered by activists as hunger—made poverty and hunger a catalyst for anti-apartheid activities, as well as one of the most effective discursive tools for advocating for change, both inside and outside of South Africa. In this context, hunger assumed an important political function, becoming a metonym for black and Coloured suffering.

As the most visceral and crushing—but also the most quotidian and widespread—of apartheid's many injustices, hunger made an obvious counterpoint to excessively disengaged forms of "pure art." This is the context in which Gordimer seeks to test her art against the revelation it provides to "hungry people" and that Brink aspires to test his against hunger's own brutally compelling logic. At the same time, and for similar reasons, hunger became a widespread trope in South African literature. Athol Fugard, for instance, describes his improvised play *Friday's Bread on Monday* (1970) as "an improvised essay into hunger and desperation in the townships," and this use of hunger as a way of visualizing and dramatizing black desperation pervades South African literature, especially black South

---

[46] Diana Wylie, *Starving on a Full Stomach: Hunger and the Triumph of Cultural Racism in South Africa* (Charlottesville, VA: University of Virginia Press, 2001), 241.

[47] Ibid., 239.

[48] Quoted in Grace Davie, *Poverty Knowledge in South Africa: A Social History of Human Science, 1855–2005* (New York: Cambridge University Press, 2015), 194.

African literature.[49] We get a sense of this pervasiveness in *A Land Apart*, an anthology of South African writing edited by Brink and Coetzee in 1986 that focuses on post-1976 writing. In the English-language section, for which Coetzee had responsibility, hunger emerges as a major theme. Joel Matlou's portrait of life in the mines, "Man Against Himself," opens with the narrator choosing the mines because "my stomach was empty" and finding similar "empty stomachs" among those working there.[50] Mtutuzeli Matshoba's dissection of police abuses of power, "Call Me Not a Man" observes that "the poverty-stricken vendors were not licensed to scrape together some crumbs to ease the gnawing stomachs of their fatherless grandchildren at home."[51] Jeremy Cronin's portrait of a man he befriended in prison describes "this undernourished frame | that dates back | to those first years of his life."[52] The section is concluded by Oupa Thando Mthimkulu's "Like a Wheel," with its refrain of "Today I'm hungry | Tomorrow it's you."[53] The cumulative impression is of the pervasiveness of hunger and malnutrition in the black experience of apartheid, and of its centrality to writing that seeks to testify to the hardships and injustices of apartheid South Africa.

In this context, the art of hunger as I have so far described it in this book—the art of hunger as a way of dramatizing aesthetic autonomy's contradictions and crises—acquires another layer of contradiction, another incarnation of crisis. In 1980s South Africa, where hunger is a widespread and discursively important effect of the apartheid regime, representations of hunger are politically coded from the outset. If aesthetic autonomy is already political in South Africa, so too is hunger. The political context of apartheid South Africa, in other words, exacerbates the contradictions of the art of hunger, magnifying the political significance of both aesthetic autonomy and the representation of hunger, and revealing that these two axes pull in opposite directions, aesthetically and politically. Suspended between realism and modernism, and between colonial legacies and anti-apartheid activism, the art of hunger acquires an inescapably political cast in apartheid South Africa.

---

[49] Quoted in Russell Vandenbrouke, *Truths the Hand Can't Touch: The Theatre of Athol Fugard* (New York: Theatre Communications Group, 1985), 104.

[50] Joel Matlou, "Man Against Himself," in *A Land Apart: A South African Reader*, ed. André Brink and J. M. Coetzee (London: Faber and Faber, 1986), 79, 83.

[51] Mtutuzeli Matshoba, "Call Me Not a Man," in *A Land Apart*, ed. Brink and Coetzee, 96.

[52] Jeremy Cronin, "Walking on Air," in *A Land Apart*, ed. Brink and Coetzee, 24.

[53] Oupa Thando Mthimkulu, "Like a Wheel," in *A Land Apart*, ed. Brink and Coetzee, 121.

3. TOWARDS AUTONOMY: THE GENESIS
OF *MICHAEL K*

The 1983 novel *Life & Times of Michael K* offers Coetzee's most sustained engagement with the challenges that apartheid South Africa poses to aesthetic autonomy. Of all his novels, it became the most prominently entangled in the debates about the function of art that were raging in South Africa at the time. South African critics attacked it for its perceived lack of utility to the anti-apartheid struggle, for the perception that, as a review in the *African Communist* complained, "those interested in understanding or transforming South African society can learn little from the life and times of Michael K."[54] The best-known critique of this sort is Nadine Gordimer's review of the novel for the *New York Review of Books*, in which she argues that "J. M. Coetzee has written a marvellous work that leaves nothing unsaid—and could not be better said—about what human beings do to fellow human beings in South Africa; but he does not recognize what the victims, seeing themselves as victims no longer, have done, are doing, and believe they must do for themselves."[55] The doubts that unite the *African Communist*'s rather vicious review with Gordimer's more appreciative but nonetheless critical reading reflect the terms of literary discourse in 1980s South Africa. The problem with *Michael K*, these reviewers suggest, is the author's abdication of his responsibility to create literature that acts in the world. Central to this apparent failure is the passivity of the title character, his refusal to "do" anything—and specifically, to take a stand within the political and historical currents that flow around him but to which he seems curiously impervious. *Michael K* therefore comes to exemplify the risk that contemporary literature will abandon realism and, with it, political action; that it will lapse into an autonomy that is indistinguishable from irresponsibility.

The tension between responsibility and autonomy that dictated *Michael K*'s South African reception also haunted its composition. Coetzee drafted the novel between 1980 and 1982, scrupulously dating drafts and hand-written emendations. Alongside the novel's manuscript drafts, composed in University of Cape Town exam booklets, Coetzee kept a small grey notebook that contains commentary and reflection on the process of composition and the direction of the manuscript. Taken together, these two parallel records of the novel's genesis suggest that Coetzee was

[54] Z. N., "Much Ado About Nobody," *The African Communist*, 97 (1984): 103.
[55] Nadine Gordimer, "The Idea of Gardening," *New York Review of Books*, February 2, 1984, <http://www.nybooks.com/articles/archives/1984/feb/02/the-idea-of-gardening/>.

surprisingly responsive to the terms of debate and the demands made upon writers in the South African literary context, and that he both anticipated and sought to avoid precisely the kinds of criticism advanced by the *African Communist* and, particularly, by Gordimer.

The earliest drafts of the novel point towards an entirely different sort of book, whose key intertext is not the hunger artists of this study, but Heinrich von Kleist's *Michael Kohlhaas*, a novella about a horse-wrangler-cum-terrorist who sets out to wreak vengeance on a local squire for his arbitrary and capricious abuse of power. In these early versions, Coetzee's Michael K seems destined to follow a similarly violent path, reacting to apartheid's injustices with the terroristic fury of his namesake. Such a reaction might not have satisfied the *African Communist*—for which K's lack of social ties proved a major problem—but it would have done much to assuage Gordimer's concerns, offering an appropriately outraged and active response to the oppression of the apartheid state.

Plans to make K into "a little avenging angel" on the model of Kohlhaas first appear in the grey notebook in August 1980, as Coetzee is embarking on a third attempt at the novel.[56] They remain a prominent feature of the grey notebook throughout the composition process, but although Coetzee experiments with drafting various outrages that could push K to action, he never attempts the terroristic response. When the crucial moment comes in the drafting process, K (and Coetzee) does not act. In fact, K never displays any of Kohlhaas's propensity for violence, instead becoming more passive, more reclusive, and less sociable as the text nears completion. As Coetzee reworks his drafts, K seems to slip out of history, eluding the intertext that promised to make him into a political agent.

In the published version, this impasse is preserved in the arrival of a rebel gang on the farm where K is tending his garden. Critics have often read K's decision not to join, or even to reveal himself to, these passing figures of history as the novel's key moment of historical refusal, what David Attwell describes as "the most politically sensitive point in the novel."[57] Coetzee's composition notes worry over this scene and its implications at least as much as his critics have done. In the published version, K feels pressed to explain himself: "enough men had gone off to war saying the time for gardening was when the war was over; whereas there must be men to stay behind and keep gardening alive, or at least the

---

[56] J. M. Coetzee, "Grey Notebook (*Michael K* and Other Materials), 1979–1982," n.d., 13, Container 33, Folder 5, J. M. Coetzee Papers, Harry Ransom Center, University of Texas at Austin.

[57] David Attwell, *J. M. Coetzee: South Africa and the Politics of Writing* (Berkeley: University of California Press, 1993), 98.

idea of gardening."[58] In early versions, however, this explanation is tinged with a sense of regret that does not survive in the published text, as he describes his decision to remain in hiding from the rebels as "a terrible defeat for me" and laments, "If I had been following my heart I would have crept away during the night and joined the men in the mountains."[59] K's sense of failure mirrors the author's own inability to turn this character into a political figure, and this shared incapacity presages the critical frustration over K's failure to take up arms, which followed the novel's publication. K's early expression of discontent and dissatisfaction with his course of action, in other words, assumes a metafictional function in the context of apartheid-era South African literary discourse, reflecting not only on K's personal political failure, but also on the novel's inability or refusal to fulfill the demands of political responsibility.

The revision process that moves *Michael K* to the edges of the South African literary mainstream is underpinned by a persistent exploration, throughout the drafting process, of hunger. While this interest keeps K lodged within the material inequalities of apartheid South Africa right up to the point of publication, the role of hunger, like K's political commitment, shifts significantly over the course of the revisions. The first version—a monologue by a narrator, Annie, addressed to her brother Albert, who ultimately evolves into Michael K—takes place against a backdrop of severe food shortages. Much of this early narrative is focused on Annie's quest to "keep you [Albert] from hunger," and this early plot, like several subsequent versions, is focused tightly on the dynamics of poverty and the struggles to survive conditions of hunger and material deprivation.[60] Annie's protestation in this early draft that "We cannot starve, Albert. I refuse to believe that people can starve in a land of plenty" echoes a widespread theme of South African anti-apartheid discourse, as seen, for instance, in the exasperated opening of *Uprooting Poverty*'s chapter on hunger: "South Africa is one of the few countries in the world which normally exports food in considerable quantities. Yet it is also a country in which there is widespread hunger and malnutrition."[61] The hunger that both Annie and anti-apartheid scholars find so outrageous is rooted in a shared, collective experience of racialized inequality,

---

[58] J. M. Coetzee, *Life & Times of Michael K* (London: Vintage, 1998), 109.

[59] J. M. Coetzee, "Life & Times of Michael K, Version 6 [Part II]," 1981, Exam Book 15: p. 117 and Exam Book 18: p. 144, Container 7, Folder 4, J. M. Coetzee Papers, Harry Ransom Center, University of Texas at Austin.

[60] J. M. Coetzee, "Life & Times of Michael K, Version 1," 1980, Exam Book 1: p. 1, Container 7, Folder 1, J. M. Coetzee Papers, Harry Ransom Center, University of Texas at Austin.

[61] Ibid., 3; Wilson and Ramphele, *Uprooting Poverty*, 100.

heightened by what will become the wartime privations of the published novel. In both cases, its representation partakes of the larger cross-disciplinary documentary project of anti-apartheid resistance, whose manifestation in literature is an exhortation to socially responsible realism. For Michael K, this shared experience of suffering and starvation promises to create the conditions for his never-realized transformation into a figure of violence, "a little avenging angel."

This collective hunger, produced by inequality and functioning as a spur to action, is the mode of hunger that I describe in Section 2 as inimical to the art of hunger, and it persists, in an attenuated form, in the opening pages of the published version, where K goes to a corner store only to find there is "no bread, no milk," and where he worries about "[falling] into that sea of hungry mouths."[62] Unlike most of the hunger artists discussed in this book, for whom hunger is an individual experience to be passively accepted (or even passively induced), K first experiences hunger in Cape Town as a threat to be resisted and as an experience that helps to fix his class and racial position within the imperiled apartheid regime. By Version 4 of the drafting process, however, Coetzee had begun to minimize the early versions' vivid descriptions of poverty and hunger. At the same time, the grey notebook begins to project an alternate form of hunger, one in which K ends the novel by "starving up in the mountains."[63] This new hunger—isolated, asocial, and singular, removed from the immediate context of poverty, and less available to political interpretation or analysis—eventually predominates. For readers of the published novel, hunger registers most prominently in K's slow starvation on the Visagie farm and his refusal of food in the rehabilitation camp—forms of hunger that break with both the collective, poverty-induced malnourishment of the novel's opening and early drafts, and the social realist mode that dominated anti-apartheid discourse and South African literature of the 1970s and 1980s.

This shift effectively writes *Michael K* into the art of hunger tradition, a fact that Coetzee recognizes when, between mid-1981 and early 1982, as he is completing the first recognizable full draft of the novel (Version 6), he identifies Hamsun's *Hunger*, Kafka's "A Hunger Artist," and Melville's "Bartleby" as key intertexts.[64] The art of hunger emerges in the drafts as the expectation of Kohlhaas-inspired political action is transformed into K's passive retreat, and as hunger as a recognizable political critique is supplanted by a more ambivalent mode that renders it individual and aberrant.

---

[62] Coetzee, *Life & Times of Michael K*, 9, 14.   [63] Coetzee, "Grey Notebook," 16.

[64] The Hamsun and Kafka texts are cited by name. The reference to "Bartleby" is more oblique, framed through a fragment presumably attributable to the medical officer: "Michaels is like that man in New York who said, 'I prefer not to'..." Ibid., 43, 60, 61.

It therefore appears as a symptom of the novel's anxious turn away from its more politically legible, historically determined early drafts—away from the external exigencies of political action and realist representation—under what appears to be the pressure of its own internal logic, the pressure of its impulse towards autonomy. Like earlier hunger artists, Coetzee turns to the art of hunger as a way of making the effects of autonomy material and legible, at the point where the novel's turn to aesthetic autonomy emerges as a crisis for the text, creating a break with the prevailing social consensus around the role of art.

4. READING HUNGER

The composition of *Michael K* evolves under the shadow of how the novel will be read, as if playing out Coetzee's dread that censorship will lead the writer to "internalize a contaminating reading." If hunger emerges from this process as a mark of the novel's autonomy, it does so in the consciousness that it will elicit responses like those of Gordimer and the *African Communist*. In the tradition of the art of hunger, autonomy for Coetzee is therefore a gesture of willed indifference towards his immediate South African audience, an act of writing against his projected readership. *Michael K* has its genesis, in other words, in the awareness that the text's claim to autonomy will be tested and ultimately rejected by its readers. Autonomy and interpretation, in this historical moment as in the art of hunger tradition more generally, evolve as opposite gestures, bound uncomfortably together in their mutual antagonism.

The novel itself thematizes this antagonistic relationship between the autonomous text and the inescapability of its interpretation, through the struggle for interpretive control between Michael K and the medical officer who narrates the second section of the novel. At stake in this tension is the hermeneutic gap between K as a radically irreducible figure—a figure of autonomy, both personal and aesthetic—and the medical officer's attempt to make him mean something. The medical officer plays out this tension in the closing scene of his section, where he imagines "Michaels" fleeing, while he chases him, yelling an analysis of "what you mean to me": "Your stay in the camp was merely an allegory, if you know that word. It was an allegory—speaking at the highest level—of how scandalously, how outrageously a meaning can take up residence in a system without becoming a term in it."[65] The conflict Coetzee imagines in

---

[65] Coetzee, *Life & Times of Michael K*, 166.

the grey notebook between "K— and his interrogator/writer" is embodied in the physical comedy of this scene, in the medical officer's dream of Michaels's comically literal flight from meaning and interpretation (and from forms of interpretation that are uncomfortably contiguous with those deployed by his academic readers).[66] Like earlier writers in the art of hunger tradition, Coetzee imagines interpretation and the confrontation with a readership as an impingement on autonomy. Read in this way, Michael K himself becomes an allegory for the imperiled and besieged fate of aesthetic autonomy in the context of apartheid South Africa, where literature, like K, is called on to be "responsible"—put to use, made to mean something.

The reading of Michael K as allegory—aesthetic or otherwise—has been influentially challenged by Derek Attridge, who argues that Coetzee's work calls for a mode of "literal reading" that, by resisting allegorical interpretation, enables an encounter with alterity through the person of Michael K.[67] In the kind of *mise-en-abyme* characteristic of Coetzee's fictions, Attridge's reading is itself inscribed within the novel: he is, effectively, picking sides in the novel's central conflict by aligning himself with Michael K in his resistance to the medical officer's (and the academic reader's) excessive and often allegorical interpretation. The medical officer's comic haplessness, and the slapstick violence of the scene in which he imagines chasing K down with his interpretation, lend textual weight to this reading, but, as Attridge himself acknowledges, the novel nonetheless allows for, even seems to require, the oscillation between literal and allegorical modes of reading.[68] In this sense, *Michael K* reanimates a tension that has long plagued the art of hunger, between the literal existence of the starving body and its disdained but irresistible reproduction of itself as metaphor and allegory.

In apartheid South Africa, however, this struggle over modes of reading is also a struggle over the role of politics. Despite Attridge's call for literal reading, without the medical officer's more systematized modes of reading we miss important aspects of K's existence. K's starvation on the farm brings this dynamic into focus: alone, in the final pages of Part I, K exhibits the symptoms of serious and prolonged starvation—a loss of appetite, "giddiness," diarrhea, the sense of "the processes of his body slowing down"—but does not make the interpretive leap that would allow him to diagnose himself as starving.[69] Coetzee himself has this

---

[66] Coetzee, "Grey Notebook," 38.

[67] Derek Attridge, *J. M. Coetzee and the Ethics of Reading: Literature in the Event* (Chicago: University of Chicago Press, 2004), 32–64.

[68] Ibid., 61.   [69] Coetzee, *Life & Times of Michael K*, 117–18.

information—he takes extensive notes on the medical effects of starvation in the unpaginated back pages of the grey notebook—but it is not K but the medical officer who makes use of it, observing immediately on K's admission that: "There is every evidence of prolonged malnutrition: cracks in his skin, sores on his hands and feet, bleeding gums. His joints protrude, he weighs less than forty kilos."[70] To read K literally and on his own terms is to fail to recognize his starvation as such, for such recognition requires the fundamentally interpretive act of diagnosis. And, as social scientists and medics under apartheid came to realize, by not interpreting his symptoms, K not only puts his life at risk, he also makes his suffering inaccessible to any kind of political reading.

By reading K's physical state as symptomatic of starvation, the medical officer is able to read K's hunger within a political narrative that has freedom as its goal. "Are you fasting?" the medical officer asks his patient, "Is this a protest fast? Is that what it is? What are you protesting against? Do you want your freedom?"[71] The medical officer sees K's starvation as a bid for freedom from an oppressive state. Following this reading, some critics have interpreted K's life in the mountains as his attempt to become a "radically free subject," as David Attwell puts it.[72] But in fact, both K and the third-person narrator stubbornly resist using the term "freedom" (or any of its cognates) to describe his life in the mountains, using the word only negatively to, for instance, speak of his inability to "kick himself free of sleep."[73] The situation in which idleness was "stretches of freedom reclaimed by stealth" from his daily life no longer pertains in the mountains, the narrator insists, suggesting that freedom is defined in this novel only through its opposition to some form of oppression.[74] Outside the grip of society and the state, K's period of starvation is portrayed throughout the first section of the novel not as a state of freedom but rather as a state beyond the poles of freedom and oppression.

In lieu of understanding his time in the mountains as freedom, this period is described as "a yielding of himself up to time," a surrender to an intensely embodied experience of temporality. Given that this stretch of time constitutes a period of starvation and that the slowing of time itself is symptomatic of malnourishment, K's idleness emerges not as a liberation from specific state structures or forms of oppression, but instead as a subjection to the dictates and rhythms of his starving body. In this sense, K's starvation in the mountains translates the art of hunger, with

---

[70] Ibid., 129.   [71] Ibid., 145.
[72] David Attwell, *J. M. Coetzee and the Life of Writing: Face to Face with Time* (Melbourne: Text Publishing, 2014), 142.
[73] Coetzee, *Life & Times of Michael K*, 118.   [74] Ibid., 115.

its decoupling of aesthetic autonomy from claims to freedom, into the political realm. Like earlier hunger artists, K becomes autonomous not by way of an assertion of freedom, but through his subjugation to his body. The medical officer, in seeking to read K's autonomy as a bid for political freedom, fundamentally misreads what autonomy means for K.

The struggle over the politics of reading K's starvation reanimates the art of hunger's ambivalence about figurative uses of starvation. To choose between the narrator's literal and the medical officer's allegorical readings of Michael K's starvation is to choose between an ethical and political understanding of the novel. While the literal can indeed produce the kind of ethical reading that Attridge advocates—reading as an encounter with alterity—it cannot produce readings that signify on the collective, social, or symbolic levels that are necessary for political discourse. Conversely, while the allegorical readings of the medical officer necessarily put Michael K's body to work in a political sense, they do so only by forcing K's isolated existence in the mountains into an uncomfortable relation with medical and political schemas. The art of hunger's attempt to insist on literal readings therefore manifests in *Michael K* as an insistence on both *Michael K*'s and Michael K's irreducible autonomy. Its inevitable breakdown into allegory and metaphor parallels the irresistible politicization of autonomy in apartheid South Africa.

Michael K—stubbornly resistant to the medical officer's political interpretations—stands at the center of this debate about the relationship between reading and politics. In fact, K's desire to escape the political leads to a resistance to reading in general. Seeking not only to not be read, but also not to read, he refuses to espouse the political and social ties that reading creates. The drafts of the novel suggest that this position evolved over time, in tandem with K's autonomy and his retreat from politics. In striking contrast to the published texts, the earliest drafts depict Albert (Michael K's predecessor) and the early Michael K as highly literate characters, engaged in a translation of *Michael Kohlhaas*. As late as Version 6, Coetzee is still writing in the grey notebook that K "must unavoidably become more bookish (vulgar realism to make him stupid & ignorant)."[75] Nonetheless, the drafts evolve towards K's illiteracy. K begins Version 4 as a semi-literate character, who teaches himself to read using the books discovered in an abandoned flat, allowing him to read and model himself on Kleist. In the published version, Coetzee retains this scene, but uses it to stage not K's education but his disinterest in literacy: Michael K, in the published text, "had never liked books"; instead, he flicks idly through

---

[75] Coetzee, "Grey Notebook," 40.

"piles of magazines...paging through pictures of beautiful women and luscious food."[76] Because of the centrality of *Michael Kohlhaas* as both the early Michael K's reading matter of choice and the explicit model for his projected political action, his gradual move towards illiteracy maps onto his retreat from politics. K's turn towards aesthetic autonomy is therefore also a turn away from both the act of reading and the potentially political act of modeling himself on literary antecedents.

K's declining literacy coincides with the emergence of references to the art of hunger in the notebooks. Where *Michael Kohlhaas* was incorporated directly into the text, however, these new intertexts entail new models of intertextuality. The published Michael K embodies, rather than reads, his intertexts. His habits and attitudes link him to other texts, but K himself never becomes conscious of them. As the intertext shifts from reading material to practice, the novel establishes a new relationship to K's literary predecessors. In the early drafts, K's reading of Kleist leads him to repeatedly describe Michael Kohlhaas as his father, suggesting a genea-logical relationship both between the Kleist and Coetzee texts and between the German father and the Coloured South African son.[77] This familial model reworks Harold Bloom's Oedipal "anxiety of influence" as a relationship not between authors but between characters.[78] It produces a kind of textual community across racial and national boundaries, in which characters can learn political action from their predecessors and filiation serves political as well as identity-forming ends.

As Paul Auster discovered, however, the staunch anti-social stance of the art of hunger resists easy assimilation into a genealogical model of textual relations, and as *Michael K* drifts towards the art of hunger, it too abandons the father-text. The art of hunger intertexts that replace it appear well after the text's conception, first appearing in Coetzee's notes as the novel is already nearing completion. They offer not a genealogical model of influence and literary descent, but something more like the "community of celibates" that Deleuze identified with the US: a model of elective affiliation between autonomous beings.[79] This shift in models of intertextuality implies a changed theory of what texts can do politically. In the early versions, K's reading of *Michael Kohlhaas* and his subsequent attempts to model himself on the German horse-wrangler show texts at work in the

---

[76] Coetzee, *Life & Times of Michael K*, 17, 15–16.

[77] J. M. Coetzee, "Life & Times of Michael K, Version 3," 1980, 1–2, Container 7, Folder 1, J. M. Coetzee Papers, Harry Ransom Center, University of Texas at Austin.

[78] Harold Bloom, *The Anxiety of Influence: A Theory of Poetry* (Oxford: Oxford University Press, 1997).

[79] Gilles Deleuze, *Essays Critical and Clinical*, trans. Daniel W. Smith and Michael A. Greco (London: Verso, 1998), 89.

world, forming political subjects through the act of reading. K's reading of *Kohlhaas* is, in other words, a model of the engaged, politically active text. As K develops into a hunger artist, this model of reading as political formation disappears, along with the sense that texts can be organized to produce genealogical or communal ties.

The published K's ignorance of his intertexts makes the novel's inter-textuality into an understanding between author and reader, to which K himself can never be privy. This is, of course, a common mode of literary allusion, but *Michael K*'s intertextuality "over the head" of the protagonist has specific social and political resonances in apartheid South Africa. K's declining literacy is the product of what Coetzee calls the text's "vulgar realism": Michael K's embodiment of the generally poor education and high rates of illiteracy that were an effect of apartheid for many black and Coloured people.[80] In contrast, the author emerges from the grey notebook as hyper-literate, linking the evolving novel to eighteenth-century and modernist works of European literature, scientific studies of starvation, and European thinkers from Bataille to Bachofen. Thus, while K's autonomy—linked to his refusal of reading—manifests as a form of historically conditioned ignorance, Coetzee's is vested in his position of highly educated privilege.

The yawning gap between the white author's and the Coloured pro-tagonist's reading practices reflects one of the most significant differences between earlier incarnations of the art of hunger, where the protagonist tends to function as an avatar for the author, and *Life & Times of Michael K.* As a Coloured man in apartheid South Africa, Michael K's experience is stubbornly inassimilable to that of his white author. The explicitly racial-ized nature of hunger in this context ensures that the art of hunger is necessarily vicarious: the experience of a victim of apartheid, as written by one of its beneficiaries. In South Africa, the art of hunger therefore becomes fraught in a new and newly politicized way: as a literary tradition, it belongs to the European lineage that is the preserve of white authors like Coetzee; as an experience—as a form of hunger—it is the province of apartheid's non-white population. David James has argued that Coetzee "aligns himself with a particular modernist credo of economy to dramatise imperialism's remnants along with the tensions and contradictions of an age of decolonisation."[81] A similar claim could be made of the art of hunger, in a context where both Michael K's starvation and Coetzee's

---

[80] A. J. Christopher, "Educational Attainment in South Africa: A View from the Census 1865–2011," *History of Education* 44, no. 4 (2015): 515–17.

[81] David James, *Modernist Futures: Innovation and Inheritance in the Contemporary Novel* (Cambridge: Cambridge University Press, 2012), 104.

modernist appropriation of that starvation are racialized positions. In an entry in the grey notebook in July 1982, Coetzee, still worrying over K's abandonment of Kohlhaas-inspired political action, writes, "His not going off with the guerillas is thematized as a lacuna in his story. It is a lacuna in the logic of his political progression, a lacuna in my own position. It is an unbridgeable gap (and must be so with all comfortable liberal whites), and the best one can do is not to leave it out but to present it as a gap."[82] For Coetzee, the abandonment of political action and the interpretive hole that this produces is an impasse that reflects the "unbridgeable gap" between the Coloured protagonist and his white author. It is a product of the attempt to think across racial categories in a context where racial difference pervades all aspects of society. In this context, the art of hunger's newly inter-racial dynamics can only reproduce the politics of apartheid. The white author's attempt to write an "autonomous fiction" still requires a Coloured character to bear the brunt of the physical suffering this entails, to live out the art of hunger through his starving body. Even aesthetic autonomy, *Michael K* suggests, is inescapably tainted by the dynamics of apartheid.

A key manifestation of this taint lies in the inequitable and dissimilar ways that autonomy is distributed in this text. For Coetzee, autonomy is above all a literary phenomenon, arising from the density of his text's allusive structure and the dialogue that his novel establishes with modernist texts that make parallel claims to autonomy. In this sense, Coetzee's claim to autonomy is a claim to a certain way of reading, culminating in a retreat from his immediate reading public into a literary tradition where autonomy remains defensible. K's illiteracy, however, ensures that the protagonist can espouse only personal, not aesthetic, autonomy. Both Coetzee's aesthetic and K's personal autonomy ultimately require the starvation—the sacrifice—of K's body. In this sacrifice, the white author seeks his liberation from a politicizing readership in the same gesture that the Coloured protagonist establishes his distance from the institutions of late apartheid society.

5. DISCOURSES OF AUTONOMY: IDLENESS AND MATERNITY

Michael K may not have access to aesthetic autonomy in the highly literary and erudite form that Coetzee does, but he seems nonetheless to achieve a provisional personal autonomy in the closing pages of Part I, as, living in

---

[82] Coetzee, "Grey Notebook," 78, July 23, 1982.

the mountains, he carefully tends his pumpkins. As Gordimer writes, K embodies "an idea of survival that can be realized outside a political doctrine... the idea of gardening."[83] When Michael K retreats to the mountains to grow a crop of pumpkins, he experiences this gardening as an ecstatic, almost religious state that carries within it the promise of self-determination, the promise that there might be other modes of life beyond the war that rages around him. This dream of a life in the mountains is also the dream of a kind of extra-political autonomy, of a life apart not just from the demands of the state, but from the demands of politics as such. But Coetzee's construction of this life outside politics keeps Michael K firmly inscribed within a set of (white, European) discursive struc-tures. He therefore imagines K's autonomy as profoundly unfree, a captive to a long discursive history tied to colonialism, which locates freedom in absolute alterity. Extending the struggle over interpretation, the discursive construction of K's autonomy foregrounds his textual boundedness to the systems he seeks to repudiate. It produces a form of unfree autonomy that, rooted in the debates over agency and dis-course of the 1980s academy, finally relocates the art of hunger to the Anglo-American university.

The ambivalence over autonomy produced by Michael K's time in the mountains emerges clearly when the novel is read in dialogue with Coetzee's scholarly essay "Idleness in South Africa," written as he was drafting the novel and first published in 1982. The essay is an exploration of European and white South African anxieties over "Hottentot" and, later, Afrikaner idleness, a preoccupation that Coetzee argues has haunted discourse about South Africa since the first Dutch settlement in 1652.[84] *Life & Times of Michael K* draws on the terms of the essay to paint Michael K's life in the mountains as analogous to the lives of idle South Africans. In the novel, K is described as idle:

> learning to love idleness, idleness no longer as stretches of freedom reclaimed by stealth here and there from involuntary labour, surreptitious thefts to be enjoyed sitting on his heels before a flower-bed with the fork dangling from his fingers, but as a yielding up of himself to time, to a time flowing slowly like oil from horizon to horizon over the face of the world, washing

[83] Gordimer, "The Idea of Gardening," n.p.

[84] The term "Hottentot" refers to the Khoikhoi people who inhabited the southern tip of Africa at the time of the arrival of the Dutch. This term is considered offensive today, but I preserve this usage in this chapter, both because Coetzee himself does so throughout the essay, and because these accounts of African idleness are less an accurate description of an actually existing people than a discursive construct produced by Dutch and British colon-izers. The term Hottentot captures the discursive and historical nature of this construct more fully than do terms such as Khoikhoi.

over his body, circulating in his armpits and his groin, stirring his eyelids. He was neither pleased nor displeased when there was work to do; it was all the same.[85]

Coetzee presents Michael K's life in the mountains as a kind of Eden that collapses the opposition between idleness and work. It reflects what, in the "Idleness" essay, he describes as South African idleness's status as an "authentically native response to a foreign way of life."[86] Imagining idleness as a site of resistance and a scandal for the system, Coetzee suggests that, for both Michael K and the Hottentots and Boers of his essay, it represents an autonomous mode of life.

In "Idleness in South Africa," this idle lifestyle links the idle Hottentot with the creative artist. Coetzee wonders, "which is better, to live like the ant, busily storing up food for winter, or like the grasshopper, singing in the sun all day, heedless of the morrow?"[87] The grasshopper, who in Aesop's fable sings through the summer and is refused food by the industrious ant when he risks starving through the winter, is often taken as a figure for the artist. At the same time, Richard Ballard has shown that the ant and the grasshopper play a recurring role in conservative post-apartheid South African discourse, where the grasshopper is imagined as the black or Coloured heir of the idle Hottentots whose laziness brings their poverty on themselves.[88] In popular usage, then, the grasshopper overlays stereotypes of black and Coloured laziness with a critique of the self-indulgence of aesthetic autonomy. Coetzee's question, which seeks to revalue both the grasshopper's purported laziness and his aesthetic practice, implicitly links the artist to the idle Hottentot. In their shared refusal of labor, both pose a scandal for their respective systems.

But even a most cursory glance at Coetzee's archive suggests that he is emphatically not an idle writer. His archive foregrounds the painstaking labor of both reading and writing that underpins all of Coetzee's written work, the voluminous research and painful, studied drafting. Often, this work is a specifically scholarly labor. In the grey notebook, for instance, Coetzee compiles the archive that lies behind *Michael K* and Michael K. In the process, he produces a kind of cipher for the text's later interpretation: notes towards an unwritten academic essay or monograph. In this sense, it is both a scholarly labor in its own right, and an invitation to future scholarly labor. It produces a counterbalance to Auster's rejection of the institutionalization of autonomy, generating instead a claim for autonomy

---

[85] Coetzee, *Life & Times of Michael K*, 115.   [86] Coetzee, *White Writing*, 35.
[87] Ibid., 19.
[88] Richard Ballard, "The Ant and the Grasshopper: Rationalising Exclusion and Inequality in the Post-Apartheid City," *Theoria* 105 (2004): 64–88.

that is fully embedded within the institution of the university and its characteristic modes of labor. Michael K's life in the mountains, outside of all institutions, emerges as the dream of the institutionalized writer for a different kind of autonomy. As K makes a claim to the art of hunger's autonomy through his mode of life and his idle, starving body, he emerges as Coetzee's projection of the person for whom autonomy is not labor.

In the opposition between his own scholarly labor and K's autonomous idleness, Coetzee replicates the central claim of "Idleness in South Africa": that idleness poses a problem for scholarly discourse. It is, Coetzee writes, "an *anthropological scandal*" that "brings him [the early anthropologist] face to face (if he will only recognize it) with the limits of his conceptual framework."[89] Indeed, the idle South African brings even "the modern researcher and writer" to the very limits of language, "present[ing] him with nothing to say."[90] This scandal of the subject about whom nothing can be said is also the scandal of Michael K, his incommensurability with the medical officer's interpretive schema, and the recalcitrance with which he confronts his scholarly writer and his scholarly readers.

In such a reading, both Michael K and the idle Hottentots and Boers mount an implicit critique of the system through their position outside discourse. In a common gesture for humanities scholarship of the 1970s and early 1980s, the outsider subject's autonomy from discourse is imagined as the site of political resistance, a space of freedom from totalizing hegemonic systems. In this sense, "Idleness in South Africa" takes its position in a tradition of scholarly political critique that incorporates such important and varied texts as Ranajit Guha's 1982 foundational document of the Subaltern Studies group, in which he lauds the "*autonomous* domain" of the subaltern, and Hélène Cixous's 1975 essay "The Laugh of the Medusa," which imagines women's alterity to phallogocentric discourse as inherently emancipatory.[91] Like these contemporaneous texts, "Idleness in South Africa" assumes that the scholarly recovery of an excluded group's mode of life promises freedom not just for that group, but for all subjects, through its capacity to throw the system itself into question.

The shifting theoretical terrain of the early 1980s, however, put the possibility of a truly free, truly extra-discursive position into question. In the grey notebook, Coetzee inserts the novel into this critical debate by

---

[89] Coetzee, *White Writing*, 22, 24, italics in original.   [90] Ibid., 34.
[91] Ranajit Guha, "On Some Aspects of the Historiography of Colonial India," in *Subaltern Studies I: Writings on South Asian History and Society*, ed. Ranajit Guha (Delhi: Oxford University Press, 1982), 4; Hélène Cixous, "The Laugh of the Medusa," trans. Keith Cohen and Paula Cohen, *Signs* 1, no. 4 (1976): 875–93.

explicitly linking K, whom he describes as a "fool," to Foucault's analysis of madness.[92] For Foucault, madness—like Guha's subaltern or Cixous's woman—is precisely that which is excluded from discourse. Foucault imagines this state as ideally free, but, unlike Guha's and Cixous's accounts of the extra-discursive other, always necessarily captured by its representation in discourse. "The liberty of madness," Foucault writes in a 1961 preface to *The History of Madness*, "can only be heard from the heights of the fortress in which it is imprisoned."[93] Derrida's response to Foucault critiques this position by arguing that the internment of madness is more fundamental than Foucault acknowledges, lying at the very foundation of discourse itself, so that "speech . . . is able to open the space for discourse only by imprisoning madness."[94] For both Foucault and Derrida, what is at stake in this debate is the possibility of a site of freedom and resistance that lies outside the coercive strictures of discourse; for both, there is ultimately no such possibility.

Coetzee, who had left the US reluctantly in 1971, remained immersed in these debates as they moved into the American academy over the 1970s and 1980s. His position in this intellectual field is reflected in the fact that he cites, not Foucault and Derrida's original texts, but Shoshana Felman's account of their debate in her 1975 essay "Madness and Philosophy, or Literature's Reason," published in *Yale French Studies*. Indeed, throughout this period Coetzee continued to read and contribute to scholarly debates coming out of the US. In 1988, his essay collection *White Writing* was published with Yale University Press, and throughout these years he continued to publish articles in major US literary studies journals, including *PMLA*, *Comparative Literature*, and *MLN*. In 1979, immediately before commencing *Michael K*, he spent a sabbatical in Austin and Berkeley, and from the mid-1980s he returned to the US academy in a series of visiting positions and guest speaking engagements at a number of US institutions, most enduringly holding a part-year appointment at the University of Chicago's Committee for Social Thought from 1996 to 2003.

Coetzee's ambivalent engagement with South African literary norms is, therefore, shot through with a countervailing investment in US academic debates, which were coming to substantially different conclusions about questions of freedom and autonomy in this period. While South African writers placed aesthetic autonomy in opposition to political freedom, American academics, in dialogue with French theory, suggested that

---

[92] Coetzee, "Grey Notebook," 69.

[93] Michel Foucault, *History of Madness*, ed. Jean Khalfa, trans. Jonathan Murphy and Jean Khalfa (London: Routledge, 2006), xxxii.

[94] Jacques Derrida, *Writing and Difference*, trans. Alan Bass (London: Routledge, 2001), 74.

discourse's totalizing power erased the possibility of any mode of freedom that imagined itself external to discourse. The question of whether it is possible to be free of discourse—of whether resistance can be mounted from some space beyond the regime of power/knowledge—became increasingly pressing as the high theory of the 1970s was absorbed into the more politically engaged theory of the 1980s. By the end of the 1980s, texts like Gayatri Spivak's "Can the Subaltern Speak?" (1988) and Judith Butler's *Gender Trouble* (1990) would formalize this growing doubt, countering the optimism of the earlier generation of political thinkers with the belief that discourse determines the limits of thought within a society, that no subject can exist outside of discourse, and that no form of resistance is therefore possible from this imagined extra-discursive position. If earlier thinkers like Guha and Cixous imagined the oppressed other as occupying an "autonomous domain" outside of discourse, in which freedom itself might be discovered or fomented, theorists of the 1980s rejected the possibility of both autonomy and freedom, arguing that political change takes place not from a position of alterity but instead, as Butler has it, "through participating in precisely those practices of repetition that constitute identity and, therefore, present the immanent possibility of contesting them."[95] Following Derrida and Foucault's intimations from the 1960s, the American academy came eventually to believe that discourse inevitably imprisons the madman who seeks his autonomy.

Coetzee's writing of the early 1980s teeters on the brink of this disillusionment with the possibility of an extra-discursive freedom. His notes on the Felman article in the grey notebook conclude with an idea for the novel's ending: "Perhaps my book ends with a great final internment of all the vagabonds of C[ape] T[own]. Like fools ever since, K lacks a language in which to defend himself."[96] This proposed ending is an allusion to the "great internment" of the mad that Foucault takes as a pivotal moment in his *History of Madness*. As Felman puts it, with the great internment, "madness is now desacralized, and through its exclusion takes on a political, social, and ethical status."[97] For Coetzee to speculate that his novel should end with such an event suggests that he envisages Michael K and his fellow "fools" as captives to the very political system from which they are excluded. Even in "Idleness in South Africa," the freedom that Coetzee associates with Hottentot and Boer idleness has no autonomous existence: it does not exist outside of the traces it leaves, the

[95] Judith Butler, *Gender Trouble: Feminism and the Subversion of Identity* (New York: Routledge, 1999), 188.

[96] Coetzee, "Grey Notebook," 69.

[97] Felman, "Madness and Philosophy or Literature's Reason," 211.

disruptions it produces, in the writing of the colonizing class, and in this sense it remains trapped within their discourse. Whatever freedom and autonomy this "authentically native" way of life entails, it registers in "Idleness in South Africa" only as a disturbance in the colonial discursive field.

While Michael K ultimately escapes from the camps in which he is interned, the novel remains in the thrall of Foucault's larger claim that modernity marks the shift from physical to discursive imprisonment. Through the scholarly labor that Coetzee's archives make visible, Michael K's apparently autonomous life in the mountains comes to embody not so much a position liberated from discursive constraints, but an amalgam of discourses, drawn primarily from colonial and apartheid archives. Through the novel's echoes of "Idleness in South Africa," Coetzee imagines K's apparent exteriority to the system in and through a set of colonial tropes. Indeed, Coetzee constructs Michael K as an amalgam of racist tropes, as when he wonders in the grey notebook, "Why isn't this man a slave to drink?"[98] The fact that Coetzee demands of himself an explanation for K's failure to wholly conform to the stereotype of the Cape Coloured people as "idle, alcoholic, and morally decadent" suggests the extent to which he is modeled on such stereotypes.[99] Michael K's personal autonomy, in other words, his status as an embodiment of the freedom granted by idleness, is also a reflection of the discursive status of Coloured people within the racist South African imaginary. Like Foucault's madman, his "liberty can only be heard from the heights of the fortress in which it is imprisoned."

In fact, Michael K is not so much determined as overdetermined by discourse, imagined not just through stereotypes of black and Coloured people, but also through (often racialized) tropes of motherhood and femininity. Throughout his life in the mountains, K is described as a mother. The metaphor is most explicit as he reflects on the aftermath of the rebels' visit, imagining himself as "a woman whose children have all left the house," a reiteration of the gendered division of labor by which K's refusal of war and politics feminizes him.[100] But it most profoundly shapes K's relationship to gardening. Although he disavows aspirations to fatherhood, worrying that "I would be the worst of all fathers," he describes his pumpkins as his children and his relation to the land as a "cord" (suggestive of an umbilical cord), figuring himself as a mother who

---

[98] Coetzee, "Grey Notebook," 37.

[99] James Muzondidya, "Race, Ethnicity and the Politics of Positioning: The Making of Coloured Identity in Colonial Zimbabwe, 1890–1980," in *Burdened by Race: Coloured Identities in Southern Africa*, ed. Mohamed Adhikari (Cape Town: UCT Press, 2009), 159.

[100] Coetzee, *Life & Times of Michael K*, 111.

is concerned above all with "provid[ing] well" for his vegetal offspring.[101] Instead of founding a rival patrilineal line with himself at the head, which he foresees would be the "worst mistake," K positions himself within the matrilineal line of his mother and grandmother, emphasizing his occupation of the land as the thread that holds him in this relation: "am I such a child, such a child from a line of children, that none of us can leave, but have to come back to die here with our heads upon our mothers' laps, I upon hers, she upon her mother's, and so back and back, generation upon generation?"[102]

Just as Coetzee reprises colonial discourses about idleness to imagine his life in the mountains, his description of K as a mother inscribes him within a set of nineteenth-century discourses about maternity and matriarchy. As Coetzee is writing the final handwritten draft of K's encounter with the rebels (Version 7), he repeatedly evokes the nineteenth-century Swiss anthropologist Johann Jakob Bachofen and his theory of "mother right" or *Mutterrecht* in the grey notebook.[103] This influential (but now largely discredited) theory claims that all societies pass through a period of matriarchy before arriving at the patriarchy that he associates with advanced civilization, developing this matriarchal organization in tandem with the development of agriculture. For Bachofen, understanding this matriarchal prehistory involves the same enormous, almost impossible, leap that Coetzee finds in scholars' confrontations with idleness. Bachofen cautions that: "The scholar must be able to renounce entirely the ideas of his own time, the beliefs with which these have filled his spirit, and transfer himself to the midpoint of a completely different world of thought. Without such self-abnegation no real success in the study of antiquity is thinkable."[104] Bachofen, in other words, generates a discourse about ancient matriarchy that, like Coetzee's account of idleness and Foucault's of madness, imagines it as extra-discursive, unimaginable within the language of scholarship and troubling to the very identity of those who try to think it.

Bachofen imagines this prehistoric matriarchy as a characteristically religious form of social organization, a theory that he develops out of existing nineteenth-century discourses about women's supposedly natural religiosity: "To man's superior physical strength woman opposed the mighty influence of her religious consecration."[105] In keeping with this

---

[101] Ibid., 104, 109, 101.   [102] Ibid., 104, 124.

[103] Coetzee, "Grey Notebook," 57, 58.

[104] Actually, Bachofen's matriarchy is often a fairly straightforward inversion of contemporary patriarchy, making its apparent unthinkability an interesting study in the power of gender norms: J. J. Bachofen, *Myth, Religion and Mother Right: Selected Writings of J. J. Bachofen*, trans. Ralph Manheim (Princeton: Princeton University Press, 1967), 81–2.

[105] Ibid., 86.

theory, Michael K's feminization develops in tandem with a new religious bent, so that, for instance, when his pumpkins ripen, he prepares his meal by praying to the earth.[106] Even the medical officer suspects a religious explanation for K's hunger, although, true to his persistent misreading of K, he imagines this spiritual food as having its source in the heavens rather than the earth: "Did manna fall from the sky for you . . . ? Is that why you will not eat camp food—because you have been spoiled forever by the taste of manna?"[107] Linking K's matriarchal Eden to both religion and agriculture, both K and the medical officer imagine his life in the mountains through the lens of Bachofen's *Mutterrecht*. In this sense, Coetzee follows Bachofen in adopting a discourse of maternal religiosity as the emblem of a radically other form of life, one that might free its practitioners from the constraints of society.

Bachofen's ideas are important enough to *Michael K* that Coetzee alters long-standing themes—such as K's father, whom Coetzee had long been figuring as Michael Kohlhaas—to make his character more consistent with the logic of *Mutterrecht*. As he warns himself in the grey notebook, "In view of the opposition, traced by Bachofen, between mother and father right, I ought to be careful about giving K both a mother and a father."[108] This passage marks the point at which K's relationship to Michael Kohlhaas is definitively severed, and it occurs as part of a shift in K's gender position: K turns his back on war, politics, fatherhood, and Kleist's terroristic embodiment of all three, in favor of a feminized, spiritualized relation to land and life. Seen from one perspective, the feminized life of gardening and idleness described by Bachofen and the writers discussed in "Idleness in South Africa" reflects a liberated position outside of discourse. In this reading, K's rejection of masculine political action is understood as a recuperation of a feminized utopia, freedom imagined as maternal. But this extra-political freedom is, as we have seen, itself only legible because of the way in which Coetzee imagines Michael K as the embodiment of a particular discursive formation that projects a fantasy of absolute freedom onto society's gendered and racialized others. Modeling K on the twinned logics of *Mutterrecht* and Hottentot idleness, Coetzee gives K a freedom that is already a kind of captivity.

The unfreedom of K's maternity is underscored by the association of motherhood with hunger, which inscribes the novel's treatment of motherhood within a narrative of bad mothers and consequent filial failure. In a notebook entry from August 1981, Coetzee toys with a possible ending to the novel: "Or else he dies—from not eating enough

---

[106] Coetzee, *Life & Times of Michael K*, 113.   [107] Ibid., 150–1.
[108] Coetzee, "Grey Notebook," 68.

for too long—thinking that if he can only recover he can take charge of his story. The story is then all about hunger: the failure of the mother to sustain the child."[109] The unexpected leap from hunger to maternal failure is striking for its disconnection from both the details of K's projected death, which do not feature a mother, and from the contemporaneous drafts, which do not deal with mothers at this stage in the drafting process. It suggests that, like Erich Neumann, whose *The Great Mother* appears on his Record of Reading, Coetzee sees hunger itself as integrally connected with the maternal, and particularly with what Neumann calls the archetype of "the Terrible Mother."[110] *Michael K* bears out this connection from its opening pages, where Michael's hare lip disrupts both the emotional and physical connection between mother and child, preventing him from "suck[ing] the breast" so that he "cried with hunger."[111] When K himself becomes mother to his garden in the mountains, the act of nurturing it repeatedly leads to hunger, such that, "as he tended the seeds and watched and waited for the earth to bear food, his own need for food grew slighter and slighter."[112] Drawing on a set of sexist tropes that blame mothers for the problems of their children, Coetzee presents Michael K's adult hunger as already predetermined by the circumstances of his infancy. In this sense, motherhood functions not as the agent of utopia, but as the source of compulsion, and hunger emerges as the unfree autonomy that exemplifies this psychological determinism.

The link between K's hunger and poor mothering is, like other facets of his character, inscribed within a complex discursive web that amplifies the sense that this state is, for K, unfree and overdetermined. Michael K's starvation forms part of the larger South African conversation about non-white hunger, bearing the traces of two prominent discourses about African hunger in twentieth-century South Africa, which explained it, as Diana Wylie argues, in terms of "habits of mothering and of agriculture."[113] Wylie quotes a Department of Public Health official lamenting that, with respect to nutrition, the "ignorance of Native mothers especially is appalling," echoing Coetzee's fascination with Anna K's inability to feed her son properly.[114] At the same time, Michael K, whose farming ultimately produces pumpkins that do nothing to nourish him, would

---

[109] Ibid., 42.
[110] Erich Neumann, *The Great Mother: An Analysis of the Archetype*, trans. Ralph Manheim (Princeton: Princeton University Press, 1963), 149; J. M. Coetzee, "Record of Reading," n.d., Container 99, Folder 4, J. M. Coetzee Papers, Harry Ransom Center, University of Texas at Austin.
[111] Coetzee, *Life & Times of Michael K*, 3.   [112] Ibid., 101.
[113] Wylie, *Starving on a Full Stomach*, 15.   [114] Dr Latsky, quoted ibid., 84.

conform to the expectations of "most of the hunger experts in this book [who] blamed African malnutrition on African farming."[115] Because these explanations for African hunger were cultural, they allowed white health officials to avoid directly examining African poverty, instead blaming Africans themselves for their malnutrition and contributing to a discourse of cultural racism that assumed African culture to be inherently flawed. If motherhood promises a utopia outside of politics and war, the association with failed mothers and racist stereotypes undercuts this possibility, dragging K's discursively overdetermined bids for freedom back into the thrall of apartheid and colonial discourse's most straightforwardly oppressive modes.

Coetzee imagines K as perpetually and inevitably hungry, forced into a life of autonomous self-sufficiency and withering appetite, as a result of his mother's failure to feed him. The radical and unchosen individualism that results from Anna's failed mothering marks the limits of K's politics. As a bad mother from a line of bad mothers, he finds himself unable to enter politics even in a nurturing role, observing of the rebels: "I would have liked to give them food, but all I fed were their donkeys, that could have eaten grass."[116] The asocial, apolitical impulse of the art of hunger, its investment in the eccentric individual, has always been a gendered position, one that relies on but seeks to abdicate the masculine. Coetzee's interest in motherhood, and specifically in bad mothers, as the source of both hunger and the exclusion from community explicitly feminizes this position. As it does so, it reveals K's inscription in a set of (often racist and sexist) discourses about maternal failure and maternal utopia, African idleness and Coloured appetite, and it translates the overdetermination of K's hunger into a position that refuses to make him an agent of political freedom.

Taken together, these competing discursive frames overdetermine the character of Michael K, repositioning his apparently autonomous existence as the accumulation of discursive givens, and producing him as a figure that, even in his liberation, remains trapped within the history of colonial and apartheid discourse. As Coetzee insists in the grey notebook, "One of the things this book is not is a record of the visions of a mad seer, someone outside and above society."[117] The key way in which Coetzee keeps K bound to society, enmeshed within it, even through his isolation, is by foregrounding his status as a product of colonial and apartheid discourses. Hunger is central to this accumulation of discourses. On the one hand, it functions as a figure for K's autonomy; on the other, hunger's

---

[115] Ibid., 226.   [116] Coetzee, *Life & Times of Michael K*, 112.
[117] Coetzee, "Grey Notebook," 48–9.

complex discursive history—as a mark of quasi-religious purity and devotion, maternal failure, Protestant abstention from appetite, and idle failure of productivity—makes it one of the central engines by which K's claim to autonomy is recast as unfree and overdetermined. Written in dialogue with the contemporaneous debates in the US academy over political agency and freedom, Michael K, in his starvation, is a figure both of extra-discursive alterity that holds out the hope of a radically other way of life, and of that hope's negation by the shifting theoretico-political consensus of the 1980s academy, as alterity came to be understood as unthinkable outside of discourse. This doubleness, in which K's autonomy is simultaneously asserted and rendered unfree, replicates the dual perspective produced by K's resistance to reading. In refusing to be read, he asserts his alterity, his claim to a freedom beyond language. At the same time, even K's claim to alterity is itself a function of Coetzee's reading, rereading, and rewriting. The oscillation between these two perspectives reveals K's autonomy to be unfree, his alterity always bound to its social moment: to the task of interpretation and the production of alterity as a function of discourse.

6. ANTI-REALISM AND AESTHETIC AUTONOMY

Through his allusions to Foucault and his foregrounding of the discursive construction of Michael K, Coetzee locates the novel within a Franco-American theoretical tradition that increasingly attacked the terms on which South African leftist and anti-apartheid discourse operated. When Gordimer criticized *Michael K* for failing to show "the energy of the will to resist evil" among the South African black population, for instance, she did so on the understanding that resistance was a position outside the ideologies and hegemonic structures of the apartheid state. In doing so, she assumed a vastly different model of political resistance than that espoused by Foucault and Derrida in their debates over madness, for whom no such position of autonomous resistance is possible. For many anti-apartheid writers, literature's role was to sacrifice its own autonomy in order to create a space in which voices of resistance from outside the apartheid system could be heard. In contrast, while the US and French practitioners of "French theory" doubted the possibility of a truly autonomous space for discourse and a truly autonomous subject, they retained, as we have seen, a lingering attachment to aesthetic autonomy. Indeed, Suzanne Guerlac suggests that the group of theorists associated with *Tel quel*—the key journal in the emergence of poststructuralist theory—should be understood as an outgrowth of modernism due to their continued commitment to the modernist principle of "esthetic autonomy (sometimes transvalued into a fetishization of text)."[118]

This investment in aesthetic autonomy survived theory's translation to the US in haphazard and uneven ways. The Shoshana Felman article from which Coetzee draws his reading of Foucault on madness, however, comes down heavily on the side of literature's special status, turning the Foucault/Derrida debate towards a defense of literature's particularity and autonomy. In Felman's reading, "literature is, for Foucault, in a position of excess, since it includes that which philosophy excludes by definition: madness . . . *The History of Madness* is the story of this surplus, the story of a literary residue."[119] In its capacity to include madness, literature also assumes madness's autonomy, its exteriority to coercive systems, becoming the only form of writing that can register in language that which is other to discourse. As such, Felman attributes to literature a characteristically poststructuralist form of autonomy. In doing so, however, this position outside of discourse loses much of its political force. By the end of her article, the politically potent discussion of madness's freedom from and imprisonment within discourse disappears in favor of an understanding of madness as that which "questions *somewhere else*: somewhere at that point of silence where it is no longer we who speak, but where, in our absence, we are *spoken*."[120] Literature for Felman is this agentless form of writing, preserving its autonomy without promising a freedom beyond discourse.

Coetzee's defense of aesthetic autonomy in this period followed Felman in tying literature's autonomy to madness. In a 1982 talk to the University of Cape Town Philosophical Society, entitled "Realism in the Novel," Coetzee evokes Foucault in linking the rise of the realist novel to the "great confinement" of the mad, "the locking up of people who deny the universality of the reality-sense asserted by the *authorities*, the authors of that reality sense."[121] For Coetzee, this coercive construction of reality is enforced both through the exile of the mad and the dominance of realism, and in this sense, they are interrelated phenomena, manifestations of a historically specific turn to the empirical. Literature that seeks to keep open a space for madness and its melding of the possible with the impossible must therefore be anti-realist, following in the tradition of

[118] Suzanne Guerlac, *Literary Polemics: Bataille, Sartre, Valéry, Breton* (Stanford, CA: Stanford University Press, 1997), 219.

[119] Felman, "Madness and Philosophy or Literature's Reason," 223.

[120] Ibid., 228.

[121] J. M. Coetzee, "Realism in the Novel" (Talk, Philosophical Society, UCT, 1982), 5, Container 114, Folder 2, J. M. Coetzee Papers, Harry Ransom Center, University of Texas at Austin.

either the escapist fiction with which the talk ends (and of which K is, at one point in the drafting process, an avid reader), or the autonomous anti-realist writing, exemplified by Kafka, with which it begins. This anti-realist literature, this literature of madness, stands outside the authorized "reality" laid down for it, sustaining its autonomy from the "official literature" and its middle-class version of life.

Despite *Michael K*'s apparent resemblance to realism, there are indications that we ought to read this text, at least in part, within the anti-realist mode advocated by "Realism in the Novel." David Attwell highlights Coetzee's frustration with the novel's tendency towards realism, locating a resistance to realism in the metafiction introduced by the medical officer's section, its capacity to "bring self-consciousness into the text."[122] As Coetzee writes while drafting Version 5, "What I need is a liberation from verisimilitude!"[123] The tension that Attwell highlights between *Michael K*'s realism and its metafictive escape from realism is evident in the dynamics I have been tracing in this chapter: between a "literal" reading of K, and the medical officer's self-conscious allegorical interpretations; between K as an autonomous figure that escapes from discourse, and our scholarly reading of this escape as merely an archive of colonial and patriarchal fantasies of otherness. This oscillation is central to *Michael K*, but in important respects, neither phase really escapes the pitfalls of realism, as Coetzee describes them in the "Realism in the Novel" lecture. The problem for him here is the "disillusionment" that Coetzee argues is "built into the realist novel" due to the fact that, "insofar as they are fictions aware of their own fictionality, they are aware that fictions, illusions cannot be sustained."[124] In this sense, the oscillation between realism and metafiction is ultimately an oscillation between different moments in the process of realism's undoing, its disillusionment.

Coetzee counters this disillusionment with a resistance to realism, grounded in K's alterity. As a "fool" whom Coetzee considers sweeping up in his own "great confinement," Michael K embodies the anti-realist mode of aesthetic autonomy, through the non-naturalist treatment of K's superhuman resistance to hunger. In the novel's closing lines, K imagines returning to the farm and fetching water from the well with a teaspoon, "and when he brought it up there would be water in the bowl of the spoon; and in that way, he would say, one can live."[125] In a literal sense, this closing image is clearly impossible: one cannot live off teaspoons of water. But while the closing scene is presented as K's own fantasy, his

---

[122] Attwell, *Coetzee and the Life of Writing*, 139.
[123] Coetzee, "Grey Notebook," 20.   [124] Coetzee, "Realism in the Novel," 9.
[125] Coetzee, *Life & Times of Michael K*, 184.

unrealistic ability to survive his own starvation pervades the second half of the novel, as K's radical new way of life coexists with the brute reality of his starvation. During this period, the narrator claims that K's "need for food grew slighter and slighter...If he ate, eating what he could find, it was because he had not yet shaken off the belief that bodies that do not eat die."[126] The implication, running throughout the scenes in the mountains and camps, that K is not the kind of body who dies without food breaks significantly from the norms of contemporary South African literary culture. As we have seen, hunger plays a central role in the commitment of apartheid-era literary culture to social realism. The abandonment of a realist hunger, therefore, constitutes a denial of the political consensus on which social realism rests, and a refusal to accept that the duty of the novelist consists in bearing witness to the suffering of the hungry.

The problem that *Michael K* poses for realism brings the novel back into the orbit of *Michael Kohlhaas*. The German novella returns here not as a model for political action but as an example of the aesthetic realm's escape from the constraints of political realism. While most of Kleist's novella is given over to a detailed account of the slight against Kohlhaas and his attempts to seek redress by legal and terroristic means, the end introduces a fantastic subplot involving a fortune-teller and a prophecy. This divergence from realism has confused critics, who, as Clayton Koelb observes, have tended "to read the story as a realistic chronicle gone astray."[127] In fact, Georg Lukács—whose advocacy of social realism underpins apartheid-era South Africa's enthusiasm for the mode—heaps considerable praise on *Kohlhaas*'s realism, but finds it "regrettable...that this masterpiece should have been disfigured by some cranky Romantic elements that Kleist incorporated into it."[128] Allied not with the politics of Kleist's heroic avenger but with the formal integration of realism with "cranky Romantic elements," *Michael K* is an anti-Lukácsian *Kohlhaas*, a rejection not just of the obligation to represent a positive political vision but of the formal requirement to do so according to the conventions of realism. If the novel declares its autonomy from politics, it also lays

---

[126] Ibid., 101.

[127] Clayton Koelb, "Incorporating the Text: Kleist's 'Michael Kohlhaas,'" *PMLA* 105, no. 5 (October 1, 1990): 1099; for a detailed summary of early critical responses—all predating the composition of *Michael K*—see Clifford A. Bernd, "On the Two Divergent Parts of Kleist's *Michael Kohlhaas*," in *Studies in German Languages and Literature: Presented to Ernst A. G. Rose by Friends and Colleagues*, ed. Robert Allen Fowkes and Volkmar Sander (Reutlinger: Hutzler, 1967), 47–56.

[128] Georg Lukács, *German Realists in the Nineteenth Century*, trans. Jeremy Gaines and Paul Keast (Cambridge, MA: MIT Press, 1993), 41.

claim to a formal autonomy, whereby the literary text is freed from its compulsion to represent the world as it empirically is.

In avoiding straightforward realism and in going beyond deflating metafiction, the novel avoids the "disillusionment" that Coetzee argues is "built into the realist novel."[129] *Michael K*, in contrast, ends not with disillusionment, but with the assertion of the outrageous fantasy that its protagonist can survive indefinitely on only teaspoons of water. This fantasy is a vehement denial of the political project of social realism and of the "authority of suffering and therefore of the body" that, in *Doubling the Point*, Coetzee would claim is "not possible to deny [in South Africa] . . . for political reasons, for reasons of power."[130] If Michael K is the kind of body who can survive starvation, then his very existence seems, impossibly, to deny the authority of the body by floating free of its most basic needs. Just as Coetzee praises *Don Quixote* in "Realism in the Novel" for its refusal of "the reality-sense asserted by the *authorities*," in *Michael K* he refuses the reality-sense that transforms the body and its suffering into authority. Transcending the authority of the body, the fantasy of the starving man who does not die functions as an assertion of the novel's aesthetic autonomy—its refusal of both the political and aesthetic demands of social realism.

Through his hunger, then, Michael K is transfigured into an exemplary anti-realist body, a manifestation of autonomy that is at once personal and aesthetic. Like its model *Michael Kohlhaas*, this novel aims to escape the "prison" of what Coetzee calls "the official literature," and to ascend instead to the freedom of "a culture which does not distinguish between myth and history"—a culture that leaves its madmen free.[131] But as Coetzee repeatedly emphasizes, there is no such straightforward escape from cultural context. On the one hand, as the medical officer's section reminds us, Michael K will always be read back into his cultural moment, his otherness interpreted on the basis of that which is intelligible within the moment of reading. On the other, he is also and just as inevitably the result of Coetzee's own voluminous reading, a product of the writer's own specific cultural and intellectual heritage. As such, there is no vantage point from which Michael K's autonomy might escape cultural determination. Where David Attwell finds in *Michael K* "an affirmation of artistic and intellectual freedom," and in Michael K a "radically free subject," I have been suggesting that what we really find in text and protagonist is not freedom so much as the unfree autonomy of the art of hunger tradition: an

---

[129] Coetzee, "Realism in the Novel," 9.   [130] Coetzee, *Doubling the Point*, 248.
[131] Coetzee, "Realism in the Novel," 11, 7.

autonomy whose refusal of social context provides not liberation, but simply paralysis.

To understand the politics of this novel, I have suggested, we need to see the space that opens up between Michael K's personal autonomy and the novel's aesthetic autonomy. This is what Coetzee calls the novel's "spiritual problem": the fact that Coetzee is "incorrigibly elitist" and "unable to move from the side of the oppressors to the side of the oppressed."[132] As a result, Michael K's autonomy fails to coincide with Coetzee's, and in the disjuncture between these two modes of autonomy, each negates the other's capacity to lead to freedom. K's personal autonomy emerges as constrained by its overdetermination by colonial discourse, which is the product of Coetzee's rigorous and scholarly commitment to understanding his protagonist through the society from which he emerges. Coetzee's aesthetic autonomy in turn produces not a mode of transcendence but, via K's unfreedom, an image of the novelist's own limitations within both the South African and the transnational academic contexts out of which he writes. Hunger's dual signification—as a politically charged site of struggle in apartheid South Africa, and as a figure for aesthetic autonomy in European modernism—is central to this political ambivalence, and central to the novel's ultimate repudiation of freedom and the political. In this sense, *Life & Times of Michael K* reanimates the art of hunger tradition in order to dramatize both the political stakes of autonomy in late apartheid South Africa, and the limits of white South Africa's attempt to build a politics of freedom.

[132] Coetzee, "Grey Notebook," 80.

Conclusion

On the Refusal of Modernism's Afters

This book has traced a history of modernism's decline and of its doubters. In post-Vichy France, the US *circa* 1968, and late apartheid South Africa, modernism's fate was precarious, its reputation tarnished, and its politics reviled. The inescapability of the political in these contexts compromised the structural conditions of the autonomous literary field on which modernism had been built. In turn, it threw into crisis the philosophical defense of autonomy and the literary legacies of modernism, which grew out of and were guaranteed by this autonomous literary field. The stories we tell about late twentieth-century literary history reflect this dilemma. According to received wisdom, the period between 1945 and 1990 saw postmodernism replace modernism in both literature and scholarship, and new waves of postcolonial literature and theory discredited the Eurocentric specter of modernism. *The Art of Hunger* has read modernism and aesthetic autonomy through the history of its supposed decline, in order to tell the story of aesthetic autonomy's failures, and, in tandem, of modernism's slump. By following the history of modernism through its dark night of the soul, it has sought to understand what happened to modernism, and how its specter continued to shape literary and academic culture through the years of its apparent demise.

In some respects, this is a strange book to have written in the second decade of the twenty-first century. In the last decade or two, modernism has seen a revival of sorts. The expansion that Douglas Mao and Rebecca Walkowitz influentially identified as the signature move of the "new modernist studies" has entailed an explosion of the modernist canon and, with it, a new impulse to apply the term to an ever-widening set of texts and movements.[1] Global modernist studies has found new modernisms in Turkey and Africa, in the Caribbean and China. For scholars like

---

[1] Douglas Mao and Rebecca L. Walkowitz, "The New Modernist Studies," *PMLA* 123, no. 3 (2008): 737–48.

Susan Stanford Friedman, this geographical expansion has also entailed a temporal one, and modernism's historical borders have correspondingly loosened.[2] In Friedman's most provocative formulations, she speculates that there might be a modernism of Tang Dynasty China.[3] Meanwhile, scholars of contemporary literature, from Mark McGurl to David James, have argued that modernism never really died, positing its return or its persistence in contemporary literary style, in the aesthetic positions that animate our literary field, or in the institutions of contemporary creative writing.[4] The literary industry too participates in modernism's revival, selling a new generation of authors, from Ben Lerner to Eimear McBride, and from Jack Cox to Teju Cole, as heirs of the modernist canon.

Underpinning this expansive gesture is often the unspoken conviction that "modernism" is a term of approbation. To call a contemporary or a non-Western work modernist often carries with it a claim about its literary value. Modernism is serious literary business (which is to say, it sells as cultural capital, although not necessarily for any great financial profit) and branding a work with this term brings it within the orbit of this serious-ness. It suggests that it is literary with a capital L, that it partakes of the best that has been thought and said. Modernism, in short, continues to signal a position in the literary field—a position of high cultural capital and low financial returns, sustained by its relative autonomy—and the expansion of the term suggests both the prestige of this position and its availability to authors who, too late or too far away, might not otherwise have occupied it. Modernism's expansion has, in this sense, rested on its rehabilitation, its renewed credibility as a form of cultural capital and as a set of literary and aesthetic positions.

More than just a sociological jostling for position, however, modern-ism's revival in the twenty-first century has hinged on a revaluation of its ethical and political implications. This revaluation has tended to take two forms. On the one hand, a new spate of leftist scholarship has continued the tradition headed by thinkers like Adorno and Jameson, insisting on modernism as a uniquely revolutionary force in literature. In the US, the scholars around the online journal *nonsite* have followed and expanded the

---

[2] Susan Stanford Friedman, "Periodizing Modernism: Postcolonial Modernities and the Space/Time Borders of Modernist Studies," *Modernism/Modernity* 13, no. 3 (2006): 425–43.

[3] Susan Stanford Friedman, *Planetary Modernisms: Provocations on Modernity across Time* (New York: Columbia University Press, 2015).

[4] Mark McGurl, *The Program Era: Postwar Fiction and the Rise of Creative Writing* (Cambridge, MA: Harvard University Press, 2009); David James, ed., *The Legacies of Modernism: Historicising Postwar and Contemporary Fiction* (Cambridge: Cambridge University Press, 2012); David James, *Modernist Futures: Innovation and Inheritance in the Contemporary Novel* (Cambridge: Cambridge University Press, 2012).

work of Michael Fried and Walter Benn Michaels, for whom modernism's autonomy persists as a last bulwark of resistance against contemporary neoliberalism's totalizing heteronomy. Meanwhile, in their recent book *Combined and Uneven Development*, the Warwick Research Collective has linked modernism with their notion of "world-literature," as the literature that "registers" modernity. They vacillate on the extent to which this registration is necessarily critical, but the examples they select certainly imply that modernism is relevant to them as "the (modern) culture that says 'no' to modernity," echoing Adorno.[5] What these groups share is a conviction that modernism offers a position from which a critique of contemporary capitalism can be mounted. Modernism's retreat from overt political engagement becomes not a refusal of politics *tout court* but a refusal of co-optation, grounded in the conviction that politics can be invested in form. Modernism is due a come back because, as neoliberalism reaches and perhaps passes its peak, modernist literary resources become political resources, carrying forward the impulses of the revolutionary twentieth century. Its seriousness is not just the seriousness of literary consecration but, more importantly for these thinkers, of real political resistance (even where that resistance is largely negative or defensive).

Against this political justification of modernism, another set of scholars have made the case for its legacy as a largely ethical one. For several of the contributors to the landmark volume *The Legacies of Modernism*, which has set the agenda for work on modernism's relationship to contemporary literature, the relationship between these two moments is determined by their negotiation of what Tim Woods calls "*the ethics of form*."[6] For writers including Andrzej Gasiorek, Peter Preston, and Woods himself, modernist formal experimentation provides the foundation on which some of litera-ture's strongest ethical claims can be built. These writers participate in a line of thought whose most influential recent proponent has been Derek Attridge. In *The Singularity of Literature*, Attridge provides an ethical justification for literature: "To respond to the demand of the literary work as the demand of the other is to attend to it as a unique event whose happening is a call, a challenge, an obligation: understand me, translate my untranslatability, learn me by heart and thus learn the otherness that inhabits the heart."[7] Although his case in *The Singularity of Literature* is not confined to modernism, his ideas are developed further

[5] Warwick Research Collective, *Combined and Uneven Development: Towards a New Theory of World-Literature* (Liverpool: Liverpool University Press, 2015), 19.
[6] Tim Woods, "A Complex Legacy: Modernity's Uneasy Discourse of Ethics and Responsibility," in *The Legacies of Modernism: Historicising Postwar and Contemporary Fiction*, ed. David James (Cambridge: Cambridge University Press, 2012), 154.
[7] Derek Attridge, *The Singularity of Literature* (London; New York: Routledge, 2004), 131.

in a companion study, *J. M. Coetzee and the Ethics of Reading: Literature in the Event*, which reads Coetzee as a belated modernist. Taking Coetzee's modernism as the prime example of his ethics of literature, Attridge grants modernism and its contemporary manifestations a privileged position in his theory of ethical reading, a position that more recent scholars of modernism's relationship to contemporary literature carry forward. For these critics, contemporary writers reprise modernism as part of a larger attempt to explore the ethical possibilities of form and of literature in general.

Both the political and the ethical defenses of modernism link its resurgence to its capacity to achieve positive outcomes in the present. Modernism comes to embody qualities that literature in general is taken to hold, and its return is taken to fill a contemporary need for a more critical, resistant, healing, or ethical literary mode. This claim to modernism's special literary quality tends to rest on its long-standing association with aesthetic autonomy. For the political critics, modernist autonomy holds open the space for critique, granting literature freedom from the coercion of totalizing political systems. For modernism's ethical defenders, it guarantees what Attridge calls the "singularity" and the "alterity" of literature, holding the text separate enough from the reader to permit a true ethical relation.[8] For both, modernism's privileged relationship to autonomy is central to its status as an honorific, and central to its value as a term that can circulate beyond the historical moment with which it is conventionally associated.

While this commitment to modernist autonomy as a force for good produces worthy defenses of literature in general and of modernism in particular, the writers of the art of hunger refuse the consolations of these positions. Because authors like Beckett, Auster, and Coetzee imagine aesthetic autonomy as unfree and anti-social, they raise difficult, perhaps intractable, questions about modernism's political and ethical functions. As I have argued throughout this book, the art of hunger is an anti-politics of literature. It is also an anti-ethics. It cannot provide a model for liberation, because it does not experience itself as free, and it cannot provide a model for social relations, because it refuses society. As a result, the modernism sketched in this book, unlike most accounts of modernism's life after modernism, is neither good nor redemptive. Returning to modernism does not offer Beckett, Auster, or Coetzee a way out of their historical impasses, or even a particularly effective perch from which to critique the systems that produce them. It does not make authors, characters, or readers ethically sound or attentive. For scholars (and I began this project as one of them) who want their commitment to modernism to

---

[8] Ibid., 2.

be a commitment to a way of living well or to an optimal political system, the art of hunger is deflating. In the art of hunger, modernism is more curse than redemption.

Deflating the claims that are made on behalf of both modernism and aesthetic autonomy, the art of hunger asks us to interrogate the processes of canonization that these claims support. Declarations of the ethical worthiness of writers like Beckett and Coetzee have been key to their centrality to the canon of post-1945 writing. At the same time, a whole theory of literature's political force has taken Beckett, Kafka, and the Melville of "Bartleby" as its central figures. My analysis, however, suggests that we might need to re-evaluate our defense of these writers, as we re-evaluate our defense of modernism itself. It suggests that whatever is compelling about writers like Coetzee and Beckett, it is not edifying in the way that most ethical or political readings of their work suggest.

In this sense, *The Art of Hunger* offers a counter-narrative of modernism's afterlives. The writers I have discussed here link modernist formal experimentation to constraint and control, as in Beckett; they tie the modernist heritage to solipsistic self-exploration and intergenerational violence, as in Auster; and they suggest that modernist autonomy is inimical to and irreconcilable with a politics of racial liberation, as in Coetzee. Above all, they understand modernism's links to autonomy not as a form of liberation or sociability, but as a practice that is essentially unfree, and one that produces unfreedom. Modernist canons and modernist concepts are central to their understanding of aesthetics, but art itself, in their hands, becomes a duty, a limit, a travail, and a restraint. If Romanticism produced the influential account of art and especially of aesthetic autonomy as a practice of freedom, the art of hunger is the strand of modernism that most polemically rejects this claim—the strand of modernism in which art's exception ends in unfreedom.

Deflating as this account of modernism and its afterlives may be, my intention here has not been to offer a critique of modernism, nor to suggest that the authors I discuss do (or should). What fascinates me about this decidedly grimmer account of modernism's persistence in the late twentieth century is precisely that it has persisted at all. The commitment of writers like Beckett, Auster, and Coetzee to the modernist legacy offers the clearest example of its on-going presence in post-World War II literary culture, but its influence is wider and deeper than the predilections of a handful of authors. As Chapters 3 and 4 of this book have suggested, modernism has profoundly structured the anglophone university in the second half of the twentieth century. Literary studies as we know it today is to a substantial extent the product of modernism and its legacies, and modernism's persistence is one of the central stories of the institutionalization of literature in the university. At the same time, the most fervent and formative literary debates of the late twentieth century took modernism as their subject or their chief example. From France in the 1940s through the transnational upheavals of 1968 to South Africa in the 1980s, the most bitterly fought debates over art's relationship to politics and society were, as we have seen, also debates about modernism. While Beckett, Auster, and Coetzee's unwavering commitment to modernism was a minority position, so too was that of those who outright dismissed its importance or its influence. For many—perhaps for most—writers in the second half of the twentieth century, modernism was a legacy to be grappled uncomfortably with, inescapable but fraught. The counter-narrative of the art of hunger brings these institutional and social histories of modernism back into focus, and it reminds us that modernism's return is not just—indeed, not primarily—a validation of its virtues.

Instead, *The Art of Hunger* suggests that modernism returns throughout the twentieth and twenty-first centuries, not because it has an exemplary solution to the problem of what art is for in the modern world, but because it constitutes an exemplary formulation of the problem itself. I have been arguing that the art of hunger emerges at moments when aesthetic autonomy's social position is in crisis. In the same way, modernism itself returns as a way of articulating the on-going twentieth-century crisis in the social function of art. Its allure therefore varies for different groups, depending on the extent to which art's social function seems to them to be genuinely in doubt. For a radical and politically engaged tradition, running from post-war members of the French Communist Party, to student protestors at Columbia in 1968, to black intellectuals in South Africa in the 1980s, art served a clearly defined social role, as part of a larger political project. For these writers, modernism held little appeal. But for other writers in these contexts, from Jean-Paul Sartre and Roland Barthes to Nadine Gordimer and André Brink, the situation was not so clear-cut. Even for many who espoused political art, the sense that art was in crisis was pervasive. For these writers, the turn to politics was imagined as a solution to this crisis, a way of making art commensurate with the demands of their historical moment. But while they rejected aesthetic autonomy in its more anti-political forms, they overwhelmingly continued to develop their ideas through reference to modernist examples. Modernism, therefore, returned as an important touchstone for writers for whom art's social function seemed precarious, in crisis, or under threat, even where aesthetic autonomy did not. Indeed, modernism for many was the dilemma they hoped to escape from, the statement of a problem whose solution they were desperately seeking.

The art of hunger is one form in which modernism returns, but, as we have seen, it distinguishes itself from the modernist engagements of writers like Sartre and Gordimer on two fronts. Firstly, for the writers of the art of hunger tradition, the relationship between aesthetic autonomy and modernism is what modernism is. Refusing to decouple their commitments to the modernist tradition and to aesthetic autonomy, they seek to carry aesthetic autonomy forward, even as its social role is thrown into question. Secondly, and as a result, the art of hunger gives up all hope that the return to modernism might be a recuperative or empowering maneuver, or that the problem that is modernism might find a solution. Instead, in tracing both the unfreedom inherent to aesthetic autonomy and the crisis that modernism articulates, the art of hunger brings into sharper focus modernism's role in negotiating larger dilemmas about the status of art at moments of social upheaval.

As a result, the art of hunger does not provide a model for political action or for ethical relation. In fact, we can learn most from these writers precisely where they refuse to provide a model for action. The tradition outlined in this book provides a useful corrective to a long-standing impulse within literary studies—perhaps especially within modernist studies—to find extra-literary benefits in the literary works we most value. If there is value in the art of hunger, it does not lie in the assertion that Kafka helps us to better fight capitalism, or that Coetzee offers a model for ethical action. The art of hunger instead asks us to see art as a social category, without transforming it into a site of political or ethical progress. Similarly, by yoking the expansive, utopian category of art to the finiteness and frailty of the experience of hunger, it highlights the distinction between the unfreedom that results from our finitude as human beings, and the oppression produced by social injustice. As such, the art of hunger illuminates the ground on which political action must be built, even as it insists that art may never be the terrain on which political battles are won. For those of us who seek a progressive or leftist politics, the art of hunger underscores what we sometimes want to forget but ought not: that our bodies themselves present constraints and limits to freedom that no political activity can wish away; and that art as we have come to understand it in the twentieth century has its own logic that may not offer a model for political or ethical action. The art of hunger, an art of anti-politics and unfreedom, reimagines the aesthetic as a site of limitation and constraint, and modernism as the privileged vehicle of this deflating aesthetics. When we inherit modernism, therefore, we inherit a problem. The art of hunger is one history of this problem: the history of art as a practice of unfreedom.

Bibliography

Adorno, Theodor. *Aesthetic Theory*. Edited by Gretel Adorno and Rolf Tiedemann. Translated by Robert Hullot-Kentor. London: Continuum, 1997.

Adorno, Theodor. "Notes on Kafka." In *Prisms*, translated by Samuel Weber and Shierry Weber, 243–71. Cambridge: MIT Press, 1983.

Adorno, Theodor. *The Culture Industry: Selected Essays on Mass Culture*. Edited by J. M. Bernstein. London: Routledge, 1991.

Agamben, Giorgio. *Potentialities: Collected Essays in Philosophy*. Edited and translated by Daniel Heller Roazen. Stanford, CA: Stanford University Press, 1999.

Agamben, Giorgio. *The Coming Community*. Translated by Michael Hardt. Minneapolis: University of Minnesota Press, 2007.

Alber, Jan, Stefan Iversen, Henrik Skov Nielsen, and Brian Richardson. "Unnatural Narrative, Unnatural Narratology: Beyond Mimetic Models." *Narrative* 18, no. 2 (May 2010): 113–36.

Anderson, Quentin. *The Imperial Self: An Essay in American Literary and Cultural History*. New York: Knopf, 1971.

Arendt, Hannah. *Between Past and Future: Six Exercises in Political Thought*. New York: The Viking Press, 1961.

Armah, Ayi Kwai. "Larsony, or Fiction as Criticism of Fiction." *Asemka* 4 (1976): 1–14.

Artaud, Antonin. *The Theater and its Double*. Translated by Mary Caroline Richard. New York: Grove Press, 1958.

Attridge, Derek. *J. M. Coetzee and the Ethics of Reading: Literature in the Event*. Chicago: University of Chicago Press, 2004.

Attridge, Derek. *The Singularity of Literature*. London and New York: Routledge, 2004.

Attwell, David. *J. M. Coetzee and the Life of Writing: Face to Face with Time*. Melbourne: Text Publishing, 2014.

Attwell, David. *J. M. Coetzee: South Africa and the Politics of Writing*. Berkeley: University of California Press, 1993.

Auster, Paul. *Collected Poems*. London: Faber and Faber, 2004.

Auster, Paul. "College Essays: Explications: The Third Poem of *Quatre Poèmes*." TS, 1966–7. Box 79, Folder 2, Paul Auster Archive, 1963–1995 Papers. Berg Collection, New York Public Library.

Auster, Paul. "Extract of Interview, Enclosed with Letter from James Knowlson to Paul Auster," September 1, 2004. Box 88, Folder 2, Paul Auster Archive, 1999–2005 Papers. Berg Collection, New York Public Library.

Auster, Paul. *Hand to Mouth: A Chronicle of Early Failure*. London: Faber and Faber, 1997.

Auster, Paul. "Introduction: The Art of Hunger." In *Hunger*, by Knut Hamsun, vii–xviii. Melbourne: Text Publishing, 2006.

Auster, Paul. *Moon Palace.* London: Faber and Faber, 1989.

Auster, Paul. *Report from the Interior.* London: Faber and Faber, 2013.

Auster, Paul. "Stele." TS, n.d. Box 67, Folder 1, Paul Auster Archive, 1963–1995 Papers. Berg Collection, New York Public Library.

Auster, Paul. "The Art of Hunger." MA thesis. TS with holograph notes. Columbia University, May 1970. Box 10, Folder 1, Paul Auster Archive, 1963–1995 Papers. Berg Collection, New York Public Library.

Auster, Paul. *The Art of Hunger: Essay, Prefaces, Interviews and The Red Notebook, Expanded Edition.* New York: Penguin, 1997.

Auster, Paul. *The Invention of Solitude.* London: Faber and Faber, 1982.

Auster, Paul. *The New York Trilogy.* London: Faber and Faber, 1987.

Auster, Paul. "TS 47 pp. Unidentified Prose," n.d. Box 22, Folder 3, Paul Auster Archive, 1963–1995 Papers. Berg Collection, New York Public Library.

Bachofen, J. J. *Myth, Religion and Mother Right: Selected Writings of J. J. Bachofen.* Translated by Ralph Manheim. Princeton: Princeton University Press, 1967.

Baker, Houston A., Jr. "Modernism and the Harlem Renaissance." *American Quarterly* 39, no. 1 (1989): 84–97.

Ballard, Richard. "The Ant and the Grasshopper: Rationalising Exclusion and Inequality in the Post-Apartheid City." *Theoria* 105 (2004): 64–88.

Barthes, Roland. *Image, Music, Text.* Translated by Stephen Heath. London: Fontana, 1977.

Barthes, Roland. "L'Écriture de l'événement." *Communications* 12 (1968): 108–12.

Barthes, Roland. *Writing Degree Zero.* Translated by Annette Lavers and Colin Smith. Boston: Beacon Press, 1970.

Beckett, Samuel. *Comment c'est.* Paris: Minuit, 1961.

Beckett, Samuel. *Disjecta: Miscellaneous Writings and a Dramatic Fragment.* Edited by Ruby Cohn. New York: Grove Press, 1984.

Beckett, Samuel. *En attendant Godot.* Paris: Minuit, 1952.

Beckett, Samuel. *How It Is.* New York: Grove Press, 1964.

Beckett, Samuel. *Murphy.* Montreuil: Calder, 1938.

Beckett, Samuel. *Nohow On: Company, Ill Seen Ill Said, Worstward Ho.* New York: Grove Press, 1996.

Beckett, Samuel. "Ping." In *Samuel Beckett: The Complete Short Prose, 1929–1989,* edited by S. E. Gontarski, 193–6. New York: Grove Press, 1995.

Beckett, Samuel. *The Grove Centenary Edition: Volume III, Dramatic Works.* Edited by Paul Auster. New York: Grove Press, 2006.

Beckett, Samuel. *The Letters of Samuel Beckett: Volume 2, 1941–1956.* Edited by George Craig, Martha Dow Fehsenfeld, Dan Gunn, and Lois More Overbeck. Cambridge: Cambridge University Press, 2011.

Beckett, Samuel. *Trilogy: Molloy, Malone Dies, The Unnamable.* London: Calder, 1959.

Beckett, Samuel. *Watt.* New York: Grove Press, 1953.

Bell, Clive. "Dr. Freud on Art." *The Nation and the Athenaeum* 35 (1924): 690–1.

Bell, Daniel. *The Reforming of General Education: The Columbia Experience in its National Setting.* New Brunswick, NJ: Transaction Publishers, 2011.

Benbow, Heather Merle. "'Was Auf Dem Tisch Kam, Mußte Aufgegessen... Werden': Food, Gender, and Power in Kafka's Letters and Stories." *The German Quarterly* 79, no. 3 (2006): 347–65.

Benjamin, Walter. *Illuminations: Essays and Reflections.* Edited by Hannah Arendt. Translated by Harry Zohn. New York: Schocken Books, 1968.

Berlin, Isaiah. *Liberty, Incoporating Four Essays on Liberty.* Edited by Henry Hardy. Oxford: Oxford University Press, 2002.

Berman, Marshall. *The Politics of Authenticity: Radical Individualism and the Emergence of Modern Society.* New York: Atheneum, 1970.

Bernd, Clifford A. "On the Two Divergent Parts of Kleist's *Michael Kohlhaas.*" In *Studies in German Languages and Literature: Presented to Ernst A. G. Rose by Friends and Colleagues,* edited by Robert Allen Fowkes and Volkmar Sander, 47–56. Reutlinger: Hutzler, 1967.

Best, Stephen, and Sharon Marcus. "Surface Reading: An Introduction." *Representations* 108 (2009): 1–21.

Bethlehem, Louise. "'A Primary Need as Strong as Hunger': The Rhetoric of Urgency in South African Literary Culture after Apartheid." *Poetics Today* 22, no. 2 (2001): 365–89.

Blanchot, Maurice. "Literature and the Right to Death." In *The Work of Fire,* translated by Lydia Davis, 300–44. Stanford, CA: Stanford University Press, 1995.

Blanchot, Maurice. *The Space of Literature.* Translated by Ann Smock. Lincoln, NE: University of Nebraska Press, 1982.

Blanchot, Maurice. *Vicious Circles: Two Fictions and After the Fact.* Translated by Paul Auster. Barrytown, NY: Station Hill Press, 1989.

Bloom, Harold. *The Anxiety of Influence: A Theory of Poetry.* Oxford: Oxford University Press, 1997.

Bonnefoy, Yves. *Rimbaud par lui-même.* Paris: Éditions du Seuil, 1951.

Boschetti, Anna. *The Intellectual Enterprise: Sartre and* Les Temps modernes. Translated by Richard C. McCleary. Evanston, IL: Northwestern University Press, 1988.

Bourdieu, Pierre. "The Field of Cultural Production, or: The Economic World Reversed." *Poetics* 12 (1983): 311–56.

Bourdieu, Pierre. *The Rules of Art: Genesis and Structure of the Literary Field.* Translated by Susan Emanuel. Stanford, CA: Stanford University Press, 1995.

Brater, Enoch. *The Drama in the Text: Beckett's Late Fiction.* New York; Oxford: Oxford University Press, 1994.

Brater, Enoch. "The 'I' in Beckett's Not I." *Twentieth Century Literature* 20, no. 3 (1974): 189–200.

Brazil, Kevin. "Beckett, Painting and the Question of 'the Human.'" *Journal of Modern Literature* 36, no. 3 (2013): 81–99.

Brecht, Bertolt. *Brecht on Theatre: The Development of an Aesthetic.* Edited and translated by John Willett. London: Eyre Methuen, 1964.

Breton, André. "Manifesto of Surrealism (1924)." In *Manifestoes of Surrealism,* translated by Richard Seaver and Helen R. Lane, 1–49. Ann Arbor: University of Michigan Press, 1969.

Breton, André. "One Cause, Two-Fold Defense." Translated by Francis Scarfe. *Transition Forty-Eight* 2 (1948): 64–75.

Brink, André. *Mapmakers: Writing in a State of Siege*. London: Faber and Faber, 1983.

Brooks, Cleanth. *The Well-Wrought Urn*. London: Denis Dobson, 1947.

Brown, Nicholas. "The Work of Art in the Age of its Real Subsumption under Capital." *Nonsite.org*, March 13, 2012.

Brown, Nicholas. *Utopian Generations: The Political Horizon of Twentieth-Century Literature*. Princeton: Princeton University Press, 2005.

Bush, Douglas. "The New Criticism: Some Old-Fashioned Queries." *PMLA* 64, no. 1, Part 2, Supplement (1949): 13–21.

Butler, Judith. *Gender Trouble: Feminism and the Subversion of Identity*. New York: Routledge, 1999.

Carruth, Allison. "War Rations and the Food Politics of Late Modernism." *Modernism/Modernity* 16, no. 4 (2009): 767–95.

Caselli, Daniela. *Beckett's Dantes: Intertextuality in the Fiction and Criticism*. Manchester: Manchester University Press, 2005.

Certeau, Michel de. *La Prise de parole et autres écrits politiques*. Paris: Seuil, 1994.

Cheever, Abigail. *Real Phonies: Cultures of Authenticity in Post-World War II America*. Athens, GA: University of Georgia Press, 2010.

Christie, Sarah, Geoffrey Hutchings, and Don Maclennan. *Perspectives on South African Fiction*. Johannesburg: A. D. Donker, 1980.

Christopher, A. J. "Educational Attainment in South Africa: A View from the Census 1865–2011." *History of Education* 44, no. 4 (2015): 503–22.

Cixous, Hélène. "The Laugh of the Medusa." Translated by Keith Cohen and Paula Cohen. *Signs* 1, no. 4 (1976): 875–93.

Clastres, Pierre. *Chronicle of the Guayaki Indians*. Translated by Paul Auster. New York: Zone Books, 2000.

Coetzee, J. M. "Address to UCT Fellows," 1985. Container 64, Folder 3. J. M. Coetzee Papers, Harry Ransom Center, University of Texas at Austin.

Coetzee, J. M. "An Exclusive Interview with J. M. Coetzee." DN.se Kultur, December 8, 2003. <http://www.dn.se/kultur-noje/an-exclusive-interview-with-j-m-coetzee>.

Coetzee, J. M. *Boyhood: Scenes from Provincial Life*. London: Vintage, 1998.

Coetzee, J. M. *Doubling the Point: Essays and Interviews*. Edited by David Atwell. Cambridge, MA: Harvard University Press, 1992.

Coetzee, J. M. *Giving Offense: Essays on Censorship*. Chicago: University of Chicago Press, 1996.

Coetzee, J. M. "Grey Notebook (*Michael K* and Other Materials)," 1979–1982. Container 33, Folder 5. J. M. Coetzee Papers, Harry Ransom Center, University of Texas at Austin.

Coetzee, J. M. "Letters to Calder & Boyars; Bach Jr. Literary Agent; McIntosh, McKee & Dodds," December 3, 1971. Container 69, Folder 1: Business Correspondence, 1969–March 1976. J. M. Coetzee Papers, Harry Ransom Center, University of Texas at Austin.

Coetzee, J. M. *Life & Times of Michael K.* London: Vintage, 1998.

Coetzee, J. M. "Life & Times of Michael K, Version 1," 1980. Container 7, Folder 1. J. M. Coetzee Papers, Harry Ransom Center, University of Texas at Austin.

Coetzee, J. M. "Life & Times of Michael K, Version 3," 1980. Container 7, Folder 1. J. M. Coetzee Papers, Harry Ransom Center, University of Texas at Austin.

Coetzee, J. M. "Life & Times of Michael K, Version 6 [Part II]," 1981. Container 7, Folder 4. J. M. Coetzee Papers, Harry Ransom Center, University of Texas at Austin.

Coetzee, J. M. "Realism in the Novel." Talk. Philosophical Society, UCT, 1982. Container 114, Folder 2. J. M. Coetzee Papers, Harry Ransom Center, University of Texas at Austin.

Coetzee, J. M. "Record of Reading," n.d. Container 99, Folder 4. J. M. Coetzee Papers, Harry Ransom Center, University of Texas at Austin.

Coetzee, J. M. "The English Fiction of Samuel Beckett: An Essay in Stylistic Analysis." Ph.D. dissertation, University of Texas at Austin, 1969.

Coetzee, J. M. "The Novel Today." TS, 1987. Container 64, Folder 7: Early Works, 1987. J. M. Coetzee Papers, Harry Ransom Center, University of Texas at Austin.

Coetzee, J. M. *White Writing: On the Culture of Letters in South Africa.* New Haven: Yale University Press, 1988.

Cohen, Josh. "Desertions: Paul Auster, Edmond Jabès and the Writing of Auschwitz." *The Journal of the Midwest Modern Languages Association* 33, no. 3 (2001 2000): 94–107.

Cohn, Ruby. "Comment c'est: de quoi rire." *The French Review* 35, no. 6 (1962): 563–9.

Columbia College. "Literature Humanities: Texts 1937–2013." Columbia College: The Core Curriculum. Accessed August 31, 2014. <http://www.college.columbia.edu/core/1937.php>.

Cronin, Jeremy. "Walking on Air." In *A Land Apart: A South African Reader*, edited by André Brink and J. M. Coetzee, 23–30. London: Faber and Faber, 1986.

Cusset, François. *French Theory: How Foucault, Deleuze, Derrida & Co. Transformed the Intellectual Life of the United States.* Translated by Jeff Fort. Minneapolis: University of Minnesota Press, 2008.

D'Arcens, Louise. "Introduction: Medievalism: Scope and Complexity." In *The Cambridge Companion to Medievalism*, edited by Louise D'Arcens. Cambridge: Cambridge University Press, 2016.

D'Arcy, Michael, and Mathias Nilges. "Introduction: The Contemporaneity of Modernism." In *The Contemporaneity of Modernism: Literature, Media, Culture*, edited by Michael D'Arcy and Mathias Nilges, 1–16. New York: Routledge, 2016.

David-Fox, Katherine. "Prague–Vienna, Prague–Berlin: The Hidden Geographies of Czech Modernism." *Slavic Review* 59, no. 4 (2000): 735–60.

Davie, Grace. *Poverty Knowledge in South Africa: A Social History of Human Science, 1855–2005.* New York: Cambridge University Press, 2015.

De Julio, Maryann. *Jacques Dupin*. Amsterdam: Rodopi, 2005.

Deleuze, Gilles. *Essays Critical and Clinical*. Translated by Daniel W. Smith and Michael A. Greco. London: Verso, 1998.

Deleuze, Gilles, and Félix Guattari. *Kafka: Towards a Minor Literature*. Minneapolis: University of Minnesota Press, 1986.

De Man, Paul. *Blindness and Insight: Essays in the Rhetoric of Contemporary Criticism*. 2nd edn. New York: Oxford University Press, 1971.

Derrida, Jacques. *Writing and Difference*. Translated by Alan Bass. London: Routledge, 2001.

Devereaux, Mary. "Autonomy and its Feminist Critics." In *Encyclopedia of Aesthetics*, edited by Michael Kelly. New York: Oxford University Press, 1998.

"Document: L'Atelier Populaire." *Cahiers de mai* 2 (July 1, 1968): 14–16.

Donadio, Stephen. "Columbia: Seven Interviews." *Partisan Review* 35, no. 3 (1968): 354–92.

Donovan, Christopher. *Postmodern Counternarratives: Irony and Audience in the Novels of Paul Auster, Don DeLillo, Charles Johnson, and Tim O'Brien*. New York: Routledge, 2005.

Durantaye, Leland de la. *Giorgio Agamben: A Critical Introduction*. Stanford, CA: Stanford University Press, 2009.

Duthuit, Georges. "Sartre's Last Class (II)." Translated by Colin Summerford. *Transition Forty-Eight* 2 (1948): 98–116.

Eagleton, Terry. "Edible Ecriture." *Times Higher Education*. 1997. <http://www.timeshighereducation.co.uk/story.asp?storyCode=104281&sectioncode=26>.

Ellmann, Maud. *The Hunger Artists: Starving, Writing and Imprisonment*. London: Virago Press, 1993.

Éluard, Paul. *Au rendez-vous allemand*. Paris: Les Éditions de Minuit, 2012.

Feenberg, Andrew, and Jim Freedman. *When Poetry Ruled the Streets: The French May Events of 1968*. Albany, NY: State University of New York Press, 2001.

Felman, Shoshana. "Madness and Philosophy or Literature's Reason." *Yale French Studies* 52 (1975): 206–28.

Felski, Rita. *The Gender of Modernity*. Cambridge, MA: Harvard University Press, 1995.

Felski, Rita. *The Limits of Critique*. Chicago: University of Chicago Press, 2015.

Ferguson, Robert. *Enigma: The Life of Knut Hamsun*. London: Hutchinson, 1987.

Ferry, Luc, and Alain Renaut. *French Philosophy of the Sixties: An Essay on Antihumanism*. Translated by Mary H. S. Cattani. Amherst, MA: University of Massachusetts Press, 1990.

Flacks, Richard, and Nelson Lichtenstein, eds. "The Port Huron Statement." In *The Port Huron Statement: Sources and Legacies of the New Left's Founding Document*, 239–83. Philadelphia: University of Pennslyvania Press, 2015.

Fogg, Shannon L. *The Politics of Everyday Life in Vichy France: Foreigners, Undesirables, and Strangers*. Cambridge: Cambridge University Press, 2009.

Foucault, Michel. *History of Madness*. Edited by Jean Khalfa. Translated by Jonathan Murphy and Jean Khalfa. London: Routledge, 2006.

Foucault, Michel. "The Birth of a World." In *Foucault Live: Interviews 1961–84*, edited by Sylvère Lotringer, translated by John Johnston, 65–7. New York: Semiotext(e), 1989.

Foucault, Michel. *The Order of Things: An Archaeology of the Human Sciences.* London: Routledge, 2002.

Foucault, Michel. "What Is an Author?" In *Aesthetics, Method, and Epistemology*, edited by James D. Faubion, translated by Josué V. Harari, 205–22. New York: New Press, 1998.

Fouchet, Max-Pol. "In Reply to Pichette." Translated by J. G. Weightman. *Transition Forty-Eight* 2 (1948): 15–23.

Fraser, Russell. "Review of *Allegory: The Theory of a Symbolic Mode* by Angus Fletcher." *Modern Language Review* 62, no. 2 (1967): 298–9.

Friedman, Susan Stanford. "Periodizing Modernism: Postcolonial Modernities and the Space/Time Borders of Modernist Studies." *Modernism/Modernity* 13, no. 3 (2006): 425–43.

Friedman, Susan Stanford. *Planetary Modernisms: Provocations on Modernity across Time.* New York: Columbia University Press, 2015.

Friedrich, Hugo. *The Structure of Modern Poetry: From the Mid-Nineteenth to the Mid-Twentieth Century.* Translated by Joachim Nergroschel. Evanston, IL: Northwestern University Press, 1974.

Fromanger, Gérard. "L'Art, c'est ce qui rend la vie plus intéressante que l'art." *Libération.* May 14, 1998. <http://www.liberation.fr/cahier-special/1998/05/14/special-mai-68-gerard-fromanger-28-ans-peintre-militant-actif-de-l-atelier-populaire-des-beaux-arts-_235995>.

Fry, Roger. *The Artist and Psycho-Analysis.* London: Hogarth Press, 1924.

Frye, Northrop. *Anatomy of Criticism: Four Essays.* Princeton: Princeton University Press, 1957.

Gallagher, Catherine. *The Body Economic: Life, Death, and Sensation in Political Economy and the Victorian Novel.* Princeton: Princeton University Press, 2006.

Gallagher, Catherine. "The Body Versus the Social Body in the Works of Thomas Malthus and Henry Mayhew." *Representations* 14 (1986): 83–106.

Gans, Herbert J. "Symbolic Ethnicity: The Future of Ethnic Groups and Cultures in America." *Ethnic and Racial Studies* 2, no. 1 (1979): 1–20.

Gigante, Denise. *Taste: A Literary History.* New Haven: Yale University Press, 2005.

Gikandi, Simon. *Slavery and the Culture of Taste.* Princeton: Princeton University Press, 2011.

Gilbert, Sandra M., and Susan Gubar. *The Madwoman in the Attic: The Woman Writer and the Nineteenth-Century Literary Imagination.* New Haven: Yale University Press, 1979.

Goldman, Jonathan. *Modernism is the Literature of Celebrity.* Austin, TX: University of Texas Press, 2011.

Goldstone, Andrew. *Fictions of Autonomy: Modernism from Wilde to de Man.* Oxford: Oxford University Press, 2013.

Goldstone, Andrew. "Relative Autonomy: Pierre Bourdieu and Modernism." In *The Contemporaneity of Modernism: Literature, Media, Culture*, edited by Michael D'Arcy and Mathias Nilges, 65–79. New York: Routledge, 2016.

Gooldin, Sigal. "Fasting Women, Living Skeletons and Hunger Artists: Spectacles of Body and Miracles at the Turn of a Century." *Body and Society* 9, no. 2 (2003): 27–53.

Gordimer, Nadine. *The Essential Gesture: Writing, Politics and Places.* Edited by Stephen Clingman. London: Jonathan Cape, 1988.

Gordimer, Nadine. "The Idea of Gardening." *New York Review of Books*, February 2, 1984. <http://www.nybooks.com/articles/archives/1984/feb/02/the-idea-of-gardening/>.

Graff, Gerald. *Professing Literature: An Institutional History.* Chicago: University of Chicago Press, 2007.

Greenberg, Clement. "L'Art américain au XXe siècle." Translated by Catherine Le Guet. *Les Temps modernes* 2 (1946): 340–52.

Greenberg, Clement. "Towards a Newer Laocoon." In *The Collected Essays and Criticism*, edited by John O'Brian, 23–38. Chicago: University of Chicago Press, 1986.

Greene, J. Lee. *Blacks in Eden: The African-American Novel's First Century.* Charlottesville, VA: University of Virginia Press, 1996.

Guerlac, Suzanne. *Literary Polemics: Bataille, Sartre, Valéry, Breton.* Stanford, CA: Stanford University Press, 1997.

Guha, Ranajit. "On Some Aspects of the Historiography of Colonial India." In *Subaltern Studies I: Writings on South Asian History and Society*, edited by Ranajit Guha, 1–8. Delhi: Oxford University Press, 1982.

Guilbaut, Serge. *How New York Stole the Idea of Modern Art: Abstract Expressionism, Freedom, and the Cold War.* Translated by Arthur Goldhammer. Chicago: University of Chicago Press, 1983.

Guinnane, Timothy W. "The Great Irish Famine and Population: The Long View." *The American Economic Review* 84, no. 2 (1994): 303–8.

Hamsun, Knut. *Hunger.* Melbourne: Text Publishing, 2006.

Hardt, Michael, and Antonio Negri. *Empire.* Cambridge, MA: Harvard University Press, 2000.

Harpham, Geoffrey Galt. *The Ascetic Imperative in Culture and Criticism.* Chicago: University of Chicago Press, 1987.

Hegel, Georg Wilhelm Friedrich. *Introductory Lectures on Aesthetics.* Edited by Michael Inwood. Translated by Bernard Bosanquet. London: Penguin, 1993.

Hemingway, Ernest. *A Moveable Feast.* London: Arrow Books, 2000.

Heywood, Leslie. *Dedication to Hunger: The Anorexic Aesthetic in Modern Culture.* Berkeley: University of California Press, 1996.

Hill, Leslie. *Beckett's Fiction: In Different Words.* Cambridge: Cambridge University Press, 1990.

Hook, Sidney. "Is Fanaticism in the Saddle?" *Columbia College Today* 15, no. 3 (1968): 90.

Hume, David. *Four Dissertations.* Eighteenth Century Collections Online. London: printed for A. Millar, 1757.

Humpál, Martin. *The Roots of Modernist Narrative: Knut Hamsun's Novels.* Oslo: Solum Forlag, 1998.

Huyssen, Andreas. *After the Great Divide: Modernism, Mass Culture, Postmodernism*. Bloomington, IN; Indiana University Press, 1986.

Jaffe, Aaron. *Modernism and the Culture of Celebrity*. Cambridge: Cambridge University Press, 2005.

James, David. "Integrity after Metafiction." *Twentieth-Century Literature* 57, no. 3–4 (2011): 492–515.

James, David. *Modernist Futures: Innovation and Inheritance in the Contemporary Novel*. Cambridge: Cambridge University Press, 2012.

James, David, ed. *The Legacies of Modernism: Historicising Postwar and Contemporary Fiction*. Cambridge: Cambridge University Press, 2012.

James, David, and Urmila Seshagiri. "Metamodernism: Narratives of Continuity and Revolution." *PMLA* 129, no. 1 (2014): 87–100.

James, Henry. "The Art of Fiction." In *Norton Anthology of Theory and Criticism*, edited by Vincent B. Leitch, 2nd edn, 744–59. New York: Norton, 2010.

Jameson, Fredric. "Postmodernism, or The Cultural Logic of Late Capitalism." *New Left Review* 146 (August 1984): 53–92.

Jameson, Fredric. *The Modernist Papers*. London: Verso, 2007.

Jauss, Hans Robert. *Toward an Aesthetic of Reception*. Translated by Timothy Bahti. Brighton: Harvester Press, 1982.

Kafka, Franz. "A Hunger Artist." In *The Complete Short Stories of Franz Kafka*, edited by Nahum N. Glatzer, translated by Willa Muir and Edwin Muir, 268–77. London: Vintage, 2005.

Kafka, Franz. *Diaries 1910–1923*. Edited by Max Brod. Translated by Joseph Kresh and Martin Greenberg. New York: Schocken Books, 1948.

Kafka, Franz. *Die Erzählungen*. Edited by Roger Hermes. Frankfurt am Main: Fischer, 2008.

Kafka, Franz. *Letter to his Father/Brief an den Vater*. Translated by Ernst Kaiser. New York: Schocken Books, 2015.

Kant, Immanuel. *Critique of Judgement*. Edited by Nicholas Walker. Oxford: Oxford University Press, 2007.

Knowlson, James. *Damned to Fame: The Life of Samuel Beckett*. New York: Grove Press, 1996.

Koch, Kenneth. "The Art of Poetry." *Poetry* 125, no. 4 (1975): 187–203.

Kock, Leon de. "A Prison-House of Mirrors?" *Journal of Literary Studies = Tydskrif Vir Literatuurwetenskap* 5, no. 2 (1989): 229–31.

Koelb, Clayton. "Incorporating the Text: Kleist's 'Michael Kohlhaas.'" *PMLA* 105, no. 5 (October 1, 1990): 1098–107.

Kristeva, Julia. "My Memory's Hyperbole." In *The Portable Kristeva*, edited by Kelly Oliver, 3–22. New York: Columbia University Press, 1997.

Latour, Bruno. *Reassembling the Social: An Introduction to Actor-Network-Theory*. Oxford: Oxford University Press, 2005.

Lazarus, Neil. "Modernism and Modernity: T. W. Adorno and White South African Literature." *Cultural Critique* 5 (1986–7): 131–55.

Leavis, Q. D. *Fiction and the Reading Public*. London: Chatto and Windus, 1939.

Lehman, David. *New and Selected Poems*. New York: Scribner, 2013.

Lisi, Leonardo F. *Marginal Modernity: The Aesthetics of Dependency from Kierkegaard to Joyce*. New York: Fordham University Press, 2013.

Löwenthal, Leo. *Literature and the Image of Man: Sociological Studies of the European Drama and Novel, 1600–1900*. Boston: The Beacon Press, 1957.

Lukács, Georg. *German Realists in the Nineteenth Century*. Translated by Jeremy Gaines and Paul Keast. Cambridge, MA: MIT Press, 1993.

Lyngstad, Sverre. *Knut Hamsun, Novelist: A Critical Assessment*. New York: Peter Lang, 2005.

McDonald, Peter D. *Literature Police: Apartheid Censorship and its Cultural Consequences*. Oxford: Oxford University Press, 2009.

McDonald, Peter D. "The Writer, the Critic, and the Censor: J. M. Coetzee and the Question of Censorship." *Book History* 7 (2004): 285–302.

McDonald, Rónán. "Nothing to be Done: Masculinity and the Emergence of Irish Modernism." In *Modernism and Masculinity*, edited by Natalya Lusty and Julian Murphet, 71–86. Cambridge: Cambridge University Press, 2014.

McGurl, Mark. *The Program Era: Postwar Fiction and the Rise of Creative Writing*. Cambridge, MA: Harvard University Press, 2009.

Mackenzie, Catriona, and Natalie Stoljar. "Introduction: Autonomy Refigured." In *Relational Autonomy: Feminist Perspectives on Autonomy, Agency, and the Social Self*, edited by Catriona Mackenzie and Natalie Stoljar, 3–31. New York: Oxford University Press, 2000.

Malthus, T. R. *An Essay on the Principle of Population, or, A View of its Past and Present Effects on Human Happiness; with an Inquiry into the Prospects Respecting the Future Removal or Mitigation of the Evils Which it Occasions*. London: J. Johnson, 1803.

Mansfield, Katherine. *The Collected Letters of Katherine Mansfield*. Edited by Vincent O'Sullivan and Margaret Scott. Vol. 5: 1922–3. 5 vols. Oxford: Oxford University Press, 2008.

Mao, Douglas, and Rebecca L. Walkowitz. "The New Modernist Studies." *PMLA* 123, no. 3 (2008): 737–48.

Marcuse, Herbert. *An Essay on Liberation*. Boston: Beacon Press, 1969.

Marx, Leo. "Melville's Parable of the Walls." *Sewanee Review* 61, no. 4 (Autumn 1953): 602–27.

Massumi, Brian. *Parables for the Virtual: Movement, Affect, Sensation*. Durham, NC and London: Duke University Press, 2002.

"Math Commune," n.d. Box 11, Folder 21, Occupiers of Buildings, Student Statements and Correspondence, Group Positions. Protest and Activism Collection, 1958–99, Columbia University Archives.

Matlou, Joel. "Man against Himself." In *A Land Apart: A South African Reader*, edited by André Brink and J. M. Coetzee, 77–88. London: Faber and Faber, 1986.

Matshoba, Mtutuzeli. "Call Me Not a Man." In *A Land Apart: A South African Reader*, edited by André Brink and J. M. Coetzee, 94–104. London: Faber and Faber, 1986.

Melville, Herman. *Bartleby, the Scrivener: A Story of Wall Street*. Hoboken, NJ: Melville House Publishing, 2006.

Members of the Situationist International and Some Students at the University of Strasbourg. *On the Poverty of Student Life, Considered in its Economic, Political, Psychological, Sexual, and Particularly Intellectual Aspects, With a Modest Proposal for its Remedy*. Detroit: Black and Red, 2000.

Michaels, Walter Benn. *The Shape of the Signifier: 1967 to the End of History*. Princeton: Princeton University Press, 2004.

Miller, Henry. *The Time of the Assassins: A Study of Rimbaud*. New York: New Directions, 1956.

Miller, Henry. *Tropic of Cancer*. New York: Grove Press, 1961.

Miller, Tyrus. *Late Modernism: Politics, Fiction, and the Arts Between the World Wars*. Berkeley: University of California Press, 1999.

Mitchel, John. *The Last Conquest of Ireland (Perhaps)*. Glasgow: R. & T. Washbourne, 1882.

Mitchell, Breon. "Kafka and the Hunger Artitsts." In *Kafka and the Contemporary Critical Performance: Centenary Readings*, edited by Alan Udoff, 236–55. Bloomington, IN: Indiana University Press, 1987.

Moody, Alys. "Eden of Exiles: The Ethnicities of Paul Auster's Aesthetics." *American Literary History* 28, no. 1 (2016): 69–93.

Moretti, Franco. *The Way of the World: The* Bildungsroman *in European Culture*. Translated by Albert Sbragia. London: Verso, 2000.

Morin, Emilie. *Samuel Beckett and the Problem of Irishness*. Houndmills: Palgrave Macmillan, 2009.

Mthimkulu, Oupa Thando. "Like a Wheel." In *A Land Apart: A South African Reader*, edited by André Brink and J. M. Coetzee, 121. London: Faber and Faber, 1986.

Muzondidya, James. "Race, Ethnicity and the Politics of Positioning: The Making of Coloured Identity in Colonial Zimbabwe, 1890–1980." In *Burdened by Race: Coloured Identities in Southern Africa*, edited by Mohamed Adhikari, 156–84. Cape Town: UCT Press, 2009.

Ndebele, Njabulo S. *South African Literature and Culture: The Rediscovery of the Ordinary*. Manchester: Manchester University Press, 1994.

Neumann, Erich. *The Great Mother: An Analysis of the Archetype*. Translated by Ralph Manheim. Princeton: Princeton University Press, 1963.

Nieto-Galan, Agustí. "Mr Giovanni Succi Meets Dr Luigi Luciani in Florence: Hunger Artists and Experimental Physiology in the Late Nineteenth Century." *Social History of Medicine* 28, no. 1 (2014): 64–81.

Nietzsche, Friedrich. *The Birth of Tragedy*. Translated by Douglas Smith. Oxford: Oxford University Press, 2000.

Ó Ciosáin, Niall. "Famine Memory and the Popular Representation of Scarcity." In *History and Memory in Modern Ireland*, edited by Ian McBride, 95–117. Cambridge: Cambridge University Press, 2001.

Orwell, George. *Keep the Aspidistra Flying*. San Diego: Harcourt, 1956.

Paulhan, Jean. *Of Chaff and Wheat: Writers, War, and Treason*. Translated by Richard Rand. Urbana, IL: University of Illinois Press, 2004.

Peacock, James. "Unearthing Paul Auster's Poetry." *Orbis Litterarum* 64, no. 5 (2009): 413–37.

Perloff, Marjorie. "'In Love with Hiding': Samuel Beckett's War." *Iowa Review* 35, no. 1 (2005): 76–103.

Perloff, Marjorie. *Radical Artifice: Writing Poetry in the Age of Media*. Chicago: University of Chicago Press, 1991.

Pichette, Henri. "Letter—Red." Translated by Jack T. Nile and Bernard Frechtmann. *Transition Forty-Eight* 2 (1948): 5–15.

Pilz, Anna. "Lady Gregory's The Gaol Gate, Terence MacSwiney and the Abbey Theatre." *Irish Studies Review* 23, no. 3 (July 3, 2015): 277–91. <https://doi.org/10.1080/09670882.2015.1054126>.

Pippin, Robert B. *Modernism as a Philosophical Problem*. 2nd edn. Malden: Blackwell, 1999.

Pryor, Sean. *W. B. Yeats, Ezra Pound and the Poetry of Paradise*. Farnham: Ashgate, 2011.

Rainey, Lawrence. *Institutions of Modernism: Literary Elites and Public Culture*. New Haven: Yale University Press, 1998.

Rancière, Jacques. *Aesthetics and its Discontents*. Translated by Steven Corcoran. Cambridge: Polity Press, 2009.

Ransom, John Crowe. "Criticism, Inc." *Virginia Quarterly Review* 13, no. 4 (1937): 586–602.

Rimbaud, Arthur. *Complete Works, Selected Letters: A Bilingual Edition*. Translated by Wallace Fowlie. Chicago: University of Chicago Press, 2005.

Ross, Kristin. *May '68 and its Afterlives*. Chicago: University of Chicago Press, 2002.

Ross, Kristin. "Rimbaud and the Resistance to Work." *Representations* 19 (1987): 62–86.

Rossinow, Doug. *The Politics of Authenticity: Liberalism, Christianity, and the New Left in America*. New York: Columbia University Press, 1998.

Royle, Nicholas. *The Uncanny*. Manchester: Manchester University Press, 2003.

Rubin, Derek. "'The Hunger Must Be Preserved at All Costs': A Reading of *The Invention of Solitude*." In *Beyond the Red Notebook: Essays on Paul Auster*, edited by Dennis Barone, 60–70. Philadelphia: University of Pennsylvania Press, 1995.

Rudd, Mark. *Underground: My Life with SDS and the Weathermen*. New York: Harper Collins, 2009.

Rudd, Mark. "Why Were There So Many Jews in the SDS? (Or, the Ordeal of Civility)." *markrudd.com*, November 2005. <http://www.markrudd.com/?about-mark-rudd/why-were-there-so-many-jews-in-sds-or-the-ordeal-of-civility.html>.

Sapiro, Gisèle. *The French Writers' War, 1940–1953*. Translated by Vanessa Doriott Anderson and Dorrit Cohn. Durham, NC: Duke University Press, 2014.

Sartre, Jean-Paul. *Life/Situations: Essays Written and Spoken.* Translated by Paul Auster and Lydia Davis. New York: Pantheon Books, 1977.

Sartre, Jean-Paul. *What is Literature?* Translated by Bernard Frechtman. New York: Philosophical Library, 1949.

Schiller, Friedrich. *On the Aesthetic Education of Man, In a Series of Letters.* Edited and translated by Elizabeth M. Wilkinson and L. A. Willoughby. Oxford: Oxford University Press, 1982.

Schopenhauer, Arthur. *The World as Will and Representation.* Translated by E. F. J. Payne. Vol. 1. 2 vols. New York: Dover Publications, 1969.

Segrè, Elisabeth Bregman. "Style and Structure in Beckett's 'Ping': That Something Itself." *Journal of Modern Literature* 6, no. 1 (1977): 127–47.

Seth, Vanita. *Europe's Indians: Producing Racial Difference, 1500–1900.* Durham, NC: Duke University Press, 2010.

Shiloh, Ilana. *Paul Auster and the Postmodern Quest: On the Road to Nowhere.* New York: Peter Lang, 2002.

Shklovsky, Viktor. "On Poetry and Trans-Sense Language." Translated by Gerald Janecek and Peter Mayer. *October* 34 (Autumn 1985): 3–24.

Silver, Anna Krugovoy. *Victorian Literature and the Anorexic Body.* Cambridge: Cambridge University Press, 2002.

Siraganian, Lisa. *Modernism's Other Work: The Art Object's Political Life.* Oxford: Oxford University Press, 2012.

Sjølsyt-Jackson, Peter. *Troubling Legacies: Migration, Modernism and Fascism in the Case of Knut Hamsun.* London: Continuum, 2010.

Sloterdijk, Peter. *You Must Change your Life: On Anthropotechnics.* Translated by Wieland Hoban. Cambridge: Polity Press, 2013.

Sontag, Susan. "Preface." In *Writing Degree Zero*, by Roland Barthes. Boston: Beacon Press, 1970.

Spector, Scott. *Prague Territories: National Conflict and Cultural Innovation in Franz Kafka's Fin de siècle.* Berkeley: University of California Press, 2000.

Stenport, Anna Westerståhl. "Scandinavian Modernism: Stories of the Transnational and the Discontinuous." In *The Oxford Handbook of Global Modernisms*, edited by Mark Wollaeger, 478–98. Oxford: Oxford University Press, 2012.

Stevenson, Randall. "Not What it Used to Be: Nostalgia and the Legacies of Modernism." In *The Legacies of Modernism: Historicising Postwar and Contemporary Fiction*, edited by David James, 23–39. Cambridge: Cambridge University Press, 2012.

Strike Education Committee and Liberation School. "For Immediate Release," May 5, 1968. Box 12, Folder 12, Strike Education Committee and Liberation School. Protest and Activism Collection, 1958–99, Columbia University Archives.

Strike Education Committee and Liberation School. "Four New Courses of Special Interest," May 1968. Box 12, Folder 13, Strike Education Committee and Liberation School. Protest and Activism Collection, 1958–99, Columbia University Archives.

Strike Education Committee and Liberation School. "Liberation Classes," May 1968. Box 12, Folder 13, Strike Education Committee and Liberation School. Protest and Activism Collection, 1958–99, Columbia University Archives.

Strike Education Committee and Liberation School. "The Future of Education," 1968. Box 12, Folder 12, Strike Education Committee and Liberation School. Protest and Activism Collection, 1958–99, Columbia University Archives.

Strike Education Committee and Liberation School. "Why Have Liberation Classes?," May 7, 1968. Box 12, Folder 12, Strike Education Committee and Liberation School. Protest and Activism Collection, 1958–99, Columbia University Archives.

Students for a Democratic Society. "Dare We Be Heroes?," n.d. Box 13, Folder 8: Students for a Democratic Society. Protest and Activism Collection, 1958–99, Columbia University Archives.

Tournier, Maurice. *Les Mots de mai 68*. Toulouse: Presses Universitaires de Mirail, 2007.

Trilling, Lionel. *Sincerity and Authenticity*. Cambridge, MA: Harvard University Press, 1972.

Troester, Änne. "'Beyond This Point, Everything Turns to Prose': Paul Auster's Writing between Poetry and Prose." *Amerikastudien/American Studies* 47, no. 4 (2002): 525–38.

Trump, Martin. "Afrikaner Literature and the South African Liberation Struggle." *Journal of Commonwealth Literature* 25, no. 1 (1990): 42–70.

Ulin, Julieann. "'Famished Ghosts': Famine Memory in James Joyce's *Ulysses*." *James Joyce Annual* (2011): 20–63.

Vandenbrouke, Russell. *Truths the Hand Can't Touch: The Theatre of Athol Fugard*. New York: Theatre Communications Group, 1985.

Vandereycken, Walter, and Ron van Deth. *From Fasting Saints to Anorexic Girls: The History of Self-Starvation*. London: Athlone Press, 1994.

Vernon, James. *Hunger: A Modern History*. Cambridge, MA; London: Harvard University Press, 2007.

Warwick Research Collective. *Combined and Uneven Development: Towards a New Theory of World-Literature*. Liverpool: Liverpool University Press, 2015.

Watts, Philip. *Allegories of the Purge: How Literature Responded to the Postwar Trials of Writers and Intellectuals*. Stanford, CA: Stanford University Press, 1998.

Wellbery, David E. *Schopenhauers Bedeutung für die Moderne Literatur*. Munich: Carl Friedrich von Siemens Stiftung, 1998.

Wellek, René, and Austin Warren. *Theory of Literature*. New York: Harcourt, Bryce and Company, 1942.

Wexler, Joyce Piell. *Who Paid for Modernism? Art, Money, and the Fiction of Conrad, Joyce, and Lawrence*. Fayetteville, AR: University of Arkansas Press, 1997.

Widiss, Benjamin. *Obscure Invitations: The Persistence of the Author in Twentieth-Century American Literature*. Stanford, CA: Stanford University Press, 2011.

Wientzen, Timothy. "The Aesthetics of Hunger: Knut Hamsun, Modernism, and Starvation's Global Frame." *Novel* 48, no. 2 (2015): 208–23.

Wilson, Francis, and Mamphela Ramphele. *Uprooting Poverty: The South African Challenge: Report for the Second Carnegie Inquiry into Poverty and Development in Southern Africa*. New York: W. W. Norton & Co., 1989.

Wilson, Sarah. "'La Beauté Révolutionnaire'? Réalisme Socialiste and French Painting 1935–1954." *Oxford Art Journal* 3, no. 2 (1980): 61–9.

Wimsatt, W. K., and M. C. Beardsley. "The Intentional Fallacy." *The Sewanee Review* 54, no. 3 (1946): 468–88.

Woods, Tim. "A Complex Legacy: Modernity's Uneasy Discourse of Ethics and Responsibility." In *The Legacies of Modernism: Historicising Postwar and Contemporary Fiction*, edited by David James, 153–69. Cambridge: Cambridge University Press, 2012.

Wylie, Diana. *Starving on a Full Stomach: Hunger and the Triumph of Cultural Racism in South Africa*. Charlottesville, VA: University of Virginia Press, 2001.

Z. N. "Much Ado About Nobody." *The African Communist* 97 (1984): 101–3.

Zagar, Monika. *Knut Hamsun: The Dark Side of Literary Brilliance*. Seattle: University of Washington Press, 2011.

Zimbler, Jarad. "For Neither Love Nor Money: The Place of Political Art in Pierre Bourdieu's Literary Field." *Textual Practice* 23, no. 4 (2009): 599–620.

Zimbler, Jarad. *J. M. Coetzee and the Politics of Style*. New York: Cambridge University Press, 2014.

Žižek, Slavoj. *The Parallax View*. Cambridge, MA: MIT Press, 2006.

Index